# SOCIAL CONSTRUCTIONS OF DEAFNESS

# Social Constructions of Deafness: Examining Deaf Languacultures in Education

Thomas P. Horejes

Gallaudet University Press
Washington, DC

Gallaudet University Press

Washington, DC 20002
http://gupress.gallaudet.edu

*Library of Congress Cataloging-in-Publication Data*

Horejes, Thomas P.
  Social constructions of deafness : examining deaf languacultures in
education / Thomas P. Horejes.
      pages cm
  Includes bibliographical references and index.
  ISBN 978-1-56368-541-5 (hbk. : alk. paper) -- ISBN 978-1-56368-
542-2 (ebk.) (print)
  1.  Deaf–Education. 2.  Deaf–Social conditions. 3.  Deaf culture.
4.  Language and culture. 5.  Language and languages–Study and
teaching.  I. Title.

  HV2430.H67 2012
  371.91'2–dc23

                  2012042855

*Dedicated to*
*Kelly Kathryn, T. F., K. M., and Mr. B*

# CONTENTS

# Preface (A "Warning")

Ideas and definitions of deafness are complicated and deeply contested, including the constraints over what ought to be socially constructed as normal, especially for a child. Social institutions such as schools play powerful and exacting roles in the creation and maintenance of social constructions such as language and culture for deaf children. Schools also provide deaf children with a unique opportunity to obtain a valuable education; however, educational outcomes for deaf children are not on par with hearing children. Issues are further complicated because efforts to define appropriate academic, linguistic, and cultural pedagogy for deaf children in deaf schools are contested by divergent ideologies of spoken English and sign language. There is a need to critically examine the larger issue of deafness within different types of deaf education to uncover emergent ideologies, paradigms, identity formations, languages, cultures, and everyday social constructions. Identifying positive constructions of deafness involves considering larger critical justice issues related to deafness through critical, yet collaborative, inquiries that have important implications for influencing the types of knowledge and identities that deaf students develop. These considerations may also lead to a greater understanding of humankind and our connections to the world. This book explores these inquiries.

Throughout the development of this book, I have painstakingly reminded myself of the adage that if we do not learn from history, we are destined to repeat it. Walking into any academic library comprising a multitude of literary works that claim to show "evidence" and justifications of certain ideals and principles toward social problems, phenomena, and/or issues is a humbling yet overwhelming experience. Libraries hold a corpus of knowledge that help us to make sense of our social world. As this book makes its contribution toward this corpus, I am mindful of philosopher George M. F. Hegel's warning that some of the history written in these libraries has permeated society, but not in ways that encourage learning from its principles; thus, society continues to repeat history.

I have no intent to (re)write history in a manner that will claim to provide the type of objective, matter-of-fact solutions in this book that will result in what Hegel forewarned. Instead, my inquiries on human history share C. Wright Mills's (1959) central task to inquire, What does it mean to be a human in today's society? What does being human mean for deaf people and its history? Where do deaf issues involving language and culture in today's society stand in the context of human history? What varieties of humans, including deaf people, prevail in today's society? What does it mean to prevail in today's society? What types of social constructions permeate deafness and its identities? I also share Lankshear and McLaren's inquiry: "Whose interests are being served in social acts of doing research? Where is this process situated ethnically and politically in matters of social justice?" (1993, p. 381). By addressing these questions, this book takes on a complex and daunting task entailing multiple micro and macro levels of analysis. In actuality, this book does not provide answers to these questions because this book is not concerned with "discovering" epistemological foundations or "holistic" forms of objectivity; rather, this book, using these questions as guiding points, focuses on revealing critical knowledge by means of discourses and "stresses the contingency of the social" to address certain social justice issues (Lankshear & McLaren, 1993, p. 410), including deafness, language, culture, and deaf education. I cannot rectify in this book all of the social injustice issues surrounding deafness; instead, I strive to frame this book in terms of a Bakhtin approach of a dialogic existence through which my writing becomes a voice to be heard within the context of social justice awareness. A dialogic discourse opens ways to better understand the diverse paradigms leading to oppressor/oppressed relationships surrounding deaf education and the importance of language/culture (or languaculture) that will become clearer as this book progresses. The goal of the dialogic approach here is to reveal the interaction of different social values, grasp history more fully, unlock critical knowledge that may have been hidden before, and expose its profound effects not only on sign language, deaf culture, deafness, and deaf education but also on human values, thought, biographies, and histories.

In the spirit of Erving Goffman (1959), I am mindful that as I write this book, no matter how I attempt to portray certain aspects of my emic identity in explicit or etic ways, I will still be influenced by certain aspects of my identity that I cannot control, and these aspects will affect each reader differently. I share Roz Ivanic's (1998) inquiry, whether you as the reader and I as the writer will get along or whether I will alienate you. However, the goal of the book is to make explicit my "experiences" and my research in a discursive approach, which will enable me to unpack knowledge and practices that may have not been visible previously because of dominant practices and ideological assumptions that will manifest as the text proceeds. As I examine my selfhood connecting to my research, it is also important to realize that the inquiries I make in this book are not extricated from my ideology. In other words, I cannot separate my inquiries from my ideology in a neat empirical, objective, value-free, and laden-free dichotomous perspective; my social inquiries are influenced by my ideology. But, I critically use my consciousness by analyzing experiences to find how my identities, languaculture, and notions of normalcy/deviance are socially constructed and, in essence, how my consciousness has become ideological. This microlevel analysis becomes a macrolevel inquiry: how has my situatedness (and that of other deaf people) contributed to the larger theoretical frameworks on deaf education?

The book is best read in a discursive manner. I consider my experiences and how these experiences are connected to my research by connecting these experiences to theoretical ideas such as identity, language, and culture. Of course, it is not possible to cover all points of interests at once; thus, certain data, themes, and important points of interests within this research will be left on the map to be explored and compared later by future researchers (Goodwin, 2002, p. 305; Denzin & Giardina, 2009, p. 29). The book unpacks a journey about my own life, that is, how I have negotiated my deafness—negatively and positively—to make sense of who I am, what it means for me to be deaf in my personal identity, and how I reveal my deafness in this world (and how others perceive me) in my social identity. This emic approach becomes an opportunity for me to consciously reveal my personal identity, my social identity, and the ways that I think society has socially constructed me by connecting these experiences in theoretical frameworks that can be understood by those unfamiliar with deafness. Theoretical frameworks, including social constructions, languaculture, and normalcy/deviance, allow me to examine my experiences explicitly in a discursive manner to seek alternative ways of looking at deafness as a social justice issue. In a way, my consciousness becomes objectified (emic to etic) so it can be connected (and understood by those unfamiliar with deafness) to theoretical concepts that elicit discursive and social justice issues at large since the "only possible objective definition of consciousness is a sociological one" (Voloshinov in Moraes, 1996, p. 23).

This book is a partial reflection about my lived experiences both personally and academically. If I could, this entire book would also be "visualized" in American Sign Language (ASL) so readers could see and feel my words. The written form of my book may complete some of the criteria of the current academic apparatus (e.g., tenure), but it does not complete some of the very sacred personal information that I want to convey to the reader by means of sign language. I am mindful that this book contains a "professional vision" (Goodwin, 1994) or "taste of a profession" where one can learn a lot about someone's writing by looking at his or her references (Monaghan, 1994). Thus, I have tried to incorporate a wide variety of "visions" and sources that are not limited to one discipline or theory because to do so is to universalize truth. Some of you may feel that this tone is coming from a postmodern framework (which I admit and recognize) and thus tautologous for your taste; however, I do not view this perspective in terms of being circular but, rather, in terms of "feedback loops" that replace static, fossilized, and objective models with conceptual frameworks (Montgomery, 1994). Studying the connections between personal experiences, histories, and theoretical frameworks provides opportunities to wrestle with canons of knowledge—a transformative type of knowledge—breaking away from the circular cult of knowledge toward a path where we can reveal  how certain frameworks construct our views of identity, language, culture, and deafness. Echoing Harlan Lane (1999), I would like to acknowledge the individuals and certain institutions that continue to claim that deaf people have neither their own identified deaf community nor their own culture and language but, rather, are confined to their deficit and unfortunate loss. It is these adverse and negative constructed ideologies that have made me even more determined to write this book as a contribution to our history.

# SOCIAL CONSTRUCTIONS OF DEAFNESS

# INTRODUCTION

The journeys that I have made throughout my life are unique in some ways, but as I meet and read more about other deaf[1] people, I have found that many of our journeys have intersected at one point or another. Including me, more than 95% of deaf children are born to hearing parents Kluwin, Moores, & Gaustad 1992; Marschark, Lang, & Albertini, 2002). Many of us start with an identity from a distinct culture, but over time, identity shifts as we become more aware of another culture—a culture that each of us has embraced quite differently (Glickman, 1993, 1996). Some of us shift identities from deaf families with a strong deaf culture into the mainstreaming world with peers from a different culture, while others grow up as the only deaf person in a family not knowing any sign language to enrolling in Gallaudet University, a university known for its use of sign language (Padden & Humphries, 2005). Others attempt to decolonize their internal oppression as a deaf person with a deficit and establish a new identify as a person with a celebrated gift, which leads to the accumulation of their true deafhood (Ladd, 2003). Numerous people become situated on the margins and/or the borderlands between the hearing and deaf cultures, and they do not feel fully welcome in either culture (Brueggemann, 2010; Valente, 2010). As I situate myself to uncover the ways that my journeys intersect with others, I use my positionality as reflective discourse (and opportunity) to delineate my identity and

---

1. For this book, the designation of *d* or *D* is not the main focus, and the word *deaf* will be used to denote an all-encompassing population immersed in deaf-specific educational programs. Constructions of d/D are highly socially negotiable, and the origins of d/D have taken on a political context; these discussions are explicated in Chapter 2.

find interconnections with other deaf individuals' positions that take on a negotiated personal and often private identity of deafness.[2]

Deaf individuals simultaneously acquire a social identity (or role) that is assigned to them and one that corresponds with how they want to be portrayed (both intentionally and unintentionally) to the rest of the world. As with identity, ideas and definitions of deafness are personally and socially complicated and deeply contested, including the constraints over what ought to be normal, especially for a child (Breivik, 2005; Brueggemann, 2010; Ladd, 2003; Lane, 1999; Padden & Ramsey, 1998; Reagan, 2002). These multiple identities and definitions can add up to quite a lot of baggage for individuals. In the social view, I have depreciated my own identity as a deaf person and have often positioned my social identity as a deviant deaf individual while, at other times, I have positioned my deafness as a unique weapon and gift that elevates me to a better status than my hearing peers.

One of the many checkpoints that significantly affected my life was the realm of education, specifically, my own experiences as a deaf student. Incidentally, as a researcher and educator, I have often revisited my past and have come to respect the importance of connecting my experiences (emic) to academic research on deafness (etic) to make sense of the multidimensional aspects of my negotiated identities and positionalities. These emic data such as my experiences make explicit translation possible to the larger etic frameworks. To be sure, most etic constructions of deafness are rooted in deviance and are seen as "essentially a medical condition" (Reagan, 2002, p. 45), mainly because dominant perceptions of deafness create a one-sided etic framework that does not celebrate differences, diversity of language, culture, and positive constructions of deafness.

The goal of this book is to provide an alternative perspective by which deafness can be seen in a paradigm that is different from deviant and/or deficient. To be sure, there have been countless books that have taken on

---

2. I am aware that by using the term *deafness*, I may be placing it in a traditional "medical" category that has often been used (and often abused) throughout history. It is the goal of this book to take that term back from the medical framework and move it to a constructive framework in which -*ness* means the state of being. This book uses a holistic approach to study the different ways of being deaf, including not only how it has been framed within the medical model but also how it has been viewed through cultural, social, and political lenses.

this task, including *Understanding Deaf Culture: In Search of Deafhood* (Ladd, 2003), *Open Your Eyes: Deaf Studies Talking* (Bauman, 2008), and *The Deaf Way: Perspectives from the International Conference on Deaf Culture* (Erting et al., 1994). This book builds on that literature to challenge traditional etic perspectives on deafness and the powerful effects of social constructions that influence the ways of viewing deafness, the language for deaf people, and what deaf education ought to look like. This book makes its contribution to the literature by focusing on languaculture (to be introduced soon) and by emphasizing that "the case of the deaf and deaf identity is not the tension, but rather, the fundamental incommensurability of the emic and emic constructions" (Reagan, 2002, p. 44). I share Cooper and White's (2009) concern that "what seems to be neglected, in many cases, is an acknowledgement of the essential role of an autobiography [my emic narrative] in the intellectual development of . . . research [etic]" (p. 168). Thus, this book makes the connection between my personal and social experiences (emic) as a deaf person and the research on deafness (etic) to reveal intersecting pathways of normalcy and its social constructions within languaculture and the realm of education.

One major challenge in locating emic experiences to make explicit is that deaf identities span a broad continuum. However, these identities "highlight both the cross-boundary interaction and internal conflicts within groups [both deaf and hearing communities] as determinants of the provisional outcome of identity" (Breivik, 2006, p. 43), or what Barth (1969) would call maintaining our boundaries. Markowitz and Woodward (1978) take it one step further, claiming that these boundaries represent deaf people as an ethnic group. Similarly, Lane, Pillard, and Hedberg (2011) have compared deaf people who use ASL to ethnic groups "with respect to language, bonding to one's own kind, culture, social institutions, the arts, history, territory, kinship, socialization, and *boundary maintenance* [emphasis added]" (p. 41). Robert E. Johnson and Carol J. Erting's *Ethnicity and Socialization in a Classroom for Deaf Children* (1989) makes an important revelation about boundaries, identities, and language: sign language has become a critical factor in the development and maintenance of a deaf person's boundaries in the deaf landscape. One strong determination of our identity as a deaf collective is built on self-recognition and social recognition by society, which stems largely from our experiences in education where schools have been sites of acculturation and enculturation to language and culture (Johnson & Erting, 1989).

## LANGUAGE AND CULTURE = LANGUACULTURE

Schools and the pedagogy of language played an important and delicate role in the social construction of my deafness; as such, this book explores the ways that they continue to play a crucial role in the social constructions of many other deaf individuals in framing their perceptions of normalcy, deviance, and what it means to be deaf. Schools not only provide deaf children with a unique opportunity to obtain a valuable education but also are typically the first sites of acculturation and enculturation to language acquisition, which becomes a precursor to culture, or what Michael Agar (1994) calls "languaculture." Languaculture reflects the inextricable relationship between language and culture in which a specific language will shape and influence culture; language and culture cannot be separated. Agar states that "[w]hen the frames coherently organize several rich points that work with people of a particular social identity, be it nationality, ethnicity, gender, occupation, or social style, then you've built a *languaculture* of the identity" (1994, p. 135), including that of deaf people. In this book, frames serve as social constructions that incorporate (and organize) language and culture into languaculture as a way to better understand their impact on one's identity.

One cannot talk about culture without dealing with the maintenance of language within a population of a particular identity and the "language play" at work when discussing what culture stands for. May adds that the role of language "as a communally shared good," serves an important boundary-marking function "as a symbolic guard of one's identity" (2012, p. 137). Think about the ways you, yourself, explain how you became part of a particular culture and the language you use to explain to others about your culture depending on the person you are talking to. Equally important is the maintenance of language by the members of one culture to strengthen their cultural boundaries (Barth, 1969). Consider a case example where two members of deaf culture converse in American Sign Language (ASL), and a third member who is not fluent in ASL joins the conversation. The two deaf members have two typical choices: (1) leave their cultural boundaries by switching their natural ASL language into an unnatural form of sign language that the third member can comprehend or (2) resume their conversation, thereby ignoring the third member, which may solidify the cultural boundary between "us" and "them." The same example can be made if two members converse in spoken English and a third member who is not fluent in English joins the conversation. Those two members have similar choices. Culture becomes an "order of things" that consists of different "ways of knowing," and this organization is accomplished through the many different forms and maintenance of language, in this case, ASL. ASL is "arguably the single most important element in the construction of Deaf cultural identity" (Reagan, 2002, p. 51); thus, this book focuses on language (both sign language and spoken English) and how it mediates the unique languaculture of deaf people.

Kathryn P. Meadow (1972) made one of the first connections between language/culture and deafness, which would later be referred to as languaculture for the deaf. This term associated with deafness is now starting to reemerge in the academic context (Allen, Meyers, Sullivan, & Sullivan, 2007; Brueggemann, 2004; Senghas & Monaghan, 2002). In this book, I argue that, although many deaf people are a part of at least one languaculture, they are a part of one dominant Languaculture.[3] They prefer either spoken-English or ASL, and their choice greatly influences their "ways of being," values, and

---

3. This l/Languaculture analysis is largely derived from James Gee's examination on d/Discourses. Like l/Languaculture, d/Discourses serve important interrelated functions, especially in the realm of education. Lowercase *discourse* indicates microlevel concepts, including storytelling, everyday conversations, and jokes, which are a part of the uppercase *Discourse* "of being in the world, or forms of life which integrate words, acts, values, beliefs, attitudes, social identities" and can be found in schools (Gee, 1990, p. 142). This book suggests that some deaf people, like many minority students, have "great difficulty accommodating to, or adapting, to certain 'mainstream' Discourses, in particular, many school-based Discourses" (Gee, 1990, p. 148). Using a functionalist perspective, one could argue that those in sign-based schools are actually part of a larger Languaculture; after all, they live in a dominant society whose values are based on hearing and speaking. Others could argue that those deaf students from generations of deaf families are a part of a deaf ethnicity and, thus, are a part of the deaf Languaculture (see Lane, Pillard, & Hedberg's *People of the Eye: Deaf Ethnicity and Ancestry*, 2011). This distinction needs to be explored further in the future.

beliefs. These Languacultures are mastered through the acquisition (not learning) of language from others who have already placed themselves in their Languaculture, usually in school as sites of acculturation/enculturation. Thus, schools become critical to the social construction of the deaf student's Languaculture (see Johnson & Erting, 1989, article as case example). Where a deaf child goes to school will be a strong determinant of his or her l/Languaculture. For example, at sign-based schools, deaf students from hearing families learn what it is like to be "deaf" from deaf students who come from deaf families. In other words, these students from hearing families become enculturated in the deaf community through other deaf students who have already mastered their Languaculture. Similarly, those deaf students who attend oral-based or mainstreaming schools with different languacultures become enculturated in the hearing community.

The nature of languaculture has only begun to be addressed by anthropologists, sociologists, and sociolinguists. Thus, I am reluctant to use the l/L distinction for two reasons: (1) languaculture first needs to be carefully explored as a theoretical foundation before moving forward to other complex levels of analysis, including the l/L aspect, and (2) determining the l/L placement can become highly socially negotiable (very much like d/Deaf). Instead, I mostly use languaculture as an important gravitating macro concept that connects many complex themes such as language(s), culture(s), identities, social constructions, and normalcy/deviance,[4] and I incorporate languaculture in the realm of institutions such as schools.

Schools set the stage to construct a specific type of languaculture for all students (both deaf and hearing) and to provide an important opportunity for students to establish a foundation in language, literacy, identity, and in essence, what it means to be human in our nation. May goes on to contend that:

> Education—and, crucially, the language(s) legitimated in
> and through education—plays a key role in establishing and

---

4. Chapter 2 provides a detailed discussion on normalcy and deviance as they relate to the study of deafness.

maintaining the subsequent cultural and linguistic shape of the nation-state. (May, 2012, p. 132)

However, for deaf children, the challenges in defining appropriate academic, linguistic, and cultural pedagogy are contested by divergent ideologies—spoken English and ASL. In essence, the constraints and constructions of what ought to be the norm to construct languaculture in deafness is so highly contested that these discussions often lead to divisive philosophies rather than a coexisting and shared collaboration on the reconstruction of deafness. Nowhere is this kind of division more true than in the realm of deaf education.

## Warning: Deaf Education Is Not So Homogenous

Before I move forward, it is critical to remind ourselves that deaf education is not so homogenous; rather, it is quite diverse. First, there are the "paradigm wars" between two whole languages in deaf education, mainly sign language-based and auditory/speech-based educational institutions. On one end of the continuum is the ASL-based bilingual-bicultural (Bi-Bi) approach, which "emphasizes the development of the natural sign language of a community as the first language, then teaches the majority language through reading" (Moores, 2010, p. 17).[5]

To be clear, the "natural sign language" as a whole language for deaf people is ASL, but not all sign-based schools teach by means of ASL. Instead, these schools may use a mixed method such as simultaneous communication (SimCom), which is a "sign system based on

---

5. I use *continuum* as an important term because these paradigms are not intended to be dichotomous or static but, rather, indicate that language for deaf people is extremely dynamic and may vary from strictly auditory/oral to a mixed method (incorporating some speech with the signs) to complete use of ASL. Moreover, ASL is also seen in terms of a diglossic continuum where ASL itself—as a whole language—also has its own continuum ranging from formal/academic to everyday "dialects" (Stokoe, 1960; Washabaugh, 1981). In addition, there may be some points during the deaf student's larger educational journey when he or she leaves one language modality to enter another language modality or even during a particular school year when a student receives primary instruction in ASL but leaves the classroom for one-hour to learn spoken English.

the syntax of a spoken language and modifications of a sign language in instruction communication or alone" (Moores, 2010, p. 17). While ASL and SimCom are two different language pedagogies, the main focus is the usage of sign language in the classroom and often incorporates continuums of ASL as a critical component within deaf education.

On the other end of the continuum, oral/aural approaches that emphasizes auditory and speech, educational institutions place spoken English as the primary language of instruction for deaf students. The most recent data from the Gallaudet Research Institute indicates that approximately 50% of deaf children are taught through speech alone, approximately 35% through sign and speech, and 11% through sign alone (Gallaudet Research Institute, 2008; U.S. Government Accountability Office, 2011). It is not clear how much of that 35% incorporate the Bi-Bi model where spoken English and ASL are taught separately and how much use a mixed method like SimCom, but one thing is for sure: as the statistics show, it appears there is a division between the usage of two whole languages—spoken English and sign language—in schools for the deaf. In this regard, throughout this book, when I mention sign-based approaches, I refer to both the bilingual-bicultural approach and the modification of ASL in the mixed methods (combining sign language with speech) because all these approaches do incorporate sign language and, to varying degrees, ASL as a whole language. For oral-based approaches, I refer to the oral/aural approach that includes auditory and speech therapy because both rely on the spoken aspect of the English language. These two diverse "paradigms" construct unique and diverse languacultures for deaf people.

Second, Deaf students are typically placed in three major types of schools: (1) oral-based schools, (2) sign-based schools, and (3) mainstreaming schools. Students will have been placed in at least one of these types of schools throughout their academic journey.[6] Significant portions of deaf students are placed in public schools (e.g., schools where

---

6. O'Brien's (2011) dissertation uncovered data that some American students who had previously experienced mainstreaming were now in sign-based schools, and this statistic increased with the age of the students. In parallel, Karen Nakamura, in a study of deaf Japanese students, discovered that deaf students who were mainstreamed into regular elementary schools then returned to schools for the deaf at the middle or high school level (Nakamura, 2006).

deaf students are assimilated with hearing students in the classroom) or what deaf education scholars refer to as mainstreaming or inclusion (Mitchell & Karchmer, 2006). Using the 2002–2003 data from the Annual Survey of Deaf/Hard of Hearing Children and Youth, Mitchell & Karchmer (2006, p. 99) found that at least 80% of the schools had three or fewer deaf students and more than half (53%) of these schools had only one deaf student. This number is an increase from 60% in 1992 (Kluwin, Moores, & Gaustad, 1992; U.S. Department of Education Office of Special Education Programs, 2006). In 2010, Dr. Marc Marschark, Professor and Director of the Center for Education Research and Partner (CERT) says that "86 percent of deaf students in the U.S. are in mainstreamed programs all or part of the day. In many cases, they are the only deaf or hard-of-hearing student in their school" (Lividas, 2010). As of February 2011, the National Center for Special Education Research (NCSE) noted that "more than three-fourths (76 percent) of students with hearing impairments were enrolled in typical schools serving a wide variety of students" (Shaver, et al., 2010, p. 7). Despite to the varying data on how many deaf students are mainstreamed, mainstreaming is an important aspect of deaf education, but it requires levels of analysis that are different from the first two types of schools. These levels include the multidimensional memberships in the mainstreamed classroom (i.e., both deaf and hearing students), the complex criteria of social identity when deaf students are exposed as the minority (as opposed to being the full majority in a contained classroom of deaf students), the role of interpreters in the classroom setting (there are no interpreters in the first two types of school), and the general background and pedagogical instruction of the teacher (as opposed to specialized training of teachers for the deaf).

Mainstreamed students are placed in schools designed for hearing students while sign language–oriented and oral-based students are placed in specific schools designed for them. More important, the mainstreaming system does not indoctrinate deaf students with a unique languaculture. The primary focus of this book is on the first two types of schools that develop unique languacultures by means of whole languages specifically for deaf students and the ways the social constructions of languaculture play a role in the identities of these deaf students. Keeping in mind that the important background information on deaf education is heterogeneous, the introduction of languaculture at schools becomes a powerful socially constructed process that connects the deaf child's cultural identity to his or her language.[7] However, the field of deaf education has undergone major changes, including "where, how, and what deaf children should be taught" (Moores & Martin, 2006, p. 3). In addition, the current deaf education system is divided by divergent ideologies into contrasting deaf educational institutions as to how "change" should occur. For example, some deaf children enter a landscape where schools for the deaf advocate for ASL, while other deaf children enter different types of landscapes where schools for the deaf advocate for oral-based education. Each of these contradictory ideologies developed by these diverse deaf educational institutions have constructed the other as the "enemy within" (i.e., not normal and sometimes deviant), including how they teach, the language of instruction, and the pedagogy applied (Cummins, 2000, p. 3; see also Cummins, 1986; Freire, 1992/2004). This clash in paradigms not only impacts deaf children and their families but also raises broader justice issues in society as to how human values, thought, biographies, and histories ought to be constructed.

My initial negative perception of sign language is an example of the type of knowledge developed through the pedagogy of the oral school, including its teachers who reinforced speaking/hearing as the primary functions of my "knowledge." My "knowledge" constructed sign language as detrimental to my learning process, which shaped my ideological perception of what it means to be "normal" in my society. The introduction of ASL in my life was a gestalt shift that opened many socially constructed categories that I had not experienced before; these experiences will be explicated in Chapter 1. Connecting the broader justice issues to my personal experience, my constructed knowledge

---

7. It can be said that parents of deaf children are often the first to choose a specific language modality for their child; however, they rely heavily on schools to reinforce the languaculture of their deaf children, often the same "native" language of their parents. For example, hearing parents will often place spoken English as the primary language and deaf parents will often place ASL as the primary language for their child; both seek schools that share their same ideology, which in turn, shapes culture for that deaf child (Erting, 1985).

and language usage reflected the powerful social relationship I had with society, including its manifested human values, paradigms, and ideologies, which further contributes to the historical understanding of our society.

Throughout my journey, my position slowly shifted from one as a person who was deviant, needing to be fixed, into a person struggling to accept his place in the deaf community as an equal, then re-regulated to the margins between two cultures. This transformation was mediated by the reconstruction of my "ways of knowing" and by the recognition that the "types of knowledge" previously constructed were not static or universal. I thought I was going to be Quasimodo for the rest of my life and that it was my place in society to carry that burden. I struggled with spoken English, never being able to "perfect" the language and, as a result, felt as if I were deficient in the shared cultural world (full of hearing members) in the knowledge that speaking and hearing were fundamental criteria of being normal. I also struggled with sign language, realizing that what I had been signing during a specific period of my life was not ASL but, rather, a variation. This realization directly impacted how I saw myself as a deaf person, and it came with a social response from the deaf community—the well-known label, "not deaf enough." Throughout my journey, I was able to challenge some key assumptions about my deafness, about the influence of my human knowledge, and about values on society's construction of various types of knowledge related to what it may possibly mean to be normal or deviant. Throughout my journey, I have experienced various constructions of normalcy and deviance and have observed how they are embedded to contribute toward the cultural production of my everyday world. Thus, society and its social constructions may have important implications when discussing how individuals are constructed in the realm of normalcy and deviance. This examination becomes a justice issue, specifically, how society throughout sociohistory plays an important role in the framing and reframing of certain individuals in the name of normalcy and deviance.

My personal experience and the incredible influence of my langua-culture prompted the inquiry for this book to examine the implications of the ever-changing constructions of my deafness by means of language and its larger place in deaf education. The inquiry specifically examines my experiences as a deaf person, which were constructed with certain "types of knowledge" that reflected certain human interests, ideologies, and meanings of the socially constructed world. It also attempts to explicate the discourses by means of my narratives to understand how society has constructed meanings about me and for me as well as how it may possibly shape the larger schemes of the social world when discussing the future of deaf generations (Cooper & White, 2009). This book raises potential implications that can follow from attempts to influence the types of knowledge and identities produced for deaf students through a reexamination of the current history and biography of deafness and deaf education to identify and analyze emergent critical justice issues.

## SCOPE OF BOOK

C. Wright Mills (1959) has claimed that for us to study history and biography (individual and social problems), we must address (1) what is the structure of the particular society, (2) where does that society stand in human history, and (3) what varieties of humans prevail in that society? These three main questions will provide a constructive framework and serve as guiding points for this book.[8] The purpose of the book also focuses on the implications of comparative languages and cultures that construct sociohistories of normalcy and deviance; the differences from other varieties of social order, including schools; and last, the possibilities that these societies could contribute positive social constructions to humankind (Mills, 1959). In this examination, the book modifies Mills's original questions to fit the framework of this book:

- What does it mean to be deaf in today's society? (*Chapters 1, 3, 6*)
- Where have the constructions of deafness by means of languaculture been framed and reframed in human history? (*Chapters 2, 3*)
- How do some social control institutions such as schools construct meanings and human values by means of languaculture

---

8. With full permission by the journal publisher, some parts of this book have been adapted from Horejes (2009a), "Constructions of deafness: Exploring normalcy and deviance within specific social representations," *Journal of Human Development, Disability, and Social Change*, 18(2), 7–22.

to shape the overall social constructions of a deaf individual? (*Chapters 2, 4, 5*)

- What are some possible strategies, if any, for our society to develop a positive and constructive construction of deafness to "prevail" in today's society? (*Chapter 6*)

By addressing these questions, I first situate myself as a "biographically situated researcher" (Denzin & Lincoln, 2003, p. 30). As a situated researcher wanting to study the micro/macro interconnectedness of various social constructions to make sense of this world, I loosely incorporate five important phases of the research process[9] deconstructed by Norman Denzin and Yvonna Lincoln's (2003) *The Landscape of Qualitative Research*. These five phases are parts of what Prichard, Jones, and Stablein call organizational discourse analysis to contribute to the "reflective understanding of the context in which researchers find themselves" (2004, p. 213). Examining these issues and questions using the five phases of the research process is central to the design of this book. Using these research processes as guiding points on my social landscape, the findings offer a unique insight on what it means to be deaf while addressing the larger justice issues of (dis)ability, diversity, normalcy, deviance, and how human values may be constructed. The book attempts to provide opportunities to recognize sites of discrimination, differences, and diversity, while acknowledging important criteria for a successful blueprint for positive social constructions for deaf students.

Chapter 1 opens with my reflections on my personal experiences to set the stage for discourse connecting these personal experiences and the research that I undertake with their importance in human history. After all, how can the reader expect to fully grasp important concepts

---

9. The five phases include (1) situating the researcher as a multicultural subject and his or her role in research, (2) framing theoretical paradigms and perspectives for inquiry, (3) selecting research strategies as methodological orientations of inquiry, (4) choosing the ways of collection and analysis, and (5) examining the art, practices, and politics of interpretation and presentation, or making sense of my own findings and how they may contribute to the overall understanding of our social world and its social problems.

that I raise without understanding my personal experiences? It is this positionality derived from feminist and critical theory (mainly inspired by minority group politics) that reveals important points of intersection in terms of my identity, where I stand in the social landscape of today's history, and my ideological position (Banks, 1996). My personal experience for the book serves as "an important relationship between the person doing the research and the research itself" (Cooper & White, 2009, p. 168). This connection includes the realm of education as important sites of acculturation and enculturation into languaculture, identity, and deafness. This chapter draws on who I am as a writer (Ivanic, 1998), one who is hoping to make a personal connection with the audience and, at the same time, set the foundation for this book by using my personal narrative as emic data that can be made useful in etic ways—that is, articulating my data so it can become academically useful information for exploring different theoretical ideas about selfhood, diversity, and humanity.

Chapter 2 opens up my research toolbox to make sense of the primary raw data from Chapter 1, in other words, framing perspectives for inquiry. By using social constructions, I examine how languaculture plays an important role in the construction of deafness and the ways that social constructions frame (or reframe) what it means to be deaf. There is not one main interpretive paradigm that drives my method of inquiry. At times throughout this book, I adopt a Marxist form of theory by including the historical and sociocultural context (materiality) to study social phenomena, and at other times, I use Michel Foucault's poststructural theory and form of discourse to warn readers that different types of knowledge will lead to different social constructions contributing to the archaeology of knowledge, specifically, deaf education. As such, I combine both a humanistic cultural studies approach (studying the lived experiences and the actualities of people's lives including mine) and a structural cultural studies approach (the constructions of identity formations on a macro level) for this book (Denzin & Lincoln, 2003, p. 35). This interpretive approach includes examining the significance of social constructions, then incorporating the epistemology of normalcy and deviance as concepts—how by means of hegemony certain social control processes construct certain ideologies of what it means to be normal and deviant.

Chapter 3 examines languaculture in deaf education, especially how languaculture plays a critical role in defining normalcy and deviance. The chapter reveals how some social institutions, including education as a social process, shape human values, ideology, identity formation, and classifications. Examining these processes offer some epistemological justice frameworks for understanding the socially produced world via "relationships of power" to construct normalcy and deviance (Kelly, Luke, & Green, 2008, p. x). The justice issues in education are a reflection on a small scale of "the conflicting purposes and tendencies which rage in society at large" (Mannheim, 1936, p. 138f). Schools, for example, serve "as the means of social sorting and preservation of the social position of more powerful segments of society" (Gallego, Cole, & Laboratory of Comparative Human Cognition, 2001, p. 957), including languaculture to form a specific sense of normalcy and identity formations to construct what it means to be deaf. Chapter 3 looks at how specific schools use certain educational pedagogies such as the use or avoidance of sign language to contribute to the overall social constructions of a deaf child.

Chapter 4 presents my ethnographic fieldwork. Using a comparative approach and a grounded theory as methodological orientations (detailed in Appendix A), this chapter examines both empirically and experimentally the larger issue of deafness in two different types of deaf education classrooms (often muddled, and not exactly dichotomous) to uncover emergent ideologies, paradigms, identity formations, and everyday social constructions. This research is examined through comparative classroom observations, including field notes and videotape analysis rooted in grounded theory, to uncover themes of social control processes, including language use, communication modality as a "dominant" criterion of normalcy, and the symbolic interactions within the classroom. The result of using these methodological orientations to study the languaculture within the school environment builds on analytical themes such as the diverse pedagogy of languages, types of classroom culture incorporated, and the implications of diverse teacher knowledge.

Chapter 5 delves into a theoretical analysis of two visibly different classrooms—a sign-based classroom and an oral-based classroom—which examines how they operate as a site of social control processes that influence languaculture. This examination on languaculture is deconstructed into three major themes: pedagogy of language, cultures in the classroom, and the types of teachers. These themes form a framework on which the data collection was based. Studying these themes may ultimately reveal the powerful role of languaculture to shape the notion of the deaf deviant student and the deaf normal student.

Finally, Chapter 6 addresses possible strategies our society could use to develop a positive construction of deafness. These suggestions are based on the findings presented in the preceding chapters, particularly as they relate to the contested terrains of normalcy and the two different types of deaf educational pedagogies. The chapter explores the divisive paradigmatic camps in deaf education and suggests underlying reasons to develop possible strategic steps toward collaborative critical inquiry, including a closer look at bilingualism. The notion of bilingualism becomes a possible way to address the confounding challenges that arise within deaf education and to provide alternative ways to redefine the languaculture for the deaf.

The goal of these interrelated chapters is to paint a larger picture of deafness, specifically, the ways that theoretical themes such as languaculture, social constructions, and normalcy/deviance located within deaf education play an important role in the reconfiguration of what it means to be deaf.

Ultimately, exploring educational institutions and uncovering the various implications of notions between and within various types of schools for the deaf can become a positive vanguard for shifts and changes not only in deafness and deaf education but also for justice issues in society as a whole.

# CHAPTER ONE

# MY JOURNEY

I am myself plus my circumstance and if I do not save it, I cannot
save myself.
　　　　　—José Ortega y Gasset (*Meditations on Quixote*, 1914)

This chapter addresses the ethical inquiry of where I am, epistemological
inquiries of who I am, and the types of social constructions that
permeate my deafness and my identity(ies) (Lankshear & McLaren,
1993). The quote, "I am myself plus my circumstances and if I do not
save it, I cannot save myself" by Jose Ortega y Gassett postulates that
it is my circumstances that construct who I am; thus, I must first locate
myself in a social landscape in a specific historical moment—the where
I am. This ethical inquiry of the where is not necessarily confined only
to a physical location, but also consciously and historically. How can
one begin to explain who they are to the reader if the reader does
not understand the author's positionality and its relevance toward this
research? The epistemological question of the "who am I?" provides
a knowledge construction of my life, my identit(ies), and how my
circumstances shape my deafness in order to "save" (or to reveal) my
circumstances. My circumstance is different than yours—but by locating
our intersectionalities of difference, we are able to possibly see some
of the tangents of our difference into a shared understanding of our
social world. My journey through constructions of deafness, including
perspectives of normalcy and deviance, began at the age of 6 months
when my family members (especially my mother and grandmother)
noticed that I was not responding to the sounds of Gumbo, our
family dog. Immediately, they considered the possibility that I had a
hearing loss. After several visits to different doctors and "specialists,"
my family received mixed diagnoses (including one from a doctor who
claimed that I was mentally retarded), but the majority of the doctors

concluded that there was nothing wrong with me and that my parents were being paranoid. One doctor advised my mother to see a therapist because he felt that she may have acquired Munchausen Syndrome by proxy; a syndrome in which mothers continually diagnose their newly born child with disorders, ostensibly for attention and sympathy from doctors.

Several more months passed, and my mother and grandmother's intuition grew stronger. They demanded a scientific explanation for why I was not responding to certain sounds. Finally, as I approached 6 months old, the doctors agreed to run more "tests." They placed me alone in a soundproof glass laboratory room with my body wired to several electrocardiography (EKG) machines in the hope of determining what was "wrong" with me. I would later learn that during this moment, my mother started to get very emotional, not because I might have a hearing loss, but because I was being examined in a quack-type experimental manner in the name of science. My mother felt that the doctors were engaging in some sort of "Frankenstein" experiment, using fabricated tools and exerting their "scientific" authority to justify their actions. After hours of testing, the doctors concluded that I had a hearing loss and told my mother that they would need to keep me overnight for further testing. Repulsed with the way they had treated me, my mother refused, demanded that they stop any further tests, and brought me home. And thus began a new journey in my parents' lives, "one that challenge[d] their understandings of themselves as parents and of what it is to be human" (Erting, 1985, p. 230).

After confirming through science their intuition that I had a "hearing loss," questions entered my parents' minds, including Will my child be "normal"? Will my child "speak"? Will my child be able to "hear"? How can I make my child as "normal" as possible? Will my child ever be able to "function" in a hearing society? How will my child be able to go to the same school as his "hearing" sister? These questions reflected their notions of what it meant to be "normal," which was based on the ability to speak and hear. For my parents, hearing loss was an indication of a lifelong deficit; the notion of hearing was a human value and a criterion for normalcy. My identification as an individual with a hearing loss constructed the cultural reality in which I was categorized. My parents looked in the Yellow Pages under the heading, "hearing loss" and found that there was a school for children with "hearing impairments." At the age of 6 months, my parents enrolled me at Central Institute for the Deaf (CID) in St. Louis, founded in 1916 and one of the premier oral schools in the world.

## CENTRAL INSTITUTE FOR THE DEAF (CID)

For 10 years, I received oral training, including extensive speech therapy at CID, where each academic subject (e.g., math, social studies, science, and so on) revolved around the capacity to pronounce terminology within these subjects, but involved little emphasis on the context or the substance of the information being taught. The school focused on speech as Erting (2003) defines it: "the form of language most people consider synonymous with underlying linguistic competence and through which most everyday human relationships are created and maintained" (p. 374). This method would be reinforced as I witnessed my family members and hearing friends using speech as their primary form of communication and as I relied on my hearing aids to connect speech with sounds.

I wanted to be hearing like them, but I was reminded of my limitations every day, either because I could not understand what they were saying or because I had to repeat what I had just said to them. The school was not assisting me to help me "master" my speech, so my parents also became my "personal" speech therapists, correcting my speech whenever possible. My understanding of the social world was centered on the immense importance of speaking as a fundamental criterion of my wholeness as a human being, or a normal human being in accordance with my knowledge construction.

Throughout my years of speech therapy, I had a strong sense that my parents and the school were more concerned with the disadvantages of my hearing loss and my inability to speak "perfectly" than with the advantages of my possible talents (including deafness). They were more focused on classifying me by means of audiological measurement and disciplining me to become "normal" based on the criteria of their ideology. All of the teachers at CID were trained in speech therapy/pathology and showed no knowledge of sign language or experience with deaf culture. Their focus was on speech pathology. I always wore a 4" x 2" mechanical device placed in front of my chest and sometimes tucked underneath my clothes. It weighed about 5 pounds, and thick wires led from it to my ear(s) (Figure 1.1).

With the use of technology and speech therapy, the school sought to "fix" me, as if I were broken, attempting to help me to hear. I did think I was going to be a hearing person someday.

My classroom during elementary school included one or two other deaf students and was a setting where our "culture in the classroom" and independence (individual/group agency) occurred strictly between the hearing teacher and each deaf student. While I would constantly have to awkwardly look at my peer to understand what he or she was saying, that individual was always fixed on the teacher and never on me (see Figure 1.2). What is also interesting in Figure 1.2 is that the student next to me is pointing at her mouth to emphasize a certain word; it was common for us, as students, to emphasize carefully, as clearly as we could, every word that we were instructed to pronounce and, somehow, by pointing at our mouths, we gave the spoken word more authority.

The awkward seating arrangement in the classroom limited my ability to engage in social interactions with other students. However, in the private spaces such as the hallway, bathrooms, and playground, I remember secretly socializing in gestures with my peers. There was something comfortable and easy about our gestures, about conveying meaning through our hands and facial expressions. It just felt more natural than speaking. Sign language/gestures seemed to be our preferred means of communicating. Most of all, I remember the

FIGURE 1.1.   Childhood years using hearing aids for communication—my mother in the middle.

FIGURE 1.2.    Speechreading my classmate during CID.

tremendous backlash from teachers who forbade us to use gestures, as if these gestures were "evil" and an indication of deviant behavior.

Every time I displayed my resistance during class by using signs/gestures, I remember being scolded and made to sit on my hands or have them tied with rubber bands to further prevent me from using them as a communication tool. The message seemed to be that my hands were not a part of me and that they needed to be controlled. I remember the forceful hands of my teachers pressed firmly on my cheekbones to direct my face toward their face as they constantly demanded that I watch and listen to the words coming from their mouths and then to repeat the words, even when I did not comprehend them in the first place. Figure 1.3 by Susan Dupor, titled *Coerce*, brings back painful memories.

I became indoctrinated to the belief that my ears and my mouth were the fundamental instruments of my education. My notions of success equated to becoming normal and subsequently becoming a hearing person or very close to one. In 1988, CID felt that I was "ready" to enter the realm of mainstreaming where I would be the only deaf person in a public school. The instance in which I learned of this determination is a memory that I remember very vividly (my mother continues to be shocked at my recollection of this memory). During school, my mother pulled me out of art class at the basement of CID and proceeded to walk with me up a flight of stairs where she

FIGURE 1.3.   Susan Dupor's *Coerce*.

sat down on one of the steps and said that I was ready academically at third grade to enter the "outside" world. Immediately, I broke down in tears and pleaded with my mother to not let me leave CID—the only environment in which I felt safe and comfortable, being surrounded with my other deaf peers. I could see the pain on her face; she wanted me to progress academically, but sensed that I may not be ready socially and personally. She asked me, "Are you sure you want to stay here [CID]?" Without thinking twice, I said yes. She finally relented, and I went back to art class, not telling anybody because I did not want them to think that I was going to become "different" from them; I wanted us all to be on the same journey together. Two years later, CID would "graduate" me at which point I embarked on a new journey in the public school system as the only deaf child at my school.

## BOY SCOUTS AND PUBLIC SCHOOL

In 1990, at the age of 10, I still had not learned sign language. I had been taught by CID that sign language was taboo, deviant, and according to one teacher, reserved for animals, specifically monkeys. This notion was further validated when one of my first exposures to sign language in the media showed a chimpanzee signing "apple" in the 1987 movie, *Project X*. By then, my perception of sign language was validated. At the age of 10, I was mainstreamed into my new world—the local public school where I was the only deaf student through twelfth grade.

But, during the same year, I met Bill Blank, a scoutmaster with CID's Troop #132, who introduced me to another new world. I was now living in two worlds: educationally, I was immersed as the only deaf person in my public school, but socially, I was immersed with other CID students and alumni who joined Troop #132 of the Boy Scouts. I juggled these two worlds until my senior year of high school—a total of 8 years. I will get back to the educational aspect of my life later in this chapter, but first, I want to highlight some of my invaluable experiences with Bill Blank and his Troop #132.

## Troop #132

When I first joined Troop #132, I realized that I was not the only person who went to a public school. Many CID alumni would also share the same isolation as mine, being the only deaf person at their schools; we shared a camaraderie. I remembered that I was always excited for Wednesday night to come—the time when we would have our weekly Boy Scout meetings, ironically, held at CID. The location was ironic because Bill Blank along with his two assistant scoutmasters were deaf, and they communicated with us in SimCom—a combined method of signing and speaking, although during that time, I thought they were using ASL. I had no idea what ASL looked like. Especially in the CID setting, the experience of deaf scoutmasters as teachers, teaching us by means of sign language, set up a sharp contrast to what I had been accustomed to.

During our meetings, we were taught on many subjects that were specifically tailored to help us obtain merit badges in categories including (but not limited to) first aid, rope-tying, government, weather-reading, science, forestry, and zoology. I learned so much through these meetings, and the next Wednesday could not come soon enough. We Boy Scouts would play for as long as we could after each meeting while my mother waited diligently as I pleaded for "just 10 more minutes" over and over.

The troop broke down into two major groups: those who were still at CID and those who were alumni of CID. CID students stayed at the residential dormitory, and the alumni commuted home where they would enter their "other world." I was always envious of those who stayed at the dorm, wishing that I could join their lifestyle. Being able to socialize 24/7 and eat breakfast, lunch, and dinner without any communication barriers would have been my heaven! Alas, I went home to my family, to my other world, where I would use spoken English and speechread (at least as much as I could understand) my family and my friends at public school. Aside from Wednesdays, Troop #132 also trained for biannual camporees where we competed against hearing troops in our district; we were the only deaf troop (Figure 1.4). We always placed either first or second (I know Troop #98 can vouch for this claim as we were always rivals). Being able to place first or second out of as many as 12–15 hearing troops was truly inspiring.

On Wednesdays and on the weekends that we would go camping, I felt the most normal. I was no longer the minority or the outcast, but one of the group. Our languages were the same, our experiences were mutual, and what it meant to be deaf was never necessary to be brought up for discussion. Instead, we learned more about each other and our own unique characteristics, not as a deaf person, but as a human. We all learned what each of us liked and disliked as well as our

FIGURE 1.4.    Some of my Troop #132 Boy Scout friends at a camporee. *Courtesy of Rob Hatterick.*

strengths (some were better at rope-tying while others were better at first aid), which made us a great team.

During the 10 years of my time with Troop #132, I became an Eagle Scout (Troop #132 held the most Eagle Scouts of any deaf troop in the United States), rose to the highest rank of our local district as Chapter Chief, and obtained the Vigil honor with the Order of the Arrow, which is handed only to those who were nominated (without solicitations for those nominations) and considered (Figure 1.5).

While my experiences with Troop #132 gave me some confidence in myself and made me challenge my traditional assumptions about deafness and sign language, my other world overwhelmingly dominated my ideology and sense of personal identity.

### Fifth Grade and On

I was the oldest fifth grader in my school and would find out that many mainstreamed deaf students were often "held back" a few years. In fifth grade, I was placed in a classroom taught by one teacher. I thought this arrangement would be an advantage for me since I would have to rely on reading only one set of lips, the teacher's. However, I soon realized my inability to understand questions from other students. I was always in the front row of the classroom (to ostensibly speechread better).

Figure 1.5.   Me obtaining the Eagle Scout Award (left) along with my childhood friend (right) and Bill Blank (middle) giving a speech about us.

Every time the teacher would allow a student to ask a question, I would immediately look back to locate that student, and by the time I found him or her, I had missed at least half of the question. Then, when the teacher would respond to the answer at length, I would not know what the question was to begin with. It did not take long for me to realize that I was lagging in all aspects of my education.

Being placed in a public school was not an advantage, despite the benefit of having one teacher; it was, in fact, a huge burden. I had to adjust my learning strategies to fit into their system rather than the school adjusting to my specific needs and talents. I did not understand most of the information being communicated by the teacher and the students. I continually had to manage my identity to come up with an understanding and explanation of my status in a new academic environment. During recess, lunch, and travel in the hallways, I would often take off my hearing aids to "hide" my stigma as a deaf person. The possibility of being rejected as a deaf person would be too traumatizing for me, so I tried to maintain my membership in the hearing mainstream by developing an identity that was not native to me (Goffman, 1968). Most of my representation of "self" came from the hearing students as I attempted to pass as "hearing." I ran and became student council president, hoping that my peers would see me as a possible leader and president rather than as a deaf and disabled individual. Being president was a testament to show others that, although I may be deaf, I was a different type of deaf person and not ordinary. I constantly played the role of master of ceremony and gave welcome speeches for various school-sponsored programs (Figure 1.6).

During recess and lunch, I used to laugh along with the hearing students, even though I did not know what they were laughing about. I wanted to pretend that I was following along conversationally. I tried to be "normal," but I felt so alienated because I constantly did not understand basic conversations and could not pass fully as a "hearing" person. I felt that I was becoming a failed product in their hearing world. I did not have any camaraderie with most of the hearing students, except for a select few who lived in my neighborhood. However, even they were reluctant to be seen socializing with me in public. I completely understood their resistance because, internally, I had cast myself as deviant and as the "other." Being deaf was my stigma; I

FIGURE 1.6.    Giving a speech at my elementary school.

started to become Quasimodo, placed in this society to carry this burden and to be the center of others' gaze and "smile ruefully . . . yes, I'm deaf. That's the way I'm made. It's truly horrible, isn't it?" (Hugo, 1978, in Davis, 1995, p. 116). I could no longer feel "normal" with hearing people around me, particularly because I was not able to use my hands, gestures, and facial expressions to portray my sense of self. Like Quasimodo, I was often made fun of and was a target for the bullies at my school. At one point, I faced a school bully to let him know that I had had enough, and in return, I was beaten for a good few minutes before staff members could pull us apart. The bully told the staff members that I had started it, which was confirmed by a few other students. However, the staff members concluded that it was both of our faults. In a meeting with the vice principal to discuss the fight, I did not understand what the bully was saying nor did I understand the vice principal. Nonetheless, we were dismissed and told to resume the day as if nothing had happened. The hallways were clear; the rest of the students were already in their classrooms, and as I was proceeding to walk back to my classroom, I broke down crying in the middle of the stairs. Coincidently, my hearing sister, who was in third grade at the time, was on her way to another classroom to give a teacher a note. She saw me on the stairs crying. I did not expect to see her, and I tried to hide my tears and told her to forget about it. Fifteen minutes later, my sister entered my classroom crying; she also was carrying this burden with me.

Both in school and at home, I was becoming increasingly iso-lated emotionally and socially. I was still struggling with my deafness and often asked God why he put a deaf person like me on Earth and whether this plan was his idea of a sick joke. My local school saw that I was failing fifth grade and intervened by calling the local special school district representative who initiated my first Individualized Education Program (IEP). My IEP would outline my academic goals, including speech therapy, social skills development, and individualized tutoring, to ensure that I would catch up with the other students. According to an "electroacoustic analysis" by my audiologist, I was a

> visual learner who uses an interpreter to comprehend the spoken word in a combination with lipreading/speechreading of the speaker. He does receive adequate amplification from his hearing aids as reported by the audiologist. Thomas voices for himself but signs to the interpreter for a preferred sign or for clarification. He effectively uses the interpreter to process information from lectures and discussions, and as needed in small group discussions, and one-on-one conversations with staff, teachers, and peers. (analysis from the Special School District of St. Louis County IEP)

I would attend speech therapy once a day for one hour every day while the rest of my peers would attend their music class; apparently, the school did not think that I needed music training since I was deaf, and therefore, the school practitioners concluded that music was not my "thing." I loved music, but not in the "normal" sense of music (Figure 1.7).

On top of my academic-related homework, I also had speech therapy homework in which I had to practice certain words with my parents daily. Although I was present at the IEP meeting to assess my failures in the public school system, I understood nothing since it was moderated by these "specialists" speaking for me and about me rather than soliciting any input from me. Their behavior made it seemed as if the school were more "concerned about the primacy of the role of experts—physicians, psychologists, administrators, social workers, and educators in devising the IEP"—than in what I wanted (Fleisher & Zames, 2001, p. 185). The school district mandated that I get an ASL interpreter for my classes.

Figure 1.7. Using headphones connected to the piano and playing a musical instrument.

Both my parents and I vehemently disagreed with having an interpreter sit in front of me and "interpret" for me due to my "hearing loss." My parents and I reminded the school that we had been told that ASL was ineffective for an oral student like me and that it would be counterproductive. Also, I was already distraught enough with my personal struggle with deafness; the last thing I needed was more stigma and more reason to be ridiculed. Ironically, during this time, many other parents of deaf children (notably on the more progressive East Coast) were fighting for their right to have an interpreter for their child.[1] Nonetheless, we came to an agreement that the interpreter be oral with no use of ASL and that I would wear a cigarette-pack shaped audiological device known as an FM system very visibly around my neck while the teacher had a microphone to transmit sound. Now, I had a FM system attached to my two already visible hearing aids. I felt that the addition of the interpreter to

---

1. In 1982, the U.S. Supreme Court in *Rowley v. Board of Education of the Gloversville Enlarged City School* decided that public schools did not need to provide interpreters for deaf students. This sent shockwaves to many parents of deaf children fighting for their right to have their child be provided an interpreter. Later court decisions muddled public school's obligation to provide an interpreter and there was no clear enforcement; finally, in 1990, the Americans with Disabilities Act was passed, specifying under Title II that all public schools must provide accommodations, including interpreters, on request.

my already technological self (hearing aids and FM system) would serve to solidify my deviant identity just in case it was ever in doubt.

My IEP would later state the following:

## 2. PERFORMANCE LEVEL AND GROWTH:

Thomas has good speech intelligibility, but needs to be careful to monitor his speech when with teachers and peers. He needs to continue to receive maintainance [*sic*] speech-language services to monitor classroom intelligibility with teachers. Teachers this year have not noted any difficulties with Thomas' speech. Intelligibility has been maintained at 80%. Teachers report that Thomas is an excellent student who is eager to learn. cooperates [*sic*] and willing [*sic*] participates in all classroom discussion. He is a prepared and organized student who is very aware of the adaptations needed due to his hearing loss in order to achieve academic success. He is doing A work in all classes. Periodic discussions by the Itinerant teacher of the Deaf with Thomas and his teachers has insured that adaptations/modifications are met in the regular classroom and that staff is aware of the impact Thomas' hearing loss has on his academic performance and comprehension of material. (from the Special School District of St. Louis County IEP)

Was I really aware that adaptations (i.e., speech-language services) were *needed* to achieve academic success? I never would really understand how and in what ways that "staff is aware of the *impact* Thomas' hearing loss has on his academic performance and comprehension of material" (emphasis mine). Did they mean that the degree of the modification of speech-language has a direct determination on my academic performance? If I was failing a subject, was my speech-language a part of the issue? Was my "intelligibility" based on speech by means of spoken English as a language? In what ways was I supposed to be "careful" to monitor my speech? Was it not intelligible enough? According to whom? How was my intelligibility "maintained" at 80%? Finally, although I relied on an interpreter, this fact was mentioned nowhere under my performance level and "growth" section of the IEP. However, accepting an interpreter would be a major turning point in my journey to reconstruct my own deaf identity in a positive way.

After meeting Leslie, the interpreter, I made it very clear to her, several times through a series of meetings, that I did not want her to sign and that all translations from the teacher would be oral. The first day the interpreter showed up "for me" was a complete embarrassment; it seemed as if I needed an interpreter to make me whole. I felt so deviant since I was being told to rely on an adult to help me reason and function in my classroom. Making the situation worse, the representative from the special school district, who would later be assigned as my academic tutor (or what the IEP called "Itinerant teacher for the Deaf"), spoke for nearly 10 minutes to the entire class, explaining my hearing loss and the purpose of the oral interpreter. According to the IEP, she would provide "introductory inservice training to all students' instructional staff . . . and classroom demonstration regarding hearing disabilities to grade level peers."

She talked about me to my grade-level peers as if she knew me better than I knew myself, and the other students in the class easily adopted the notion that I was incapable of speaking for myself. She left out all the pain and sacrifices I had made to "fit in" to the classroom and, instead, explained that I had a "hearing disability" and that the hearing aids, the FM system, and the interpreter were necessary to make me successful—as if I required these foreign accommodations to successfully "complete" me. By speaking for me, I felt that she, "the expert," attempted to take on the role of my identity as if I were incapable of explaining who I was as a deaf person. Her presentation was a missed opportunity for her, a hearing individual, to educate the other hearing students and teachers that being deaf was okay.

Soon thereafter, I realized that only I could reconstruct my identity in a positive way. I informed her that she was dismissed from her duties as a tutor and that I never wanted to see her again. This instance was the first time I tried to claim authority in terms of my issues. This burden was mine only to keep, and I alone should decide how it ought to be presented to the rest of the world. During my adult years, I went through my old IEPs and would soon learn that my "teacher of the deaf" also provided "consultation" each week to instructional staff members regarding my "hearing disability," including "(1) Hearing disability/audiogram; (2) Preferred mode of communication; (3) Impact of hearing disability on academics; (4) Environmental adaptations necessitated by hearing loss; (5) Amplification and use of residual hearing; (6) Impact of hearing disability on speech/language development; (7) Literature/articles/newsletters regarding children with hearing disabilities included in general education classroom; (8) Notetakers, captioned films, TTY; and (9) Interpreters, interpreting services" (from an IEP from the Special School District of St. Louis County).

Most of the annual goals involved my "hearing disability" and "speech" as major criteria of success while the interpreter (the most important accommodation for me at the time) was dead last and described only briefly. If there were any literature/articles/newsletters regarding children with hearing disabilities as a "guideline" for staff members to use, I would assume that it was sure to be presented in a one-sided view based on the medical language and IEP being framed in the medical model.

All the while, the oral interpreter proceeded to mouth word for word what the teacher was instructing. Having an interpreter as a third party to my educational learning was a new accommodation that I had never before experienced. The constant speechreading through which I was still able to catch only less than half of what she said proved to be a disaster. I also found myself falling asleep toward the end of the day after intensively speechreading what I could, guessing other words, and connecting the words I could understand to make meaning. A classic example involving you as the reader comes to mind. Go ahead and fill out the words in blanks:

> The problems that confront p _____ in raising
> ch _____ from in _____ to adult life are
> not easy to s_____. Both fa_____ and
> m _____ meet with many d _____ in their
> concern for satisfactory pro _____ from the
> e _____ stage to later life.

Are your words the same as the words below?

> The problems that confront **poultrymen** in raising **chickens** from **incubator** to **adult** life are not easy to **solve**. Both **farmers** and **merchants** meet with many **demands** in their concern for satisfactory **production** from the **egg** stage to later life.

This example is a classic exercise given at many "deaf sensitivity" workshops to indicate that speechreading is guesswork and requires a lot of creativity. My experience was no different in the classroom. Additionally, the FM system was ineffective; daily, I would get static white noise—caused by things such as the microphone rubbing against the teacher's shirt or his breathing—which would startle and distract me.

After several months, the interpreter could see that the current method of accommodation was not effective and subtly offered to sign while mouthing the words. I obliged. I had nothing to lose; I had hit rock bottom, so I figured I would try sign language, with the expectation that it would also fail me. As I look back now, I wondered whether my "teacher of the deaf" played a role in communicating with my current interpreter to make that adjustment (as suggested in the ninth responsibility listed for her above).

Ironically, I embraced sign language in my other world with my other deaf friends, notably during Boy Scouts, but I did not think that it was functional to place sign language in the hearing-dominated world. As soon as the interpreter started signing, I knew that it would be a major distraction for the other students, but I no longer cared since I had become used to being deviant. I would continue to read the interpreter's lips while picking up the signs attributed to the speechreading. Once she started signing, I could tell immediately that the students were quickly drawn to the signs as some sort of alien language. For me, the immediate impact I had with sign language in my educational instruction struck in the core of my consciousness as a deaf person. I had almost forgotten how important signs and gestures were to me during my childhood at CID, but because I was the only deaf student in my public school, I did not think to demand that the public school incorporate sign language into my academic program. I was now able to really understand what the teacher was saying. I was actually learning! No longer was my ability to comprehend speech used to measure my academic success. It was now a question of how well (and how fast) I could learn sign language that would determine my academic success. I took off the FM systems and never looked back.

I started to embrace sign language as an integral component of my academic instruction, deaf cultural identity, and perception of normalcy. Sign language not only had an emotional and educational impact on me but also gave me more leverage as a "normal" person. I was no longer struggling to adapt to the hearing society, but rather, by using sign language, I found avenues to enable the hearing society to adapt to me. My confidence soared and sign language became my "special" weapon, as if I were somehow equal in different ways (often personally feeling superior) to those hearing students. I also could feel that they looked at me as uniquely different in a positive rather than deviant way. This change would be validated as many of them would come up to me asking me how to sign particular words. I would have a unique relationship with some of them by communicating with them through signs. My school started asking me to perform poems and songs in sign language in front of the entire school. In fact, during the end of fifth grade, the music choir learned a song using some sign language and performed this entire song not only to me and my parents but also to other students' parents, school administrators, and the superintendent of the entire school district. Interestingly, the song was about "love in every language," and it was sung in various languages, including German, Italian, Spanish, and ASL, as though ASL was equally as important as the other languages!

I found success through sports and extracurricular activities. Now, I was finally "speaking" back and feeling normal. Suddenly my horizons were broadened and my two worlds and languacultures merged: no longer did I commute my deaf identity from two worlds; I was integrating my identity in both worlds. At the end of fifth grade, I was the goalie of my undefeated soccer team. I remember vividly trying to be the best athlete on the team so I could prove to my hearing friends that I was as good as them, if not better. This determination would also reflect in my academic performance. I strove to earn high scores on all tests and assignments because I needed to constantly remind all hearing people that my deafness was not a "bad" thing and was, perhaps, an advantage. Deafness was no longer my disability; I no longer felt disabled. Now, I was normal, accepted, and natural. Of course, looking back, there were a few experiences that were powerful enough to shift my sense of normalcy back to viewing my deafness as a deficit.

When I entered sixth grade at Ronald E. McNair in 1991, I was assigned to a homeroom teacher who was hard of hearing at best (I was still not sure whether the school consciously placed me with this teacher on purpose), but it proved to be a disaster. The teacher would express to me his frustrations as a person on the margins (neither hearing nor deaf) and his distaste for the "rest" of the world, and he asserted that he and I would become comrades. My classmates constantly mocked him, made comments that he would not understand, and in a way, cast him as deviant. As a result, I tried to disassociate myself from the teacher. When that did not work, I explained to my parents that I wanted a different homeroom teacher. After a few meetings with the administrators, I was reassigned to another teacher with whom I felt much better emotionally, but I still was not happy with my surroundings.

Although I was assigned a new homeroom teacher, I would have different teachers with different peers in each subject. I was more comfortable with my deaf identity in certain classrooms but was not comfortable in other classrooms, depending on the teacher and the peers. I often found that I felt more comfortable with female teachers, and many of my peers were girls who appeared to be sympathetic to my "hearing loss." Nonetheless, I would regularly pretend that I was sick with some sort of stomach muscle cramp and make my mom pick me up so I could avoid having to deal with my school. I was looking forward to Brittany Woods Junior High school because I knew sports was an important influence at the school, and the better you were athletically, the better your reputation at school. That sports focus could be an opportunity for me to use my athletic skills as leverage to become "normal" and to mask my deafness. An emphasis on athletics seemed to be my game plan, but then, something major happened in 1991–92 that would make my deafness a far less important precursor to my identity—the Rodney King beating (1991) and the trial itself (1992).

While the Rodney King beating occurred during sixth grade, racism was not a big issue, but entering junior high school in seventh grade, it seemed a whole different world. I was now entering a school whose population included mainly Black people (nearly 95%) while the rest were White. Before entering junior high school, I never thought about race as a part of identity formation. It just never factored in my mind; identity had always been centered on hearing versus deaf. This new intersection of oppression opened my eyes to new worlds. My peers and I were more aware of racism, the historical oppression of Black people, and the power inequality in society.

The Rodney King situation produced a heightened awareness of racial issues at the school. I now became a double minority, deaf and White, which posed a few advantages and disadvantages for me that I constantly had to negotiate as an individual. The more I aligned myself as a deaf person, the more I was "connected" with my Black friends as being a part of an "oppressed" group and a minority at large. It made sense to me: if I interacted with my White friends, then being White was "cancelled out" and what was left was my deaf identity. Thus, I sat with my Black friends most of the time on the premise that we were all members of an "oppressed group," regardless of how, and my deafness would be masked. This strategy worked to my advantage; I would sit with my Black friends nearly every day during lunch (which would continue throughout high school). They were much more tolerant of my deafness than my White peers. I learned to play Spades and Craps (allowed back then) and learned to dress like them and talk like them. I gained a lot of respect from the majority of my school. When I won president of the Student Council in seventh and then in eighth grade, my closest competitor who was White came to me and directly said that the only reason I won was because I was deaf and that they voted for me out of pity. I suppressed that specific moment and denied it, but today, I do wonder.

High school was similar to junior high school, but the race issues were much more intensified as I left a school of about 400 students and entered a school of nearly 1,500 students. Many of my White friends with whom I grew up went to private schools, and my parents were determined that I would have a better education at these private schools than at the public school. However, when I found out that these private schools would not provide an interpreter, I immediately defended myself to my parents and emphasized that I needed an interpreter to understand and learn academically. I was empowered enough to voice my own accessibility needs and my parents respected that.

At my high school, I continued to be a "double-minority," being among the 5% of White people at the school. My parents initially saw the public school as a disadvantage to my learning, but it became a tremendous advantage, both academically and emotionally. My Black friends and I were not privileged, did not have power, and did not live within the dominant ideology of what was normal, and we knew it. This mutual understanding is what led to a shared camaraderie and respect for one another as human. There were some problems, though. When it came to athletics at my high school, race became a major factor. I enjoyed playing basketball and football, but those sports were traditionally reserved only for Black people. If you risked playing these two sports, then you risked stigma. I wanted none of that. One of my White friends played both basketball and football; his nickname was "Snowball" and he appeared to embrace that moniker. Instead, I played soccer (4 years), wrestled (3 years), and played tennis (2 years)—sports that were reserved for White people. It is safe to say that I made varsity on all of those teams basically because we did not have a junior varsity team or any competition among those in the "White" sports (Figure 1.8).

In high school, I felt the most normal ever. I was content with my integrated identity: my identity with my hearing world (academically, athletically, and socially) as well as my deaf identity in my deaf world through Boy Scouts and with many deaf friends who were also mainstreamed at other high schools. There were times when I would have to drive 20–30 miles just to meet with deaf friends; we rotated locations where to meet up and were notorious for staying up during the wee hours, talking and catching up. We did not have the luxury of telephones to converse during the week, so weekends were our opportunity to catch up and to get our "deaf fix"—sign language. While

Tommy is known around school for his achievements on both the Varsity Soccer and Wrestling teams. Outside of school, Tommy is an active Boy Scout, earning the prestigious Eagle Award at age thirteen. To get the award, Tommy volunteered nearly forty hours of community service, planting various flowers throughout U. City.

freshman   SPOTLIGHT

FIGURE 1.8.   Blurb about myself in my freshman high school yearbook.

there were times that we would communicate by means of TTYs, the conversations were very one dimensional and did little to fulfill our need and desire to catch up face to face and, again, to use sign language. Before long, it was time to enter the realm of college.

## ARIZONA STATE UNIVERSITY

College was a whole different ballgame. As a senior in high school, I visited three schools that I was interested in and was accepted to. One of my top (if not *the* top) criteria for a school was its accessibility. What good was my education if I did not have access to it, I thought to myself. This insight was something I would have not figured out earlier on in my deaf education. At this point, I knew I did not want to endure the politics of accessibility that I had so far had to mediate to arrive at where I was today. Thus, the first people I met with at these schools were the disability resource specialists who would be in charge of my accommodations, specifically, ASL interpreters.

At one of the schools, one specialist was blind and another was a person in a wheelchair. I remember immediately disassociating myself from them because I did not want anybody else to "speak" for me; however, I felt that I had no option—until I visited the third school, Arizona State University, whose specialist was a deaf person who was fluent in ASL. I felt relief knowing that I would not have to take the same path that I had taken before, having the "other" speak for me. Of course, later on, I would soon realize that many specialists, regardless of disability, were able to understand the importance of an ASL interpreter as an effective accommodation, but I did not know it at the time. I was being very guarded about what I wanted in terms of access.

Once I met with the specialist at Arizona State, she informed me that I would be having lunch with a few other Arizona State students who were also deaf; I was shocked. "Arizona State has deaf people?" I asked her. I thought that all (if not most) deaf people went to either Gallaudet University or Rochester Institute of Technology, which most of my St. Louis friends had attended. She smiled and said that Arizona State had approximately 40–50 deaf people who used

ASL interpreters. I was flabbergasted! I knew I was home once again, despite being among strangers. As long as they were deaf, I was home (Schein, 2003).

I knew this transitional moment from high school to college would be scary, and I did not know what to anticipate because my transition from CID to public schools had proved to be traumatic (and continues to be to this day). That summer, my entire family and my grandparents took a road trip from St. Louis to Phoenix. After arriving in Phoenix and unpacking all my stuff, to be housed in a dorm at Manzanita Hall full of hearing students whom I had not met, I was ready for whatever I would face.

I still felt guarded and wanted to get beyond my first experience with an interpreter in a college class. My first interpreters were Lori and Patty. Their signs were quite different; I was shocked by their fluent and natural ability to sign. I had never encountered interpreters of that caliber. I had never met any deaf person of that caliber, let alone an interpreter! I asked where they got their training in sign language, and they both looked at each other and smiled, "We're Codas." Puzzled, I asked, "What's a Coda?" They answered, "Our parents are deaf. We're Children of Deaf Adults. Our first culture was the deaf culture." Holy shit! Adults who had hearing using sign language and acknowledging that they belonged first in the deaf culture?! It was at this point that I realized my positionality as a deaf person was so far away from "the" deaf world and that my "deaf world" was actually an in-between world. I was not fully deaf yet. This realization was affirmed when I learned that my "ASL" (also spoken by my Troop #132 scoutmasters and my deaf friends in St. Louis) was actually PSE (Pidgin Sign Language) and that I was more closely aligned in the hearing world than in the actual deaf world. There were some hearing people that were more "deaf" than me out there (Mudgett-DeCaro, 1996).

I found myself reverting to the hearing world—the world that I felt I knew the most, not necessarily the most comfortable. Thus, I joined Sigma Nu, being the only deaf fraternity member, but took a lot of pride knowing that all 50+ active members of the fraternity unanimously accepted me as a brother (if one dissented, I could not become a brother). It was during this time that I met my future wife, only we did not know it at the time (we would get married nine years later). When we first met, she asked what was with my accent, and I told her that I was deaf. She did not believe me, saying that she had met a few deaf people before and none spoke as well as I did. I proceeded to show her my two hearing aids and jokingly asked, "Do you think I would wear these hearing aids to pretend that I am deaf to impress you?" She was convinced. I also hung out with mostly hearing people. Although I knew there were a large number of deaf students, I stayed away from them, but did occasionally become involved in some of their Deaf club meetings (Collegiate National Association for the Deaf) and functions. I was going back to being a commuter—commuting between both worlds, leaving one identity behind as I entered a world. I still relied heavily on my fluent interpreters to convey academic information, which was one of the few connections to ASL and the world of sign during this time.

It was toward my junior year in college that I would meet Pat, who would become a lifelong mentor for me. I took his "Political Deviance" course and remember clearly that he was very reluctant to accept me as a student because he felt that the interpreter would not be capable of capturing essential information and effectively being able to convey it to me. Although he would not admit it, I think he was concerned that I, as a deaf person, could not succeed in his class. After I aced the midterms, his concerns went away and he realized a lot of things. I became empowered as an equal, but that did not last long.

I decided to apply to study abroad in Ireland for one year; I got accepted to University College Cork, and all of the courses I took there would fulfill all of the credits I needed to graduate with a B.A. from Arizona State. I had gotten initial approval from Arizona State, and they were going to provide and pay for an interpreter. Things were looking up until a few months before my departure to Ireland, when I got a letter from Arizona State deciding to reject my request for accommodations to study abroad in Ireland for one year. The letter still encouraged me to go and proceeded to outline how much money I would have had to pay out of my pocket for these inter-preting accommodations—a total of $30,000. This traumatic experi-ence immediately crumbled any notion that being deaf was a positive gift. I was shocked that Arizona State would view this opportunity as a financial burden and that it would consider that anybody going to study abroad representing the university was a bad thing. I was immediately back in the mind-set of having a disability, realizing that they were looking at the financial "hardship" of having to provide an interpreter rather than looking at the potential positive benefits of my being able to study abroad. I was extremely angry at myself, at God (once again asking whether this situation was his idea of a sick joke), and at the rest of the world. I was no longer successful and no longer "normal," and I felt that I was just an expendable commodity. My dream of studying abroad was gone, but I finally collected myself to write a complaint to the Department of Education, Office of Civil Rights; surely, they would side with me and cast Arizona State as being wrong by unethically overlooking my human gifts and justifying their actions in terms of only financial reasons. Legally, I felt that the Americans with Disabilities Act (ADA) of 1990 could have been applied to my case because ASU was my primary university and the International Program office [IPO] was run by ASU. All of the credits I would take in Ireland would be considered ASU credits. I could not understand why ASU ought to be exempt from the ADA even though I would physically be in Ireland, my credits and my financial payments were being paid directly to ASU, not overseas.

A few months later, I got a copy of a letter[2] (sent to me as a third party) from the Department of Education, which was addressed to Dr. Coor, then president of Arizona State University. In it, OCR described my situation in detail, saying that I had applied for the Study Abroad Program at University College Cork in Ireland, had been accepted, and was expecting accommodations to be made for an interpreter but had been turned down by Arizona State. However, after studying the situation, OCR analysts had concluded the following:

> Upon reviewing the information provided by the complainant and the University, as well as current OCR policy information, and available case law, it is OCR's determination that Section 504 and Title II protections do not extend extraterritorially.

2. The full letter can be found at http://www.nacua.org/documents/OCRComplaint_SignLanguageInterpreter.pdf

> In other words, it is OCR's position that neither Section
> 504 nor Title II requires the University to provide auxiliary
> aids and services in overseas programs. Nor does either stat-
> ute otherwise prohibit discrimination on the basis of disabil-
> ity in overseas programs. As such, we have concluded that
> the University's refusal to provide and or pay for interpreter
> services for the complainant while participating in the Study
> Abroad Program in Ireland is not prohibited discrimination
> under the laws OCR enforces.

I thought to myself, "What in the hell is going on here?" I would have to
bear the expense of these interpreter services—something that a college
student could not afford. I would learn much later (approximately 8 years
later, in 2009) that the letter became a standard for other universities to
follow, but I did not know until later. Immediately, I felt that I was
being put in my place as a disabled person and told not to challenge
long-standing policies that I felt were not justified. It was then that I
realized how powerful ideological beliefs were—not only of certain
individuals who questioned me at first but also of larger institutions such
as schools and much more powerful institutions such as the Department
of Education, Office of Civil Rights, the same institution that was
supposedly established to foster justice! During my senior year, I became
a realist real fast; I had to stop worrying about my stigma on a microlevel
and start figuring out how I was going to make it in the real world,
which was full of Kafkaesque processes that would continually speak for
me and claim authority over my life. I envisioned myself getting a job
and having to "educate" everyone else that I was just normal, but at the
same time, fear that I would be their Quasimodo. I considered passing
as "hearing" and not requesting any type of accommodations to get by,
but I realized that I would lose valuable information. Was it worth the
sacrifice? It was fifth grade all over again.

Pat saw my frustrations and convinced me to apply for my masters at Arizona State. He knew I was not done with Arizona State
emotionally. Once I got accepted, he became my academic mentor.
During these two years, he carefully and slowly helped me realize that
I was not the problem; it was the social circumstances that continued
to exacerbate my disability as being a problem. Throughout the many

nights of long conversations in his office and home, he was able to help me deconstruct my identity; by doing so, I was able to analyze the deep-seated ideologies that I had established pertaining to who I constructed myself to be. Pat provided me with academic resources and then discussed at length with me these important theories and concepts to make the connection between the academic and my personal understanding of myself.

## Work in the Deaf World

After my masters in Justice Studies, I was ready to work, but I no longer wanted to associate myself with hearing people because they had abused me to the point where I could not handle it anymore. I was ready to encounter the "deaf" world. I wanted to work for (and with) deaf people, so I moved to California to work as a community advocate for one of the largest deaf agencies in the United States, which proved to be a very powerful experience for me. Almost everyone at the agency was deaf—the CEO, the human resources director, the payroll specialist, and even the janitors. I was baffled, but in a very good way. Whenever I had a payroll issue, I could easily go to that person and converse in sign language; my office had no telephone, but it had video phones that enabled me to contact an interpreter virtually to make calls; and my office door was equipped with a "doorbell" that would flash the lights in my office to get my attention. My job was entirely accessible, and the main form of language used in my workplace was ASL. I would provide speeches in ASL for work-sponsored events. I was breathing ASL everyday (Figure 1.9).

It was about time! I was not disrespecting my primary language— Spoken English—but I felt that ASL needed to play a larger role in my life and that I needed to have better "balance" in my two worlds. I was tired of being viewed by deaf people as someone who was privileged because I could speak. I also vowed that I would never use my voice; I operated in "voice off" mode. I wanted to be enculturated entirely into the deaf world as I never had before. Whenever my coworkers and I went out for lunch, I always ordered by writing on paper, gesturing, or pointing at the menu. Since the deaf community was so small, I also hung out with my coworkers socially during nights and weekends. I

FIGURE 1.9.    "Speaking" in front of an audience.

was "passing" as deaf and it was working well; I was finally home again, so I thought.

I ran into an old friend from Arizona State who was visiting a coworker. This person immediately saw a different side of me and asked why I did not use my voice. I tried to quickly comment that I no longer needed my voice and changed the subject. No such luck. My newfound deaf friends immediately asked whether I could speak, and I signed, "I used to." They probed as if they wanted to know where I stood in terms of a deaf identity within the deaf boundaries, just as my parents had first imagined similar questions to see where I stood within the hearing boundaries. Apparently, my deaf friends had fallen short in "screening" me to determine whether I was welcome in their boundary. Often, when meeting for the first time, the first question deaf people ask of other deaf people is where they went to school. This question serves as a criterion to determine "automatic" membership in the deaf world (Padden, 1980). They had not asked me for that information, until now. "So, did you go to a deaf school?" They used a specific sign for school to denote institution—indicating an important emphasis of a state deaf school containing residential dorms and in which it is assumed that ASL is used. I answered that I had gone to a deaf school (signing the same sign they did), which was technically right since CID did have residential dorms. Then, of course, they asked a second question, "Which school?" so they could see whether they knew anybody from that school to make the "deaf" connection and to identify me as a deaf person. I said that it was in Missouri, and immediately, they said, "Oh, Fulton, Missouri?" where the state school for the deaf was. I knew my answer to this question would answer many questions and open the floodgates to other inquiries of my selfhood. "No, in St. Louis," I replied. "Oh my god!!! You went to an oral school! You can speak!" exclaimed my friends in a mix of shock and bewilderment as to why they did not "catch" this fact earlier. My friends proceeded to list a few of my childhood friends whom they had met in other circles (mostly from National Technical Institute for the Deaf at Rochester Institute of Technology) and asked whether I knew them. I said yes, at which point they immediately said that since those people were all very "strong" oral, you must be too! My "passing" as deaf was now "spoiled"; I started to be (re)relegated once again to the margins.

One coworker confided in me, and she asked, "Can you really speak good? Like a hearing person?" I said, "Yes, but not like a hearing person. I can speak *enough if I have to*," signing the last four words with emphasis. She replied, "I'm jealous. I wish I could speak like that. You have a gift, Tommy. Don't let them get into you." I understood what she meant, but at the same time, I did not want to show my privilege. A few days later, word had spread at work that I could "talk." I still ignored this chatter and proceeded to try to "pass," hoping this awkward situation would go away. During lunch one day at a restaurant, this same coworker who had supported me proceeded to sign me her order and requested that I verbally give her order to the server in front of my other coworkers. At first, I said that I would not speak for her. She was adamant and said, "Tommy, if I had this ability to voice, I would use it. Do not be stubborn." I caved in and voiced for her, which was the first time I had used my voice in front of my coworkers. The server nodded as he acknowledged the order, and my coworkers stared in amazement as if I had performed a magic trick. It was now official. I no longer was in the margins but, rather, was a deaf hearing person and/or a deaf person who could speak.

Previously, I had not worn hearing aids while working for the deaf company, which had been a personal testament that I could "purge" my "sounds" out of my brain, no longer have to wear hearing aids, and finally feel "natural" again—without "adding sounds," a feeling similar to a drug addict finally being free of the need for drugs. Not using my hearing aids during this time had been completely overwhelming: physically, all my life, my brain had been accustomed to receiving sound (static) signals from my hearing aids, so when I took them off, my brain reacted to the absence of these sounds, which caused mild vertigo. Emotionally, however, I felt I could now be seen as human, not as a cyborg or a robot. Feeling relegated once more to the hearing boundaries, I put my hearing aids back on and my vertigo went away, but I no longer felt natural anymore. I continued to advocate for my deaf consumers, who did not seem to not care about my "new" hearing aids as long as I could do my job. They also did not seem to care about their newly found discovery that I could talk and would use my voice while advocating. Let me explain.

During work, I had been struggling to make progress with hearing agencies by means of interpreters over the video phone (video relay services). Many of the hearing agencies were confused with the interpreter as the "third party" and could not directly identify with me as being in a position of authority to deal with business-related issues. For example, I would have a deaf consumer who had a question about his credit card bill, and I would proceed to call the credit card agency, through the interpreter, on the behalf of the deaf consumer. Almost always, the agency representative would state that he or she could not divulge information about the consumer (which I could understand, but what other choice did I have?). After I would explain at length the whole process—about the purpose of the relay service and that the interpreter was there as a third party and that I was an advocate for a deaf consumer—we could finally get down to business. The process sometimes took 30 minutes and I had only 1 hour maximum for each consumer per day. Also, this third-party route was not always effective because the agencies would question my ability to discuss terms such as equity, certified deposits, prorated interest, and so on.

However, that awkwardness would soon change when I requested a voice telephone for my office and began using it to conduct business with hearing agencies for my deaf consumers. Instead of having the interpreter sign for me, I would use my voice, speaking directly to these agencies, and the interpreter would sign back to me what they were saying. Often, the agencies had no idea that there was a third party (interpreter) present. I was sad to realize that my ability to advocate improved specifically by making progress with these agencies much more quickly. I started to speak and sign at the same time to interpreters who mingled around the building. Also, my consumers gained renewed respect for me when they found out that I could speak; my sense of privilege was at work once again—or so I thought, until I was called to the CEO's office.

The CEO graduated from Gallaudet University and had a PhD. I had respect for her, and she carried a reputation of being fierce and blunt. I had an idea what the meeting was about. "So, Tommy, I learned that you are using your voice in this building?" I explained the reasoning why I used my voice for consumers and clarified that the interpreters on the video phone were also interpreting my voice so the consumer was also able to understand effectively what I was saying. This explanation seemed to reassure her just a little, but she made it extremely clear that there was a zero-tolerance policy on voicing. I would be allowed to use my voice only for that particular type of scenario, but I could not use my voice while I signed to deaf and/or hearing coworkers. It was then that I realized this place no longer suited me, so I began applying for different jobs (in both the deaf and hearing worlds) and to different universities (for a PhD), including Arizona State. (Apparently, I was not done with them.) Arizona State immediately replied, saying that they would offer me a "full-ride" tuition-waived four-year ticket along with a graduate assistantship with a doable financial stipend. They had me sold.

As I prepared to leave for Arizona, what had been an amazing 1-year experience with the agency in California was marred toward the end by two coworkers. We had developed a close friendship before they found out my background as a person who could talk, at which point, they concluded that I was "hearing" (using the sign for "hearing," not over the chin, but in front of the forehead to indicate that I was a deaf person who wanted to be hearing—that I was a hearing wannabe when in fact, I really wanted to be accepted as deaf. In this aspect, they also classified me as a deaf wannabe—here they placed me once again on the margins of not being fully accepted in both worlds. Their conclusion was a major blow to my identity as a deaf person. I was being told by these two coworkers (both of whom had gone to deaf schools and had graduated from Gallaudet University) that I was "not deaf enough." I had lost two potentially good friends because of boundary maintenance. One of the last things I did before leaving the agency was an exit interview with the human resources director. I told him everything—my struggle to "pass" as deaf, finding myself once again relegated to the margins, tiptoeing along the borderlands only to be pushed into the hearing boundaries by my coworkers with whom I had once confided. The human resource director sat there in amazement; "I am so sorry, Tommy. I had no idea." I said to him, "Now you know. Thank you and good-bye." Arizona State, here I come.

## Arizona State—Again

Once arriving at Arizona State, I realized immediately that I needed my hearing aids back again. I had "tested" myself to see how long I could last before getting vertigo without hearing aids and had pushed my threshold. However, without the aids, I found myself either speaking too loud or not loud enough or not being able to speechread (the little bit of sound I heard with the hearing aids helped tremendously with picking up words). Becoming a cyborg once again by using my hearing aids on a daily basis, I met with Pat and told him that I did not want to talk about the Ireland episode and was ready to make sense of all this craziness that I had gone through all my life. He planted a seed that would grow into my dissertation. My dissertation, with his guidance, became a self-fulfilling journey into my life to make sense of its circumstances.

As Pat provided guidance, he advised me to first explain my "story" through my own eyes and then to provide theoretical ideas to help explain the oppressive implications of my experiences, including growing up in school as the only deaf student. I never imagined that I would be able to really examine how my story, as primary data (emic), could be made explicit (etic) so it would make sense to others. Now, I was able to really try to "tell" my story in a way that did not have a negative tone (as I would have done a few years prior) but, instead, could provide a healthy platform for discourse on ideas and themes that would make sense to the reader. There were times where the writing became too emotional and Pat would instruct me to slow down and take a break. The dissertation was the result of Pat's being a patient, open-hearted, and mindful mentor to an often lost, frustrated, and embattled student trying to make sense of his "disability."

Toward the end of my dissertation, I came to realize that my deafness was a gift to me (as opposed to the world). My dissertation was a much needed enlightenment about my life. Looking back during this time throughout my doctoral phase, it was Pat's unselfish dedication, incredible patience, and immense support that made me realize that he was genuine—that he was not just helping me because he "had to" but because he truly wanted to and he cared about me. Most of all, he had faith in me and, in retrospect, gave me faith and encouragement every step of the way. The product of the dissertation is now this book. With his help, I got hired at Gallaudet University. Apparently, I was not done with the deaf world either.

## Gallaudet University and Beyond

I first arrived at Gallaudet in 2010 with my wife, my mother, and my mother-in-law. I had to pick up some paperwork to fill out from human resources and was going to be quick, so they stayed in the car. As soon as I left the car, I took off my hearing aids. I was going to try to "pass" as a native deaf person. After all, I was now at Gallaudet University, the mecca of the Deaf! The first impression I made on people was not going to be one of a faculty person who wears hearing aids! After being greeted in ASL by a few people at human resources, I proceeded to obtain my paperwork and went back to the car where my family was awaiting. My wife saw me put my hearing aids back on and inquired, "Why'd you take them off?" I told her that she would not understand and that I was right for not using the hearing aids on campus. As it turns out, she was right to question me because she wanted to understand my identity and where I situated myself at Gallaudet University—I was still managing my identity (Goffman, 1968) that I was still working on as a deaf person at Gallaudet.

When the semester started, I was shocked to see the wide array of identities on the campus. The faculty, students, and staff members represented every system on the communication continuum—from fluent ASL to oral only. I also saw many people using hearing aids and cochlear implants. This Gallaudet was not the Gallaudet that I grew up envisioning. That Gallaudet was a radical school that denigrated anybody who used any form of technology and that promoted the "ASL or the highway" philosophy. This image of Gallaudet soon went out the window, and I realized that Gallaudet was not as homogenous as I had thought.

When I arrived in my first class, I was met with an ASL interpreter, and I immediately told her that I would be using ASL and that an interpreter was not necessary. I had relied on an interpreter for 9 years in the academic classroom at Arizona State, so I was quite proud to become "independent" from a third party. The interpreter quickly said, "Oh, Dr. Horejes, I realize that, but I am here to voice interpret for a deaf student." I was baffled, "I'm sorry, Ma'am, what kind of interpretation does this deaf student need?" The interpreter proceeded to tell me that the student was hard of hearing and that he would rely on voice to understand my lectures.

My world turned completely upside down as I thought, Where the hell am I now within my boundaries? I had assumed that teaching and being immersed at Gallaudet University would solidify my positionality as centered in the deaf world. In addition to the student who needed a voice interpreter, I had students who wore hearing aids, had cochlear implants, were new signers, had attended state deaf schools, had deaf families, and were from other countries. I realized that my boundaries were forever fluid and that I had been looking for my identity in the wrong places. There was never going to be a static and discrete home for my identity as a deaf person. It was a surprising realization to make, especially at Gallaudet.

Embracing and accepting this part of my consciousness, I have since taught various deaf-related courses such as "Sociology of Deaf People" and "Multicultural Perspectives: Contesting Identities in Deaf Education." Describing my personal experiences with deafness as being fluid, it was my goal to share and help students realize this valuable lesson, which I wish I had learned a long time ago: that being deaf is forever a dynamic and ongoing mediation of boundaries. The constant discussions on what it means to be deaf in my classroom were reflective of realizing that constructions of deafness were fluid. I often would share with my students my emic experiences on what it meant for me to be deaf. I have been told directly by several students that I was not deaf enough because I wore hearing aids (see *Hearing Aids Are Not Deaf* by R. A. R. Edwards, 2010), but after informing the student that I used hearing aids to help minimize my tinnitus, her perception changed; my choice was no longer a purely attitudinal choice. That recent discussion about my hearing aid was a small reflection of the many different assumptions that deaf people make when discussing identity.

Gallaudet University is also in the midst of a cultural and identity transformation. There are unprecedented numbers of new signers entering Gallaudet with the hopes of gaining an education, learning sign language, and negotiating their long-standing identity in their new social surroundings. The arrival of many new signers has been a welcome sight for some students, but for other students, it has been seen as a threat to their cultural boundaries. In my second semester teaching at Gallaudet (2010), there was a controversial article published in the student newspaper, *Buff & Blue*, titled, "Who Is Gallaudet?" The author, Elena Ruiz, raises an inquiry: "Why are we wasting our time kowtowing to the needs of ASL-inept and unwilling students rather than taking them by the collar and demanding to know why they are infiltrating our cultural grounds with their spoken language and visible resistance to ASL?" Ruiz speaks of Gallaudet as a deaf space that requires "language immersion at all times. Cultural representation at all times. No more wasting time coddling the hearing students or the Deaf students victimized by the hearing system who are not yet fluent users of ASL. It is time to rise up and unite, to recreate Gallaudet as a deaf embodiment."

However, what Elena Ruiz may have failed to understand is that a deaf embodiment is in itself a social construct and that many deaf individuals will experience embodiment quite differently as this chapter about my own life experience has indicated. The variety of deaf embodiment was affirmed by the deputy to the president and the associate provost for diversity who responded to the article by hosting an ongoing Dialogue on Language and Communication at Gallaudet. Educational backgrounds of those attending varied from deaf schools to mainstreaming programs. Linguistic backgrounds ranged from deaf people who were fluent in ASL to deaf people who were new signers to hearing students who were fluent in ASL. The narratives by various students during the dialogues were so dynamically diverse, their embodiment so unique, yet many shared a common thread— the importance of their language in their culture. The dialogues were set up in groups of five to six peers with one facilitator in each group. Each group discussed shared issues such as what ought to be the "climate/culture/community" of Gallaudet, which invoked different responses from students, including the lack of support or welcoming environment for new signers/ASL learners; fear of the loss of ASL and deaf culture as a result of inclusion, mainstreaming, and cochlear implants; and the need to respect all cultures and language abilities. One recurring theme that I observed was the impact of language on deaf culture and how their language represents a unique embodiment of what it means to be deaf. Gallaudet has an opportunity through the Dialogue on Language and Communication program to reveal the different ways that each deaf experience, including language and culture, contributes to the overall social construction of deafness; it is the collection of these experiences (emic) that can be incorporated into theoretical themes (etic) to organize these important experiences and reach a greater understanding about what it means to be deaf. More importantly, understanding the socially constructed embodiment of deafness and the impact of languaculture serves to create awareness of what it means to be deaf. This book continues these inquiries.

When visiting my deaf community in St. Louis and my friends from Troop #132 who have remained in St. Louis all this time, I have been asked why I have not gotten cochlear implants. These friends have also noticed my signing becoming more "fluid" like a "native" deaf person. I remember thinking that by being involved in Troop #132, I had solidified myself in the deaf world, but then I realized that my deafness became contested depending on my situatedness. No matter where I went, my cultural boundaries would shift, but the major factor in these shifts was my manipulation of language—whether I chose to use ASL, spoken English, or a variation of both. It was the usage and maintenance of language that made my culture malleable.

Looking back to my journey between the two worlds and its intersections, I wondered, if I had learned ASL earlier on, how would have my life been different? What social constructions would have developed? If I had not met Bill Blank, what would have become of me? If I had not gone to work for a deaf agency, how would I have understood the importance of entering the margins and then coming back into particular worlds? How would my positionality at Gallaudet have shaped my understanding of selfhood? So many questions!

Being positioned in a certain boundary contingent on time and place surely was important in addressing these questions. For example, my parents got a letter from the director of CID in 1984 saying that the "FDA approved an electronic ear implant" (now known as the cochlear implant), but it was not recommended for children. However a few years later, they switched their stance, and today, more than 90% of the children at CID have at least one cochlear implant.

If I had been born later, I may have gotten a cochlear implant, and that experience would have constructed me differently. If I had not decided to stay at CID for two more years and had gone on to public schools, who knows? I may have left the deaf world and immersed myself as a complete hearing deaf person. These possibilities are some of the contingencies of the social that might have socially constructed my identity and what it meant for me to be deaf. Throughout my journey, I realized that I am who I am because of my circumstances including experiences I have actually had.

# CHAPTER TWO

# SOCIAL CONSTRUCTIONS

If you ask any American to describe men, you are likely to get responses such as "masculine, strong, athletic, aggressive, breadwinner" as descriptions of the "normal" male. But if you add the word *gay* to the question, you are likely to get answers that describe a "gay male" with words completely the opposite of the traditional perception of a man and, instead, resemble descriptions of females such as "feminine, sensitive, emotional, and non-athletic" as the "normal gay male." If men or gay men go against the "bingo checklist" of their socially constructed identity, they are perceived as deviant (Rubington & Weinberg, 2008).

If you ask any American what he or she thinks about the word *deaf*, you are likely to get answers such as "unable to hear," "unable to speak," "uses sign language as gestures," "lives in a silent world," and so on. Just recently, I asked my deaf students in an "Identity and Culture" course to write a few sentences on what being "deaf" meant, and almost all referred to being deaf as being unable to hear, not in a negative way, but rather as a matter of fact, thus, reverting to the medical model for these ontological definitions of deafness.

More and more Americans are viewing cigarette smokers as deviant and "uncool," but these same socially constructed labels were assigned to nonsmokers in the 1950s. What do men, gay men, deaf people, and cigarette smokers have in common? They are members of socially constructed categories that have changed throughout our history and will continue to change depending on culture as well. James Banks's *The Social Construction of Difference and the Quest for Educational Equality* crafts how certain groups with labels such as race, mental retardation, and giftedness "are socially constructed categories . . . used to reinforce the privileged positions of powerful groups, established practices, and institutions" (Banks, 2000, p. 23). Thus, social constructions are powerful, yet critical to understanding our social world. Social constructions play an integral role in ideology by defining norms, values, ideas, and language.

Many members of deaf culture have a positive emic construction of their identity, but it is the dominant etic construction that often casts them as deviant (Reagan, 2002, p. 44). These etic constructions include paternalism and deficit thinking and are driven from the medical model while emic constructions include a focus on deaf people as a part of a cultural and linguistic minority. It is this paradigm clash that continues to dominate conversations about deafness and what it means to be human.

James Gee uses color as a social construction to show how something so visual such as color "in the physical world is a spectrum of continuously graded shades running into each other with no discrete boundaries . . . [yet] in every language there is a *prototype* (or typical instance) associated with each basic color term" and that each culture has its own ways of "cutting" off colors as an absolute based on certain social constructions of what color ought to look like (1993, p. 272). Gee uses the Dugmun Dani language in New Guinea as case in point to indicate that in their language they only have "light/bright" and "dark/dull" as their basic color terms while the English uses 11 levels as "cutoffs." Gee's point was that we socially construct meanings including something so fundamental as color as ideological concepts. He then uses this language construction to illustrate that language becomes an important driver toward social constructions to construct culture (languaculture), ideological assumptions, values, and in essence, what it means to be human. Social constructions permeate, maintain, and reinforce certain ideas and values about language and culture for deaf people, that is, which language ought to be the "norm" and which language is attributed to "success." The maintenance of language, in turn, influences the type of culture within any specific group, generating what is referred to as languaculture. The notion of languaculture and its contribution to socially constructed categories of deafness is a recurring point throughout this book. The goal for this chapter is to demonstrate how language and culture are socially constructed with the help of two concepts: normalcy[1] and deviance.[2] Studying langua-culture and its social constructions in turn reveals certain ideological assumptions about what it means to be deaf. This chapter focuses on five major topics: (1) examining the significance of social construc-tions; (2) connecting the useful exploration of normalcy and deviance as a concept; (3 and 4) applying the framework of social constructions, first to disability, and then to deafness, including the regulation and maintenance of languaculture by means of normalcy and deviance; and (5) exploring social constructions in a discursive and critical approach for developing positive social constructions.

## Significance of Social Constructions

Before considering normalcy and deviance as concepts that regulate and maintain a social construct, it is necessary to first define social constructions. Social constructions are knowledge bases (epistemology) that create the larger consciousness of a reality, or what I could call ideology. Ideology—the study of ideas—is rooted in paradigms, or theoretical framework of a discipline consisting of theories and laws, and in its knowledge framework. This knowledge framework is socially

---

1. Some American reference works have found that although "normality" is the preferred word, "normalcy" is also accepted. Like Lennard Davis (2002), I use the -cy form rather than the -ity form of the word because the -cy denotes a political state usage of the suffix (e.g., democracy, aristocracy, and plutocracy). Throughout this book, I use Davis's (2002) definition of normalcy to mean a process of "the political-juridical-institutional state that relies on the control and normalization of bodies" (p. 107). In this book, I include institutional state schools as also being part of that process. Normality refers to the "alleged physical state of being normal" with little emphasis on the political and/or social connection to the nor-malizing process (Davis, 2002, pp. 106–107).

2. Throughout this book, I use Lauderdale and Amster's definition of deviance as "[d]eparture from social *norms* [emphasis added]; traditionally defined by soci-ologists and psychologists as the violation or transgression of *norms* [emphasis added] and expectations" (2006, p. 123). Deviance consists of ideas on abnor-malcy, lacking "norms," a deficit, and/or possessing characteristics that do not "fit" in the categories of normalcy. In this respect, normalcy and deviance cannot be separated; thus, the purpose of and relationship between the terms *deviance* and *normalcy* throughout this book becomes important.

produced by a group—as a form of epistemology—to "make sense" of its everyday world (Habermas, 1972).

By examining the features, processes, and characteristics of ideologies and their paradigms, one does not need to look beyond the social constructions and epistemology that permeate them. These epistemological properties vary in diverse cultures, countries, and histories as they shape humankind. In addition, they are what Ferdinand de Saussure (2006) calls "signifiers" in that they represent symbols and epistemological makeups of individuals. Once a signifier is established in a specific time and place, it almost always proceeds to change, though usually very slowly; more important, it actually becomes what it signifies and, ultimately, becomes a paradigm. A paradigmatic shift in a social construction usually requires what the signifier represents to change. For example, the Earth (as a signifier and epistemological property) used to be flat (signified as a social construction) but now is round; groups reconstructed what had been signified as flat so it was now round by redefining knowledge and its epistemological properties (Commerson, 2008).

Thomas Kuhn used the duck-rabbit illustration (see Figure 2.1) to show how meanings of objects can shift; the same object (signifier) can be seen (or signified) as either a duck or a rabbit. By looking at the nose on the right of the figure, you can see the rabbit, but if you turn your focus on the nose on the left of the figure, you can see a duck.

These two epistemological paradigms (duck and rabbit) are reflected depending on the knowledge and types of evidence that are primarily given and regulated. More specifically, the figures or the lines enable a

FIGURE 2.1. Thomas Kuhn's duck-rabbit optical illusion.

gestalt shift that allows the viewer to perceive and signify the environment as either a duck or a rabbit, even though the environment (the signifier) remains the same. For example, if you were to turn the figure 90 degrees counterclockwise, you would see a different angle of the duck-rabbit optical illusion (Figure 2.2). The signifier (the figure) has remained the same, but it becomes signified differently. Do you now see a small human face staring at you on the upper side of the figure?

Thus, social constructions become important (and dangerous) when studying any social phenomena—whether they involve colors, figures, or identities of people (e.g., male, gay, deaf)—because they contribute to our ideologies.

Social constructions include (but are not limited to) shared norms, values, belief systems, social consciousness (and false consciousness), social phenomena, social institutions, and culture that becomes *situated* to the type of knowledge that in total constructs the social reality of our society and its meanings. Meanings include what ought to be considered normal and what social practices are idealized within that society. These meanings are reflected throughout history and have gained "great suggestive power" (Waldschmidt, 2005, p. 192) situated in specific histories and specific contexts.

Figure 2.2.   A different angle of the duck-rabbit optical illusion.

Within each social construction, the type of knowledge situated in the historical setting becomes the major force that drives the overall construct of reality (Mannheim, 1936). To study this type of knowledge, one must locate the epistemic forces that create these knowledge constructions. Using these epistemic forces then, one can deconstruct how social constructions become important features of ideology in numerous ways. George Herbert Mead (1934) used social interactions as symbolic representations that enable children to socially construct the "other," and Goffman (1959) used stigma to indicate how, despite trying to manage their social identity to be presented to the world, the labeling of someone as discredited socially constructs their (spoiled) identity. Other scholars use madness (Foucault, 1965/1998), capital (Bourdieu, 1992; Marx, 1867/1996), rationality (Weber, 1968), solidarity (Durkheim, 1893/1977), race (Ladson-Billings & Tate, 1995; Montagu, 1997), writing (Derrida, 1974), sexual orientation (Butler, 1993; 2000), and disability (Delvin & Ponthier, 2006; Mercer, 1973; Oliver, 1990). These examples used epistemic forces to provide explanations of certain processes and mechanisms that contribute to a social construction of a social phenomenon in society. Through these epistemic forces, these social constructions become powerful mediating forces within a framework.

For this chapter and book, I select the notion of normalcy and deviance as epistemic forces by which to fully comprehend the social construction of deafness. Studying the permeating changes of normalcy and deviance as concepts provides ways to understand the type of knowledge socially constructed in society and to explore how social constructions are created and maintained through the powerful roles that normalcy and deviance play. In this respect, the notion of what ought to be normal (and in turn deviant) helps construct the "types" of norms, what values are "good," and what ideas are considered important to the overall social world. In essence, these epistemological paradigms based on certain social constructions produce and reproduce ideology.

## Theoretical Ideas in a Social Construction: Normalcy and Deviance

Throughout history, there are many examples of individuals who have been categorized through various constructions and social representations: some individuals have been categorized in the name of race (e.g., the "one-drop rule" for African Americans by which having only a drop of African American blood would make one an African American), ethnicity (the blood quantum laws for American Indians), sex (having certain physiological properties), and disability (having limitation in a major life activity). Others may be categorized by social constructions in the name of religion (Christianity, Judaism, and Islam in the Middle East and Catholicism and Protestantism in Ireland/ Northern Ireland), location of origin (Hutu/Tutsi tribes in Rwanda), and social status (Confucianism's four divisions in China) to name a few. These social control processes and social representations influence the constructions of normalcy and, at the same time, construct ideas of deviance. The measurement of normalcy may also be attributed to physical, intellectual, emotional, economic, social, physiological, and societal influences as forms of social representations and societal dynamics (Davis, 1995).

The concept of normalcy is rooted in the "ideal of a 'well-mixed' distribution of people within the social environment, a distribution that can always change" depending on the current power relations of that era (Waldschmidt, 2005, p. 195). This change process permeates new moral boundaries of deviance and often moves certain people to reassigned boundaries of abnormality while others return to the center of society or the centered axis of normalcy. At the same time, moral boundaries of deviance are redesignated with newly constructed definitions of normalcy.

Simultaneously, societies also construct the ideology of abnormalcy with specific sets of constraints (i.e., biology, physiology, intellectually, and so on). These boundaries are developed not only through careful documentation but also through ostensible examinations as valid casual inferences to reach toward (proclaimed) validity. Validity is then transmitted through social control agencies and institutions. These institutions then situate the body or objective subject as a strategic instrument to perpetuate the types of discourse through moral boundaries and their movements. These boundaries, then, become formalized through a documentation of reality, whether through medicalization or legalization of societal norms. In the end, the documentation of validity becomes a site of social control through which social stratification is used as a strategy to construct the "order of things" in the name of ideology at that given time. That order of things, however, is continually changing by means of paradigmatic shifts in our social consciousness (Marx & Engels in Bunge, 1999).

For example, Peter Conrad and Joseph Schneider (1992) examined how medical institutions, in the name of science, continually re-created deviance designations. In Conrad and Schneider's book (1992), *Deviance and Medicalization: From Badness to Sickness,* they used several case examples, including the changing definitions of alcoholism and homosexuality, to examine changing moral boundaries of deviance. In addition, they pointed out the significance of "medical ideology [as] a type of social control that involves defining behavior . . . because of the social and ideological benefits accrued by conceptualizing it in medical terms" (p. 245). The medical professionals determined whether the patient was "dangerous," or "sick" and how to provide "treatment" that served as "social control functions . . . including roles as information provider, gatekeeper, institutional agents" (p. 244). This process allowed the medical professionals to redefine alcoholism and homosexuality as a disease, a societal condition, a "natural" process, or some combination. Specifically, during the 1960s, the American Psychiatric Association (APA) classified homosexuality as a sexual disorder in the *Diagnostic and Statistical Manual of Mental Disorders II (DSM II)* (APA, 1968). In the *DSM III* (APA, 1980), homosexuality was classified as Homosexual-Conflict Disorder, replacing an older label—Sexual Orientation Disturbance (Conrad & Schneider, 1992, p. 208). These sociologists claim that, by associating homosexuality with the term *disorder,* the APA continues to perpetuate the current perspective of homosexuality as being far from anything on the normalcy spectrum and that the homosexuality label is still categorized in the current *DSM IV* (APA, 2000) despite APA's stance that it is no longer a "disorder." Presently, the APA includes the diagnosis of "Sexual Disorder Not Otherwise Specified" for someone with persistent and distress about his or her sexual orientation.

Currently, the objectification and normalization of the regulated or re-categorized individual through regulations such as the DSM enables institutions and their agents to become "specialists" (i.e., medical and legal social agents). Specialists play a shared role in the classification of these individuals that further shapes ideologies of normalcy. The power-relationship between the "normal" and the "deviant" becomes part of the hegemonic process supported by relevant institutions, agents, disciplines, vocabularies, and types of discourses that arise from oversimplified dichotomies (Lauderdale & Amster, 1998). Hegemony is one type of social control that allows ideology to shape and form dominance on the "order of things," including what it means to be normal (Nader, 2002, p. 47). Annamarie Oliverio and Pat Lauderdale (2005) explain:

> Hegemony is an order in which a certain way of life and thought dominates, in which one worldview permeates customs, politics and religion, especially their intellectual and moral connotations. In simple terms, hegemony involves all the processes and strategies which develop a society's (or the world's) 'common sense.' (p. 157)

To be sure, the notion of normalcy is not examined as "good" or "bad" social control processes, but rather, these processes contribute to our ideology of normalcy, and these ideas become "common sense" for certain apparatuses. The regulation of influence and authority by means of power and knowledge suggests that "this influence is expressed both in the concepts and institutional arrangement of the social structure," including normalcy (Feinberg & Soltis, 2004, p. 50). Antonio Gramsci, (1971) who developed the concept of hegemony further, uses "ideological hegemony" to note that these constructs of normalcy and deviance become "common sense" and objectively given. Thus, the "hegemony of normalcy" becomes a theoretical idea with which to examine the various social control processes embedded in the cultural production of the everyday world in critical historical moments (Davis, 1995, p. 49).

Again, social constructions consist of knowledge bases (epistemologies) that shape ideology. Particularly, ideology is rooted in paradigms that drive its knowledge base as a social construction. Thus, one of the many ways to study social constructions is to look at the notion of normalcy and deviance in terms of theoretical ideas. What it means to be normal and deviant in a certain historical moment provides an opportunity to study the social processes of epistemology and how it ultimately permeates ideology as well as its social constructions.

As people enter legal, educational, and medical institutions in America, they are often categorized as a case, client, and commodity that can be calculated, divided, and documented. These populations, then, are defined and constructed into a legal, educational, and medical discourse attributed within the categories of normalcy in the name of ideology. The constructions of normalcy become a social control process, and there is "probably no area of contemporary life in which some idea of a norm, mean, or average has not been calculated" (Davis, 1995, p. 23). The configurations of normalcy, although in different disguises in various historical eras, continue as a paradigmatic mechanism and permeate theoretical ideas of progress, ideology, and the order of things. For example, craniometry of the normal and abnormal skull in the nineteenth century was replaced by intelligence testing for the twentieth century as a means by which to configure normalcy (Gould, 1996). Normalcy also plays a role in the time and place of the historical era; for example, a Black woman in Africa does not experience racism until she sets foot in America, and there was a time and place in which Irish immigrants were not considered White (Johnson, 2000). Race, in this aspect, becomes a socially constructed category using the features of the skin as an epistemological property and as objectively given.

These epistemological properties influence the constructions of normalcy and deviance. Thus, the measurement of normalcy is attributed to physical, intellectual, emotional, economic, social, physiological, and societal influences as epistemological properties (Davis, 1995). The epistemological definition of normalcy varies with respect to the time and place of the historical era. It is not frozen in time but, rather, is a chronotope, a time-space matrix that governs the meaning of narratives and other linguistic acts (Bakhtin, 1981). Thus, an examination of normalcy and its ever-changing epistemological properties is a chronotope and a part of the ongoing discourse on justice, humanity, diversity, and deviance (Horejes & Lauderdale, 2007).

Expanding on Banks's (2000) approach to examine social constructions of difference (particularly race, giftedness, and mental retardation), I add the following case examples to show the mechanisms and social processes situated to craft certain type of epistemic knowledge and its social constructions:

- African American individuals in the 1600–1800s were each counted as only three-fifths of a person when officials tallied the total population of each state (for electoral purposes). This approach reflected a view that African Americans were lower in the ranks of the human race because of their physical ethnic features, despite having the same biological properties as other humans. This view also justified the legalization of American slavery and the common ideology that African Americans were inferior to Whites. For Whites to aid and abet escaped slaves as they attempted to go to the North was considered unlawful under the Fugitive Slave Laws of the 1850s, but a few years later, slavery itself became the crime (Lauderdale & Amster, 1998). Even after slavery ended, Paul Broca, an anthropologist, used craniometry (measurement of brain skulls) as a measurement of intelligence among various races and concluded in the name of "science," namely, quantitative empiricism, that African Americans had lower intelligence than Whites. Broca's work in 1873 would be validated by medical institutions and would further reinforce the hegemony of normalcy, that is, what it meant to be an African American.
- Michel Foucault studied how medical institutions were able to use negative ontological descriptions of certain individuals to maintain "reason" during the Classical age. Foucault uses the Paris Hôpital Général in 1656 as an example of medical institutions' ability to use their power and knowledge to determine the types of correction and medicalization directed toward those who were poor in Paris. With their power of authority, the medical institutions were able to "confine" certain groups that were considered not a part of the "administered society" (Foucault, 1965/1998). This type of social control seeks to regulate the individual by means of a system of institutional experts authorized to isolate, modify, and provide health standards they define and administer as a strategy to further increase their own domination as a medical authority. Foucault also pointed out that during the Renaissance in fifteenth-century France, madness was ontologically regulated by a narrow

definition of what it meant to be "mad" during an era of "reason" through the use of power/knowledge in the criterion of "truth" (Rabinow, 1984, p. 142). In this respect, the notion of madness and reason are socially constructed as binary opposites. Those who were classified as "mad" were confined in the hands of a "semijudicial structure, an administrative entity . . . with the already constituted powers" within the legal institution in the name of reason (Foucault, 1965/1998, p. 40; Rabinow, 1984, p. 125). In Michel Foucault's *Discipline and Punish* (1977/1995, p. 26), this form of power and control exercised over the "mad" subject "is not conceived as a property, but as a strategy, that its effects of dominion are attributed not to appropriation, but to dispositions, maneuvers, tactics, techniques, and functionings [*sic*]." Thus, the human body or "political technology of the body" is disciplined as a tool and mechanics of power that is a "diffuse and multiform instrumentation" of control (Tagg, 1988, p. 70). Also, the constructions of reason and madness are categorized as a site of social control in an attempt to "maintain the coherency of the conflicted/fragmented subject" in his or her pursuit in defining normalcy (Erevelles, 2002, p. 25).

- Mohawk Correctional Facility is an American institutional facility dating back to 1825 when Oneida County, New York, constructed its poorhouse under the public welfare system as a refuge for society's homeless paupers. It later housed criminals, physically handicapped persons (a word they used during this era), epileptics, "insanes," and other disability populations. Through time, this facility became specialized with specific treatments for various categories of deviance. During this period, public attitudes toward "feebleminded" people began to change, linking them with crime. For the "insane," the Utica State Lunatic Asylum was created in 1837 and then followed by special institutions for the blind and for deaf mutes in the early 1900's. As a result of a huge societal backlash against "institutions" for containing certain populations as a form of "progress" and the staggering economy resulting from World War II, the facility specialized for the next 50 years in services only for those with severe mental retardation (a word that would be considered extremely offensive today). In 1988, in response to a rising population of criminals, it became a medium-security correctional facility (Prison Talk, 2004).

- H. H. Goddard, who is considered the father of intelligence measurement and who introduced the term *moron*, relied on the Intelligent Quotient (IQ) as a measurement of intellectual normalcy and as a "manifesto of conservative ideology" (Gould, 1996, p. 376). He relied on a scientific measurement called the Binet Scale to determine IQ and established a testing program on Ellis Island, New York, to measure the intellectual levels of immigrants. Goddard concluded that immigrants were more feebleminded than the American White population. His project resulted in high numbers of deportations and inspired the Immigration Act of 1924. As then-President Calvin Coolidge signed that Act, he proclaimed that "America must be kept American" (Gould, 1996). This IQ measurement through the Binet Scale (and placement of normalcy in the socially constructed Bell curve) not only further defined immigrants as "feebleminded" but also would serve as a standard measurement to identify people with questionable disabilities for which many were sterilized during an era of eugenics in the 1920s, supported by then-President Woodrow Wilson and the U.S. Supreme Court (see *Buck v. Bell*, 1927; *Williams v. Smith*, 1921). Numerous states still have eugenics laws (Lombardo, 2009). The Binet Scale, now modified as the Stanford-Binet Scale, is still used in some states as a scientific measurement to determine whether one qualifies for the death penalty (a person with an IQ of lower than 79 is not considered eligible for the death penalty because death in that situation is considered "cruel and unusual punishment" (see *Atkins v. Virginia*, 2002). In this respect, the quantified claim of intelligence serves to provide sites of power and opportunity for categories that deviate from that central locale of "average" intelligence.
- Jean-Jacques Derrida comprehensively discusses human exploitation through the apparatus of writing and uses the Nambikwara Brazilian tribe to portray how the European settlers dehumanized and exploited the tribe (see also L. T. Smith's *Decolonizing Methodologies*, 1999, for a similar comparison of the indigenous populations in New Zealand). Using the tribe as objects of social

control, Derrida deconstructs their speech to their inability to write "as a leap, as the instantaneous crossing of a line of discontinuity: passage from a fully oral language, pure of all writing—pure innocent—to a language appending to itself graphic 'representation' as an accessory signifier of a new type, opening a technique of oppression" (Derrida, 1974, p. 120). In this respect, the notion of "writing" became a site of social control and a staple of "civilization." As a result, these indigenous societies that do not possess the ability to write (as a feature of normalcy) have been measured as incapable of functioning and reasoning and cast as the "other." Derrida also has examined how language has been used as a mechanism of multiple signifiers that have become a product of meaning, the order of things, and values. Thus, writing became a measure of what it means to be normal and "civilized."

As these examples indicate, the construction of normalcy is shaped by hegemonic processes at important historical moments (Ladd, 2003). The regulations of epistemological properties serve as a tool for social control institutions to shape the boundaries of the "status quo" within certain populations to maintain a particular hegemony. Once an individual is categorized in a specific population, she or he is assigned a defined set of rules and norms to maintain her/his current role. Theoretical ideas such as the boundaries of normalcy offer ways to examine how social constructions as a framework become critical in studying social justice issues. Social constructions include gender (Code, 1991; MacKinnon, 1994), race (Banks, 1996; DuBois, 1897; Hooks, 1994), class (Merton, 1968; Sutherland, 1949), gender/race/class as intersecting social constructions (Bettie, 2003), disability (Oliver, 1990), blindness (Scott, 1969), and mental retardation (Mercer, 1973). This hegemonic process that constructs epistemological claims includes the population of disability and deaf people as social constructions (Horejes, 2009a; Horejes, 2009b, Lane, 1995).

## SOCIAL CONSTRUCTIONS OF DISABILITY

Disability has been studied under many different socially constructed models, especially medical, educational, and legal apparatuses. It is significant to note that "until the 1980s, historical assessment of disability came almost exclusively from those outside of the disability community: educators, doctors, and policy makers" (Burch & Sutherland, 2006, p.128). Thus, for more than 200 years, the politics of disability has become an archaeology of knowledge controlled and researched by nondisabled people. The archaeology on disability has been socially constructed predominately from an ostensibly static and discrete perspective (Sayer, 1992, p. 178). The epistemology of disability, as part of the attribution of normalcy, is connected intimately to an ideology of humanity and selfhood.

The classifications of disabled individuals start as soon as they are born; the medical institutions (i.e., hospitals) immediately rely on scientific measurements as an "objective" measurement to modernize and normalize the sociohistorical identities and diversity of disability. This type of scientific knowledge is ostensibly founded "on a rational, empiricist, objective, and seemingly enlightened approach" (Collins, 1999, p. 272) to diagnose and control these populations. These populations are readily labeled, mislabeled, examined, and documented through rigorous standardizations, including the diagnosis as a biomedical norm often that needs to be "fixed" in time and place. Frequently, ostensible methods are developed with the goal of finding "cures" or "remedies" to enable categorizing individuals closer to the realm of normalcy in the name of the specific ideology of what is normal. The "specialists" in the medical institutions rely on the examination of scientific language and research as well as reconstructions of the "historical, archaeological, ethological, and philosophical wealth of information" (Derrida, 1974, p. 28) to shape disability in the name of normalcy.

The examination is a social control process of normalizing the disabled individual into a case, a client, and/or a commodity that can be fixed, divided, and documented (McIntosh, 2002). Furthermore, the examination is disciplined through power and control to scientifically construct disabled people in a medical and legal discourse historically and biologically. In *Discipline and Punish* (1977/1995), Michel Foucault explains that bodies are rendered docile when being manipulated or, analyzed, and they become powerless to the forces of authorities who are trying to control them. This process is accomplished by placing deaf, blind, physically handicapped, mentally ill, and other persons into one category (disability) without considering their unique identities and their cultures as important priorities. Also, these individuals with specific disabilities, including deafness, are objectified into one particular category without appreciating possible differences (e.g., some may benefit better with sign language while others may benefit better with auditory/oral approaches and their preferences of assistive listening technology). Some scholars in the Disability Studies field contend that the medical and legal institutions normalize the body using specific terminology, which is often stigmatizing (DePoy & Gilson, 2004, p. 17; Horejes & Lauderdale, 2007; Hughes & Paterson, 1997).

For these scholars, the stigmatization of the people with disabilities by a school of "experts" also constructs certain knowledge about disability as a necessity for intellectual, social, and economic frameworks in the legislative agent of government as an ideological state apparatus (Brown, 2003; Hughes & Paterson, 1997; McIntosh, 2002). It is not the disability of the body that is being focused on but, rather, the scientific power to describe the physical body as a target for the exercise of power. Hughes and Paterson (1997) purport that "disablement has nothing to do with the body and that impairment is in fact less than a description of the physical body" (p. 330). Thus, the individual is epistemologically defined as deviant, not because of disability, but, rather, because of the medical and legal language develops into a "type" of knowledge that renders the individual as deviant.

Is it possible that the person was never disabled in the first place? According to Davis (1995), "The 'problem' is not the person with disabilities; the problem is the way that normalcy is constructed to create the 'problem' of the disabled person" in that specific historical moment of that society" (p. 24). For example, in medieval times, a physical "deformity" was considered in some countries to be a punishment from God; however, a physical limitation in another country during that same period was considered special, even superior to the normal spectrum. Two cases in point: in India, for example, individuals with multiple arms were compared with the god Vishnu. In a Mexican village, blindness was not considered a disability (Gwaltney, 1970).

The medical and legal language, as the power to name bodily dysfunctions, creates the "problem" for the disabled person through disciplinary techniques of bio-power that produce and optimize the capabilities of the body, developing its economic utility and ensuring its political docility (Hughes & Paterson, 1997). Using disciplinary techniques of bio-power as scientific language to examine the body, it becomes devoid of history and culture. This process makes it difficult to grasp the "confinement" or "mind colonization" of these individuals, especially if it happens "slowly and incrementally over many years" (Nader, 2002, p. 127).

Institutions as a form of control typically use disability as if it were universal, homogenous, and normalized as "a science of connections" without respect to the local context (Nader, 2002, p. 210). Hughes and Paterson (1997) discuss how disabled people have been cast in the role of the other. Social control institutions also often create anthrocentric notions of the law by classifying people with disabilities epistemologically with neglect to cultural or historical considerations (Nader, 2002). The anthrocentric definition of disability and the formal apparatus of how to define and accommodate people with disabilities are perceived as a "social problem made by trained experts who may depart quite substantially from public perceptions of social problems" (Lauderdale, 2003, p. 19). This perception includes the realm of special education.

Alfred Binet, a French psychologist, devised the first formalized test of intelligence in 1905, which the French government used to identify "those children whose lack of success in normal classrooms . . . [warranted] some form of special education" (Gould, 1996, p. 179). Binet and the minister of public education claimed that intelligence could be ranked on a linear scale of intrinsic merit that would establish locales of comparisons and labels (Gould, 1996, p. 182). In the United States, Henry Goddard's work on IQ testing helped to "lay the foundations for special education; it computed a distribution around a norm and assigned those children who fell a specified number of units below the norm to specialized institutions" (Lane, 1999, p. 85). Psychologists Rudolph Pintner and Donald Paterson (1915, 1916, 1917) were the first to administer IQ testing to deaf children and found that with the "verbal IQ measures which they were using, the deaf as a group were scoring in the mentally retarded range" (Vernon, 2005, p. 226).

Binet's techniques have evolved over time into less crude testing measurements that are used now when legitimizing current educational policy with claims of a fair education in a least-restrictive environment for the student with disability and other minority populations (Donoghue, 2003; Foster & Kinuthia, 2003; Glickman & Gulati, 2003; Hall, 2002; Hoffmeister, 1996; Lane, 1995). The legitimization of educational policies can be seen through Supreme Court cases such as *Brown v. Board of Education* (1954) and *Mills v. Board of Education of D.C.* (1972). These pivotal cases claimed to reject the "separate but equal" ideology; however, it would take "another 21 years after the Brown decision before students with disabilities were guaranteed the right to any education at all" (Shapiro, 1994, p. 340). In 1974, these court cases led to the creation of educational policy laws notably one of the most important policies for those with a disability: the 1975 Education for All Handicapped Children Act (Pub. L. No. 94-142), which was amended to become the Individuals with Disabilities Education Act (IDEA, Pub. L. No. 101-476). Some scholars argue that President Ford signed Public Law 94-142 in response to a 400% increase of students in the mentally retarded category from 1948 to 1966 (Donovan & Cross, 2002, p. 22). Simply put, this legal reform may have been in response to the socially constructed definitions of mental retardation. Nonetheless, the main purpose of the IDEA was to ensure that students with "disabilities" were equally able to receive a high-quality education in the least-restrictive environment, which was interpreted to mean a public school classroom. This type of least-restrictive environment supports the American ideology of equality and the "strong cultural values of individualism and egalitarianism" (Nash, 2000, p. 214; see also Fordham, 1988).

The philosophy behind the least-restrictive environment was to place children with disabilities in the "least drastic or most normal setting appropriate as possible" (IDEA Pub. L. No. 101-476). This philosophy "reflects on the medical/public health sub model and reflects the psychological sub model in its requirements for a nondiscriminatory evaluation of the student (including a psychological evaluation)" (Turnbull & Stowe, 2001, p. 201). These assessments produce social and cultural constructions of intelligence, school success, and school failure that have nothing to do with the nature of things but, rather, are the product of social arrangements that contribute to the overall institutional framework of the school and its ideology of what a successful/failed student is, which are based on these wrong and/or incomplete assessments (Mehan, 1993; Spencer & Marschark, 2010).

Special education relies on policy and social control processes such as assessment in the name of ostensible scientifically based research to categorize and frame students with disabilities. It uses measurement of student identification and achievement that "has been a ticket to resegregation and isolation" (Shapiro, 1994, p. 340). Some scholars contend that if such institutions continue to "separate the special from the general education system, we [society] will never confront the uncertainty, think about real innovations and change" (Tomlinson, 1995, p. 5; see also Sekula, 1981). This concern applies to many specific populations in the realm of special education. Thomas Hehir (2002) reaffirms that "unlike some disability populations, such as students with significant cognitive disabilities, educational programs for deaf children have existed in the U.S. for over 150 years" (p. 5). Lennard Davis (1995) adds that "the beginning of what we now call 'special education' started with deafness" (p. 52). Examining deaf education and languaculture will contribute the larger implications on humanity, including its complex identities and how it is are regulated within the realm of normalcy.

Language choices and their maintenance are driven by hidden curricula, the "types" of teachers (i.e., their academic background and language preference), and "culture" within the classroom. Hidden curricula "involve various interests, cultural forms, struggles, agreements, and compromise" as well as the language choice to be used for instruction, which further contribute to understanding instructional ideology (Margolis, Soldatenjo, Acker, & Gair, 2001, p. 16). The epistemology of language relies heavily on the pedagogical definition of "effective" communication (specified as being achieved by either sign or spoken English) as an important factor in determining the type of school in which the deaf child is placed (Meadow-Orlans, 2003, p. 40). The relationship between language and learning is "interwoven in any classroom, but for the deaf students it has most often functioned to impede academic success, not secure it" (La Bue, 1995, p. 164).

Language as a part of communication and educational pedagogy serves to "influence how and what knowledge and identities are produced within and among particular sets of social relations" (Giroux & Simon, 1989, p. 239). Communication for deaf people has been a tool to regulate language as knowledge and as a "form of stigmas lacking a typical human characteristic," and an indicator of shaping languaculture for deaf children (Jones, 2002, p. 54).

These efforts to define disability specifically and in general further solidifies what it means to have a disability and functions as a way to maintain society's ideological domination; these populations provide similar social constructions of the deaf and their sign language.

## SOCIAL CONSTRUCTIONS OF DEAFNESS

There are two predominant socially constructed views of deafness (as there are with disability): one as a difference (normal) and the other as pathology (deviant) (Wixtrom, 1988). A person who perceives a deaf person as a pathology (deviant) might "define deafness as a *pathological condition* (deficit or a handicap which distinguishes *abnormal* deaf persons from normal hearing persons" (Wixtrom, 1988, n.p.). On the other side of the continuum, someone who perceives a deaf person as a difference (normal), might "define deafness as merely a *difference*, a characteristic that distinguishes normal deaf persons from normal hearing persons" (Wixtrom, 1988, n.p.).

The most dominant perspective on deafness (usually by outsiders of the deaf community) sees deafness as a deficit (Reagan, 2009; Wixtrom, 1988). This perspective is accomplished by using an etic construction of deafness; in contrast, a perspective on deafness as a culture is rooted in emic constructions (Reagan, 2002). A lot of these social constructions have to do with the role of sign language as a precursor for culture; thus, languaculture.

One of the earliest studies on sign language and deafness as a social construct can be traced back to a quote in William C. Stokoe's 1960 article, "Sign Language Structure: An Outline of the Visual Communication Systems of the American Deaf." While this classic article would lay the foundation for American Sign Language (ASL) as a "whole" language comparable with English, Stokoe also gave room for a lengthy quote by A. S. Lunde whose 1956 paper at the American Sociological Association gave note to the "Sociology of the Deaf." In the quote, Lunde states:

> Among the other factors enforcing the *social isolation* [emphasis added] of the deaf from the hearing world is *public opinion* [emphasis added], as expressed in the attitudes of the hearing majority. These appear to be similar to the fear and hostility patterns which appear in other dominant-minority relations; there is the assumption of the inferiority of the deaf and the stereotype of the deaf as "dumb." (Lunde in Stokoe, 1960, p. 15)

Lunde goes on to detail that there is nothing inherently wrong with the biological notion of deafness, but rather, it is the environmental conditions that construct deafness as "dumb," and as a result, a person affected by this construction has been "often taken as an individual adrift in a hearing society" (Lunde in Stokoe, 1960, p. 12). Placing deafness in a social construction framework gave rise to studying deafness in ways other than through the medical framework; instead, there were other epistemological ways of studying deafness, including its sign language and culture (to be explicated further in Chapter 3). The regulation of sign language has played a powerful role in the reconstruction of cultural identities for the deaf. The notion of languaculture emphasizes that it is the modification of language that reconfigures culture and how it will be seen by society (Agar, 1994).

When two individuals engage in a conversation in sign language, it is often said that outsiders (namely, nonsigners) "gaze" at the conversants. The "gaze" is not directed toward the person as a human but, rather, directed toward sign language as a thing of exotic beauty, which is reinforced by classic remarks by the gazers such as "Wow, that is so beautiful," even if the signed conversation was about what to do this upcoming weekend. Often, nonsigners say, "I want to learn sign language" as if they assume that learning it would be a simple task. It is interesting to note that more and more hearing students at universities are taking sign language as a foreign language. In fact, from 1998 to 2002, there was a 432% increase in students taking ASL (Cornwell, 2005). ASL-based teachers have told me that many of the

ASL students who completed the class did not realize how complex it was, but were glad they took the course and said they had learned a greater appreciation of diverse languages, including sign language.

As an academic, I often present at conferences on perceptions of language; I sometimes use sign language (allowing the interpreter to voice for me), but then switch languages to use my voice. Immediately, I solicit the audience's thoughts in a discussion. Many of these people have admitted that they felt the authority of knowledge had shifted from the interpreter to the speaker. When I was using only sign language, many of the audience members felt that, initially, the interpreter was the primary source of authority and, thus, tended to look at the interpreter instead of me, the speaker. But after I used my voice, their eyes immediately were drawn to me as one in a position of authority. This seemingly simple change in language usage represents an enormous gestalt shift of a paradigmatic thought process. This small example that I have given here reflects the larger perception of sign language in our society and suggests that "ASL is a language that has been misunderstood, misused, and misrepresented over the last 100 years" (Hoffmeister 1990, p. 81).

During the European Enlightenment (eighteenth century), sign language became revered as a positive and remarkable component of language. Writing and speaking were considered forms of sign language; in fact, writing was considered a "language of mute signs" because the author could not speak per se (Davis, 1995, p. 59). Scholars during the Enlightenment contended that writing was an apparatus of recorded and archived texts and that all knowledge acquired by means of writing was derived from "nonhearing knowledge acquisition" passed on for centuries, while sign language was viewed as "the" novel source of information in which the author was the sole authority of information (Davis, 1995, p. 63). One of the first, if not the first, document written by a deaf person is by Pierre Desloges, a deaf man living in Paris, who wrote a book in 1779 defending the use of sign language in the education of deaf adults. Desloges believed sign language to be "the most natural means for leading the deaf to an understanding of languages, nature having given them this language to substitute for the other languages of which they are deprived" (Desloges in Lane, 2006, p. 35). Nonetheless, the embodiment and hegemony of writing and speech as language continued to be solidified as a "hearing" phenomenon; sign language was to be reserved only for those who could not speak. That approach would not last long for deaf people, however, because they would soon be told to eradicate their sign language in favor of speech, despite the earlier claims that sign language was a positive indicator of knowledge acquisition. In this respect, the language for deaf people shifted and, in turn, also shifted what ought to be the culture for deaf people and what sign language ought to mean for members of society.

More and more parents seem to agree on the positive contribution of sign language, reflected in the fact that more and more hearing babies are being taught "baby signs." However, note that the majority of deaf babies are prevented from signing. Maureen Klusza, a member of the deaf community called this situation the "greatest irony" and depicted two babies side by side, one hearing and one deaf. The hearing baby is signing "I love you," but the deaf baby is shackled in handcuffs (see http://www.cafepress.com/moeart for the image). Thus, languaculture is a critical indicator of how the regulation and reappropriation of sign language not only impacts the deaf community, its educational pedagogy, and the rise of new professional organizations as well as new forms of knowledge but also impacts the larger society.

The notion of what it means to be a normal deaf individual has taken on a political aspect by society as explicated in the first part of this chapter, but in addition, what it means to be a normal deaf individual within the deaf community also becomes political. Certain members of the deaf community feel that others in that community have placed them socially on the "margins" of the boundaries of deafness by identifying them as people who are "hard of hearing" (Brueggemann, 2010). Others in the deaf community feel that as hearing children of deaf adults, they are both hearing *and* deaf, or "hearing-deaf" (Mudgett-DeCaro, 1996).

The evolution of technological devices for the ear also has provided diverse perspectives concerning what it means to be deaf and normal. The Stealth Secret Sound Amplifier (SSA) was invented by Kagan Unlimited, Inc., in the early twenty-first century as an assistive listening device. The Stealth SSA was designed to look identical to the Bluetooth earphone designated for hearing users. However, it is not a phone but, rather, a disguised hearing aid. It was developed to replace the hearing aids of the twentieth century (which previously replaced the "audiophone" of the nineteenth century) so the individual with the "hearing loss" could mask his/her "disability"; by using the Stealth SSA, he or she would be perceived as normal like any other Bluetooth user. This device further reinforced the perspective that hearing aids are stigmatized products. According to the company's website, "If mention of a conventional hearing aid makes you feel self-conscious, consider the first personal audio amplification device that combines an ergonomic design with a discreet, professional look" (Kagan Unlimited, 2009). This perspective on technology for deaf people is not new. See Figure 2.3 for examples.

Today's form of technology include miniature hearing aids, Stealth SSA®, and the SoundBite™ (a device that transmit sound through one's teeth and bones), all intended to minimize the visibility of assistive devices for deaf people during the twenty-first century. The SoundBite™ Hearing System transmits sound picked up with a small microphone in the ear canal to a unit that snaps around a back tooth that then transmits the sound through bone conduction to the cochlea. The device has been called the "greatest resonator yet produced" and is yet one more effort in the pursuit of ostensible normalcy (Bentler, 2009, p. 38). These current forms of technology also include cochlear implants. Cochlear implants are becoming much more popular; more than 90% of the deaf

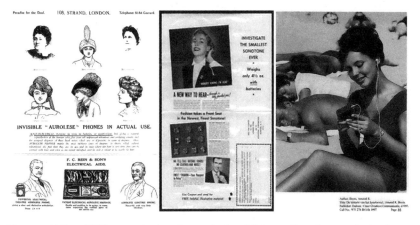

FIGURE 2.3.  Different devices intended to hide or disguise one's deafness during the nineteenth and twentieth centuries.

children in the two different classrooms that I observed were using them (see Chapter 5). This change suggests that students still wearing hearing aids in the classroom (10%) have now become a minority and often cast as "different" from their "normal" deaf peers with cochlear implants.

The notion of what it means to be deaf is based on social constructions including attitudes on language and technology to shape cultural identities. These attitudes on language and technology are driven by ideological notions of normalcy and deviance linked to a given historical time and place. These ideological notions of normalcy also influence the ongoing debates on what it means to be deaf within the deaf community. Breivik (2005) in *Deaf Identities in the Making: Local Lives, Transitional Connections* chronicles two women and their struggles with identity in two different "borderlands" as both provide a view of the margins of their deaf boundaries. Carol C. Padden (1980) was among the first to outline the criteria for what a deaf community ought to entail, including demographic, linguistic, political, and social implications. This effort gave rise to the complexity of deaf/ Deaf (or d/D) as a socially constructed category. Ironically, the notion of d/D was first raised by James Woodward (1975)[3], who attempted to simply categorize 'd'eaf as a medical/audiological model and 'D'eaf as a social, cultural, and political model as a simple way to distinguish two popular models of deafness. Nonetheless, it has now expanded into a paradigm of identity formation (Napier, 2002). Namely, 'D' is now a cultural identifier of those who are "inside" the boundaries of deaf culture, including those from traditional schools for the deaf, those with deaf parents, and those who are fluent in ASL; simply put, those who are 'D'eaf with a capital *D* consider themselves proudly as a part of deaf culture. In terms of languaculture, they emphasize sign language to solidify their deaf culture. On the other side of the spectrum (although this claim is debatable) the 'd' identifier represents those who generally have a deficit perspective of being deaf, including those who do not know sign language.

---

3. In Padden and Humphries's popular book, *Deaf in America: Voices from a Culture,* they incorrectly cite the origin of d/D to Woodward's 1972 article when it fact, it was 1975 that Woodward makes this distinction (See c.f. 6 in Nonaka, 2004).

This "spectrum" is debatable because there are now members who claim to be 'D'eaf but do not sign fluently; however, they claim the 'D'eaf status because of their similar experiences of oppression and their positive attitude toward being deaf. One particular member has been identified as being in "a culture *neither* but *also, and* but *or*—a culture made up of immense and intense imagination, illustrating deaf identity in the making" (Brueggemann in Valente, 2010, p. xiii). Edwards (2010) points out that some members consider those who wear hearing aids as not "deaf enough" and thus marginalized to the lowercase 'd'eaf regardless of their language use. It could be argued that James Woodward could have easily decided the other way around that *D* would refer to those populations being studied from a medical view and that *d* would refer to those being studied from a social/cultural/political view. Indeed, the notion of d/D described above is confined to certain countries such as America (Erting et al. 1994; Lane, 1989) and Great Britain (Skelton & Valentine, 2003). In Ireland, those who claim the 'D'eaf status are those deaf people who can speak well enough to interact with hearing people and who feel that being able to speak is an important function of being a successful and normal individual, while Irish 'd'eaf members rely on traditional forms of sign language as a way to communicate (LeMaster, 2002). Thus, the Irish view of d/D is the complete opposite of the American traditional view of d/D. The reason why I mention traditional is because there is now an emerging group of young deaf leaders who are pushing for the eradication of assigning d/D, taking a "who cares" attitude and emphasizing that deaf people are already an oppressed group and that to include the d/D as a social construction is to further oppress the deaf community (Deaf Youth USA, 2010). Thus, in addition to the d/D notion becoming hotly contested, the very definition of "deaf community" as a social construct continues to be socially negotiated.

In Graham T. Turner's article *How Is Deaf Culture?* (1994), he raises some fundamental concerns of Padden's criteria of a deaf community, especially Padden's "oversimplification" of culture. According to Turner, Padden uses a "bingo card" model to screen what a deaf community ought to entail, as if there were a universal checklist for these types of determinations. Turner, then, met with a series of respondents, including Yerker Andersson (former professor of sociology at

Gallaudet University and former president of the World Federation for the Deaf), Trevor Johnston (professor of linguistics), Leila Monaghan (professor of anthropology), Ben Bahan (professor of ASL and Deaf studies at Gallaudet University), and Paddy Ladd (professor of Deaf studies). Each respondent provided unique social constructions and perspectives on deaf culture and community that seemed to raise more problematic questions than answers, but Turner summarizes these respondents' observations as an opportunity to engage in an intellectual form of discourse that is necessary to better examine (carefully) deafness and its social constructions.

Just like Turner's exploration and the approach of the Dialogues at Gallaudet (see Chapter 1), discussions on studying deafness, specifically, languaculture and what a "community" means, need to be carefully examined. By using normalcy/deviance as a tool of measurement, it is possible to reveal the powerful role of social constructions. However, questions remain: What does it mean to be deaf? Which embodiment of deafness ought to be "the norm"? For some people, being deaf equates to a hearing loss that needs to be "fixed" while other people construct being deaf as normal and natural. For some people, being deaf depends on languaculture, their position within d/D, and the type of technology they use. It is important to remember that these ideologies change with respect to time and place in a specific historical era. For example, in villages in the Amazon basin of South America and on Martha's Vineyard in North America in the nineteenth century, most hearing members viewed their deaf counterparts as equal/normal and used sign language to communicate with them. In a small Yucatan village called Chican, being deaf is not a social issue. Deaf people in Chican are viewed as equally important members of the community and considered mainly in terms of gender status and occupation—males as farmers and females as homeworkers (Johnson, 1991). In contrast, Europe and the United States in the late-nineteenth century and into the mid-twentieth century viewed deafness as a defect and a type of deviance that needed to be "fixed" by means of audiological methods, including speaking and hearing rather than using sign language (Davis, 1995, p. 89).

There is not one answer, but with the use of reflectivity, careful discourse, and conceptual ideas of normalcy and deviance, it can become possible to understand the contributions of social constructions, the intersections and "visions" on deafness. This revelation is important not only within the discourse on deafness, using normalcy and deviance as concepts, but also in the examination of how these ideas connect with the larger implications of selfhood and humanity.

## EXPLORING SOCIAL CONSTRUCTIONS IN A DISCURSIVE APPROACH

Throughout sociohistory, the changing designations of deviance and normalcy have influenced not only individuals but also how these processes have contributed to the hegemony of that society. Studying social constructions of deafness offers a layer of analysis focused on the larger critical justice issues, including emergent ideologies, the impact of identity formations (including stigmas), and everyday social constructions. The examination of these theoretical ideas also raises some potential limitations. Thus, it is essential to address important criticisms and to examine certain theoretical ideas and frameworks.

This chapter first explored the notion of social constructions in terms of regulation of epistemological knowledge and how these constructions are diffused and exercised in the foundations of history, culture, and the "order of things." The discourse then connected these analyses to the social construction of deafness. Discourse, here, becomes a mode of language and praxis that constructs human identity, reasoning about humans, social life, and the archaeology of "disciplines" such as medicine, law, sociology, psychology, disability, and in this case, deafness. The praxis of power (which is inseparable from knowledge) becomes a form of strategy in constructing disciplines and the "order of things." The construction of epistemology is mainly about who or what disciplines/institutions have the power/knowledge to normalize and maintain certain "truths" throughout relevant history.

For some scholars, this theoretical perspective leads to a negative connotation of power through domination (Gane, 1986). However, a major misconception of power is "negative power: seeing power only in terms of a sovereign figure who always prohibits or says no" (Foucault in Wickham, 1986, p. 157) as a form of negative control. This research, however, examines the "regulation" of power as a strategic process of social control institutions to construct certain types of knowledge. These ideological state apparatuses use power as a form of strategy to produce their own social constructions of normalcy and deviance. Instead of focusing on a notion of negative power, this book strives to find strategies to examine certain types of knowledge and social control processes, including the constructions of identities in the name of normalcy and deviance. Equally as important is to present examinations and discourses in the reflective symbolist tradition by means of performativity to elicit further constructive discourses through which to examine dialogues that may have not been possible in this historical moment.

Performativity gives the reader the opportunity to acknowledge certain epistemological processes through constructions of normalcy and deviance as dynamic categories to possibly unravel discrimination and oppression within these processes (Butler, 2000). Thus, to uncover "hidden knowledge" constructed by certain ideological apparatuses, there need to be discussions of social justice issues, including possible sites of discrimination and oppression through power (Guinier, 2001). Equally important is to recognize that these social justice issues vary across the range of deaf people (i.e., accessibility and impairment mean different things to different people); thus, understanding different dimensions of normalcy and deviance becomes essential (Beckett, 2006, p. 97).

Rather than establish claims and theoretical ideas about certain "universal truths," this discourse is a form of social practice, "which suggests the importance of understanding the practice of subjectivity" (Cooper & White, 2009, p. 169). This discourse includes recognizing the dynamics of epistemology as a situational and partial force in shaping types of knowledge and experiences. When analyzing epistemology by means of discourse as social practice, relevant data are viewed as situational and partial with the spirit of eliciting meanings and uncovering types of knowledge that may be critical in understanding specific implications of normalcy and deviance, including in social control institutions.

Social control institutions are formed by consolidating power to construct a formal-rational framework of systems of thought, or "rational logical interpretation of meaning" (Weber, 1968, p. 789). These systems of thought can become part of a hegemonic process that "has resulted in the neglect of diverse disabled cultures, which homogenize the identity of disability as a collective where values, heritage, and history are normalized" (Horejes & Lauderdale, 2007, p. 18). The theoretical discourses in this book strive to be reflective as they discuss the importance of a diverse range of values and sociohistories. It is both the silenced people and semiconnected actors in certain social control institutions who offer possible strategies in bringing "to the surface stories of those whose voices have not been heard, those who have been oppressed or disenfranchised" (Pugach, 2001, p. 443). From this perspective, using personal examples of marginalized groups can "give life to history" as this book makes the connection between personal experiences toward research (Cooper & White, 2009, p. 168). These reflective examinations can help us understand reflective collaborative discourses in the pursuit of social justice.

It is important to "acknowledge the complex and contradictory histories" when discussing certain populations (McRuer, 2006, pp. 151–152). This process also necessitates comparing groups with and without the labels of deafness/disability to understand the multitude of constructions of normalcy and deviance for these groups. It is critical to examine these ideas when discussing the constructions of normalcy and deviance to gain a better understanding of the ways certain populations are being disenfranchised. This examination includes people defined as having disabilities within the realm of special/deaf education and even within the deaf community as important sites of analysis.

Throughout the sociohistory of deviant and disabled subjects, they are maintained as static categories that are created by social control institutions and state agencies through often stigmatized and objectified terms such as *mad, crippled, deformed, dumb, feebleminded, defective,* and *insane* (Goffman, 1968; Longmore, 2003). These deviance designations have been recategorized as disabled, someone with mental illness, hearing impaired, or with a hearing loss, yet they neglect diversity or unique histories and identities. This process also includes designations maintained by special and deaf education social control institutions.

It is critical to realize that the ways of being deaf as a "norm" are shaped by socially constructed ideology. In general, deaf people remain fixed as the signifiers, and it is the signified, including the placement of sign language, that ascribes meaning and their placement in the socially constructed world. The notion of deafness (like Thomas Kuhn's duck) is an object of study. The power of social constructions driven by notions of normalcy and deviance continue to shape and exacerbate the ways that deafness ought to be viewed, especially in deaf education. The "general social milieu of the nation . . . and changes in the educational philosophies or theories regarding deafness have repeatedly combined to shape the education of deaf children" (Moores, 1992, p. 7) and further solidifies the paradigm of certain educational philosophies, including the pedagogy of language for the deaf. Examining the importance of social constructions as a theoretical framework, Chapter 3 takes a look into the archaeology of deafness that consists of contrasting paradigms within deaf education, its historical social constructions, its ideological perceptions on languaculture, and how these paradigms play a role in constructing normalcy and deviance for a deaf student. Chapter 3 provides the connection between theory and history to raise another level of analysis on the ways that deafness (specifically deaf education) has been socially constructed.

# CHAPTER THREE

# ARCHAEOLOGY OF DEAF
# EDUCATION AND LANGUACULTURE

Deaf children at an early age might be unconcerned with languaculture, social representations, social constructions, politics, and ideology. However, they are developing members under ideological state apparatuses such as schools, which are embedded with specific histories and cultures that will assist in constructing and organizing their life and its meanings (Althusser, 1970; Erting, 2003). Schools, as social institutions, often determine the status of children and the type of languaculture for the deaf child. This chapter supports Tim Reagan's (2002) call for a need of an "archaeology of deafness" to locate the ways in which deafness is constructed, reconstructed, and maintained. Specifically, an archaeology of deaf education would reflect historical and philosophical notions of social constructions as a way to study the knowledge construction and reconstruction of deaf education, especially when discussing what it means to be deaf and, in essence, human. Such an archaeology creates important sites of knowledge construction for deaf children because schools are often among the first to introduce the deaf child to the world of languaculture, knowledge construction, and a view of their identity as a deaf person.

Rather than present a history of deaf education that may be static and lead to linear interpretations of selected historical "facts" with little room for multiple perspectives, I offer an archaeology that reflects the socially constructed ideas that have become "factual." It is these "facts" that require further digging (deconstruction) to uncover hidden knowledge and meanings that may provide ways to view the same "fact" differently and, in turn, enable different ways of thinking about the larger social implications. In a way, an archaeology may present only a version of history of deaf education as it implies more than one side to history. Two examples come to mind that show how an analysis can capture the dangers of "history" and the importance of an "archaeology." Michel Foucault's (1975) analysis on a case study of Pierre Rivière and Charles Goodwin's analysis of the video on the beating of Rodney King provide important alternative aspects of history.

Pierre Rivière was accused of fatally beating three members of his family, but as soon as he defended his actions in the name of God and wrote his reasoning "all down as best" he could, his testimony was scrutinized by the medical and legal apparatus (Erevelles, 2002, 2005; Foucault, 1975). While the murders were "fact," the reason behind them became socially negotiable; the very inherent meaning of reason was being debated. The medical view indicated that Rivière was a sick individual who ought to be viewed as a "monster." Rivière's own "reason" for murder was a result of "madness," which should be left to be handled by medical experts. The legal view juxtaposed that he was a cold, calculated murderer and that his "reason" was justified by his testimony that outlined how some members of his family were "evil" and that he was consciously doing a higher moral good; thus, he should be handled by the legal system. Which position ought to be the most "legitimate" perspective on Pierre Rivière? Without an archaeological examination of Pierre's case by means of a Foucaultian analysis, his case perhaps may not reveal the importance of the different "disciplines" claiming to write history about his "reasoning." Instead, Foucault was able to use an archaeology of Rivière's case to illustrate the power dynamics wherein certain authorities mediate information as being objective and factual. An archaeology allows the audience to see the power structure and the dangers of "experts" in redefining something inherent such as "reason." This larger level of analysis becomes much larger than just the Rivière case; it now becomes an issue of regulating and maintaining the type of knowledge construction about reason and humanity.

Charles Goodwin's (1994) "Professional Vision" provides a brilliant comparative analysis of archaeologists in the field and "experts" in the courtroom, each using their unique professional vision to make sense of the same data by means of coding schemes. First, Goodwin compares several archaeologists using their own coding schemes to provide different information based on the same dataset (dirt). Using these coding schemes, archaeologists are able to draw their own conclusions about the texture, color, and even taste of the dirt. Goodwin then compares their technical approach to examining dirt with the Rodney King videotape as "experts" use different coding schemes to provide different information based on the same videotape clip. The videotape recounting the Rodney King beating by the Los Angeles Police Department is used to develop two main perspectives toward one "fact" (the videotape). The videotape, as an object of knowledge, created intensive examinations by "experts" to deconstruct the actions by these LAPD officers, mainly, "a brutal, savage beating of a man lying helpless on the ground versus careful police response to a dangerous 'PCP-crazed giant'" (Goodwin, 1994, p. 606). During the Rodney King trial, the grainy videotape was often examined in still frames, cropped, and zoomed to dissect the actions of certain LAPD officers; both perspectives were able to come up with various "evidence" that the officers were either engaging in police brutality or defending themselves in response to a dangerous man who was not cooperative. Although history tells us that the police officers were found not guilty of police brutality, Charles Goodwin was able to warn the audience that there is much more to just the factual conclusion of the Rodney King case. More important, Goodwin raised the larger, broader issues of negotiating data by means of coding schemes that socially construct entirely different perspectives of a single phenomenon.

Michel Foucault and Charles Goodwin were able to subtly warn the audience that to "organize the perception of nature, events, or people within a profession carries with it an array of perceptual and cognitive operations that have far-reaching impact" (Goodwin, 1994, p. 609). This powerful statement goes to show how dangerous matter-of-fact assumptions by "professions" can become when they build history that is derived from unique perceptions that lead to larger implications of certain phenomena, whether they are actions or events. I use their warning when discussing history; specifically, deaf education. Who ought to write a "history" of the deaf? Describing the background of Gunther List, a hearing scholar from Germany (the first country to develop oral-based education for deaf people), Baynton states that List is adamant that he, as a hearing scholar, not only has the right to be

> involved in writing deaf history, but that they [hearing scholars] have an obligation to be involved . . . [because]

> deaf history—any minority history—cannot be understood separate from the history of the majority who controlled society's major institutions . . . that the history of the deaf people is part of hearing people's history because of what the latter have done to the former. (Baynton in List, 1999, p. 113)

This perspective is quite an interesting one and has great merit in terms of "writing" deaf history. I could use my background to show why I should not "write" deaf education based on the premise that I did not learn sign language until my adolescence, but like Baynton has mentioned about List's background, I do contribute to the histories of deaf education. However, instead of writing a "history" or "literature review" of deaf education from a particular perspective, I want to provide an archaeology of deaf education and languaculture and then make the larger connections by means of a deconstruction of these histories and languacultures.

Like Foucault and Goodwin in their analyses, the goal is to reveal possible alternative ways of looking at "facts" through mediated meanings of certain social constructions on deaf education, that is, through a sociology of deaf education. To be sure, countless historical literature reviews or collections of articles pertaining to the sociology of deafness have already been written (Andrews & Leigh, 2004; Bauman, 2008; Branson & Miller, 2002; Higgins & Nash, 1987; Komesaroff, 2002; Ladd, 2003; Lane, 1999; Lunde, 1960; Nash & Nash, 1982; Van Cleve, 1999), but there needs to be more deconstruction using themes (or discourse) within genealogy/archaeology and epistemology of languaculture. Such a deconstructionist analysis will show how the "facts" within deaf education are diffused, practiced, and exercised in the foundations of history, culture, and the "order of things" as a part of the larger discourse on deafness. Specifically, the varying perspectives and pieces of evidence constructed by these "professions" will reveal how they came to support oral-oriented language usage (oral-based schools) and sign-oriented language usage (sign language-based schools).

Historically, the paradigm wars that construct diverse languacultures within deaf education, mainly those supported by sign-based and oral-based educational institutions, present evidence to make a case for the most normal avenues to a child's education. The con-structions of what it means to be deaf have been understood "as an ideological system of normalization" (Horejes & Lauderdale, 2007, p. 20) that continues to build on a complex archaeology of deafness. Such constructions shape the life reality of individuals by framing cer-tain social representations and dynamics of deafness and identity. It is not enough to provide a simple clean-cut literature review depicting deaf education; instead, what is needed is an archaeology to uncover different deep-seated perspectives and how certain "ideas" become ideological.

## DEAF EDUCATION AND LANGUACULTURE

The school environment can provide deaf children with a unique opportunity to obtain a valuable education and to establish a foundation in language (Hall, 2002; Lane, 1999; Little & Houston, 2003; Sacks, 1989). Unfortunately, the "history of deaf students' poor academic achievement indicates a problem in the definition of appropriate academic and linguistic classroom environments for these students" (La Bue, 1995, p. 166; see also Bowe, 2003; Swanson, 2007). Historically, the quality of deaf education has exhibited low standards (Hoffmeister, 1996; Janesick & Moores, 1992; Lane, 1999; Lou, 1988) and currently, the academic performance of deaf children continues to lag behind hearing peers in language, cognition, and learning (English & Church, 1999; Marschark, Convertino, & Larock, 2006; Marschark & Spencer, 2010; Traxler, 2000). Marschark, Lang, and Albertini (2002) indicate that

> on average, 18-year old deaf students leaving high school have reached only a fourth to sixth grade level in reading skills. Only about 3 percent of those 18 year olds read at the same level as the average 18-year old reader, and more than 30 percent of deaf students leave school functionally illiterate. (p. 157)

The above statistics were clarified in a more recent publication to indicate that rather than "on average," there were approximately half of all 18-year-old deaf students that leave high school with a fourth to sixth grade level (Marschark & Spencer, 2011). Deaf scholar Frank Bowe (2003) adds that

> 25% of deaf and hard of hearing students each year are at risk of being identified as low functioning deaf as adults because they read at less than second-grade level . . . and 30% were eligible for colleges. But 70% of those who enrolled in two and four year colleges dropped out without receiving a degree. (p. 488)

More recently in February 2011, the National Center for Special Education Research (NCSE) noted that:

> With regard to academic achievement, a gap existed between the academic achievement of student's with hearing impairments and their peers in the general population in reading, mathematics, science, and social studies. Higher percentages of student's with hearing impairments scored below the mean across subtests compared with the general population. (Shaver, 2010, p. 28)

These low-average academic achievement levels "are not results of learning deficits inherently associated with deafness but of problems in the communication practices" within deaf educational settings (Johnson, Liddell, & Erting, 1989, pp. 89–93; Kelly, Lang, & Pagliaro, 2003; Luckner & Bowen, 2006; Luckner, et al. 2005; Luckner & Muir, 2002; Marschark, Lang, & Albertini, 2002). To be sure, there are scholars who have questioned the reliability and the validity of some assessments on student achievement (Qi & Mitchell, 2011). Further complicating the challenges in defining and measuring appropriate academic, linguistic, and cultural pedagogies for deaf children, there are "paradigm wars" among two dominant educational pedagogies: (1) the oral-oriented pedagogy in which the deaf child is fully integrated with other deaf students with the goal to be eventually mainstreamed in a public school possibly being the only deaf student in that school using aural/oral methods that include auditory and speech therapy and (2) the sign-based pedagogy in which the deaf child is fully integrated with other deaf students often throughout their K–12 education with other deaf students using a combination of ASL, mixed methods, and/or spoken and written English in the educational setting.

While there is a wealth of scholarship regarding deaf education, these two paradigms are emergent forces in the deaf community when discussing ways to advance the lives of deaf students in the realm of deaf education. These two paradigms are reinforced by an archaeology of archived data supporting both sides of the spectrum; they both have "evidence" with "valid" justifications to claim one paradigm more "effective" than the other, through which each may have promoted a form of social inequality toward the other. Scholars in deaf education have taken different "professional visions" to examine deaf education using these two opposing paradigms as a framework for analysis in their attempt to solidify ideology about what it means to be deaf and how deaf children should be taught in the deaf educational institution. The various types of professional visions allow these paradigms to "organize knowledge, shape perception, and structure future action" as a social control process (Goodwin, 1994, p. 628). These paradigms are "linked to historical communities of researchers . . . [who have] assumed that social reality is objective, orderly, and rational" (Gabel & Peters, 2004, p. 587).

When a deaf child is born in America, current medical institutions determine as biological fact that the child has a sensory loss (hearing). The current social representation of deafness becomes complicated when their deafness is represented in the normal/deviant category in the name of ideology. The ideological decision of language placement then becomes a major representation/signifier of the deaf child's place on the normalcy continuum. Recent examples of these professional visions on languaculture are two "recruitment" videos developed by proponents of the two paradigms: (1) Alexander Graham Bell Association for the Deaf and Hard of Hearing and (2) California State University–Northridge (CSUN) Department of Special Education and Deaf Studies in collaboration with the National Center on Deafness (NCOD). Both proponents produced a video targeted to recruit first-time parents of deaf children to accept their particular ideologies with respect to educational and linguistic considerations. The video of the

Alexander Graham Bell Association is titled *Dreams Spoken Here*[1] and CSUN/NCOD's video is titled *Through Your Child's Eyes: American Sign Language*.[2] The titles reinforce the two contrasting professional visions of languacultures: one relying on the spoken language and the other on American Sign Language through visual means. The videos provide narratives from parents who have experienced raising their deaf child in a unique languaculture, and they are used as evidence that their choice was the most successful choice for their deaf child. The videos also include footage of deaf children using their unique languaculture to depict their "normal" lives. These two videos reflect the ideological positions of the proponents of the two paradigms, both of whom strongly feel that their method is the most effective avenue for a child's education, including the type of languaculture the deaf child ought to adopt to be acculturated/enculturated.

While deafness has been around since the birth of civilization, it was not until the last 250 years that language pedagogy for deaf people became a site of social control, public debate, and social inequality (Moores, 2010). However, languages, whether signed or spoken, are "organized in essentially the same way at all levels of linguistic structure" (Neidle, 2002, p. 92), and "the acquisition [of ASL] is strikingly similar to the spoken language acquisition process in normally hearing children" (Coryell & Holcomb, 2007, p. 387). Both English and ASL are recognized as official, whole languages that include their own linguistic rules, classifiers, and syntax as well as carry the same potential for acquisition. Although the two languages may be perceived as the same linguistically, they are definitely perceived and signified differently. Spoken English has been considered the hegemonic language in America for all children, hearing and deaf, while sign language has not been welcomed at the same level as spoken English when it comes to determining language usage for deaf children. Language choice, then, becomes a matter of ideology by means of hegemony of certain groups to "reproduce and legitimate their domination," including

---

1. *Dreams Spoken Here* can be viewed at http://www.oraldeafed.org/movies/index.html
2. *Through Your Child's Eyes: American Sign Language* can be viewed at http://www.csun.edu/~tyce/

manipulating language as "natural" and "God-given" (van Dijk, 1997, p. 25). For deaf children, there are two diverse languacultures, each with its own resulting implications: for the constructions of oral-based schools, to talk is human; for the constructions of sign-based schools, to sign is human. How did these two diverse languacultures for deaf children originate?

The formalization of sign language within the realm of education is often attributed to the French priest, Abbé Charles Michel de l'Epée (circa 1712–1789), who has been dubbed the father of deaf education. In 1760, he established the first school for the deaf in Paris, France, called the National Institution for Deaf-Mutes, which grew from 68 pupils in 1783 to over 100 pupils by his death in 1789 (Lane & Grosjean, 1980, p. 122).[3] Epée's school would later become the model for many schools, including the first permanent school for the deaf in America—the Connecticut Asylum for the Education and Instruction of Deaf and Dumb Persons (now the American School for the Deaf [ASD]) in Hartford, Connecticut. The school was founded in 1817 by Thomas Hopkins Gallaudet, a Congregational minister, and Laurent Clerc, a deaf Frenchman who had been a student and a teacher at the school in Paris. ASD graduates became successful teachers and leaders of the deaf community. By century's end, they had been instrumental in helping to establish some 30 schools for the deaf throughout the United States (Buchanan, 1999). In 1864, the Columbia Institution for the Instruction of the Deaf and Dumb and Blind, under the leadership of Edward Miner Gallaudet (the son of Thomas Hopkins Gallaudet) was established as an institute of higher education for the deaf, now known as Gallaudet University. The college had five students in its first year and, by 1890, more than 300 (Buchanan, 1999). This era was considered by the deaf community to be the golden era of deaf education in America; however, the golden era would be short-lived due to the emerging paradigm of oral-based pedagogy in deaf education.

The formalization of oral-based instruction in deaf education began in Germany during the late 1700s through the efforts of Samuel

---

3. For an extensive historical narrative documenting Clerc's impact on deaf education, I suggest Harlan Lane's (1989) *When the Mind Hears: A History of the Deaf.*

Heinicke, who is recognized as the father of oral/aural education. By the early 1800s, Jean-Marc Itard, the resident physician at the National Institution in Paris, took Heinicke's aural/oral approach and went on a crusade for the linguistic annihilation of sign language. He gained immense support from various social control institutions. Itard gave two presentations to the Society of the Faculty of Medicine in 1808 titled "On the means of providing hearing to deaf-mutes" and "On the means of providing speech to deaf-mutes" emphasizing that

> speaking is a prompt and necessary consequence of the functioning of hearing; that once a deaf-mute had been taught to hear, he must be aided and taught to listen to himself; that the development of speech will be the more prompt and more complete the less the subject is able to use manual sign language. (Itard in Lane & Grosjean, 1980, p. 137)

In that fateful speech, Itard maintained that manual sign language did not complete the deaf individual as a whole, but rather, that the development of speech would restore the fragmented subject into being whole and finally normal.

At the second National Conference of Principals of American Institutions for the Deaf and Dumb in 1872,[4] Alexander Graham Bell reiterated Itard's vision "to show the reasonableness of the belief that deaf-mutes may be taught to speak like other people" (Bell, 1872a, p. 157), and this vision was "validated" by his Boston experiment in which "evidence" is outlined in Bell's article "Visible Speech as a Means of Communicating Articulation to Deaf-Mutes" in the *American Annals of the Deaf and Dumb* (Bell, 1872b). In the very next article of the same volume. B. D. Pettengill states that "[a]ttempts made, in

---

4. From 1868 to 1884 the organization was known as the Conference of Principals of American Institutions for the Deaf and Dumb, and from 1884 to 1933 as the Conference of Superintendents and Principals of American Institutions for the Deaf and Dumb. In 1933, the name Conference of Executives of American Schools for the Deaf was adopted, and in 1980 the name was changed to Conference of Educational Administrators Serving the Deaf. In 1996 the name was changed to its current name, the Conference of Educational Administrators of Schools and Programs for the Deaf.

any quarter, to decry the language of signs, to restrict its use in the instruction of deaf-mutes, or to discard it altogether, are, in my view, mistaken and unreasonable" (Pettengill, 1872, p. 21).

In the Ninth Convention of American Instructors of the Deaf and Dumb on August, 1878, Dr. Fay, a well-respected leader in deaf education, supported Pettengill's position to safeguard sign language and that it "germinates in his social instincts and by living lives, as naturally as easily, as does speech in the intercourse of hearing children. It is as real as genuine, and any other language is to him labored and foreign" (1878, p. 71).

At the fourth National Conference of Principals of American Institutions for the Deaf and Dumb held on May 26, 1880, Dr. Isaac Lewis Peet, principal of the New York Institution, disagreed with Itard and Bell's notion of speech as necessary to be more a more complete person:

> You may teach a deaf-mute to articulate distinctly and read from the lips distinctly every word, every syllable in the English language, and yet, if you could not make him understand the meaning of those words and their force in a sentence, you would have accomplished nothing whatever in his real education. *You have simply made a parrot of him, teaching him to speak words he does not understand* [emphasis added]. (Peet, 1880, p. 180)

Sister Mary Ann Burke, then principal at St. Mary's Institution, with nearly 20 years of experience in deaf education at the time (she would eventually amass 40 years total in deaf education), acknowledged the historical debates between speech and sign language, but she made it clear that, despite her support for sign language, the strong influence of oral-oriented approaches in deaf education and in society—"after so many learned articles have been written, heated discussions, and arguments held"—was too strong to ignore (Burke, 1880, p. 172). In response to these attempts by both sides in the paradigm wars to provide supporting "evidence," she said:

> the time has been when thoroughly-practiced teachers in signs could scarcely restrain themselves within the bounds of

> moderation in condemning what seemed to them the utter
> folly of attempting to impart oral speech to those who were
> congenitally deaf. Other teachers, again, equally skilled in
> teaching vocally inveighed, with a like bitterness against the
> use of signs. (Burke, 1880, p. 172)

Recognizing the division between these two "types" of teachers that
reflects a particular ideology of language for the deaf, Burke proposed a
solution: a "combined method" that was becoming a buzzword among
the deaf education professionals during this time. According to Burke,
the "two methods [spoken and signed] may be combined, by mutual
concessions, into *one single system* [emphasis in original], embracing
the advantages of both" (Burke, 1880, p. 172). It is not clear whether
Burke was proposing a system of signs and spoken English together as
simultaneous communication or whether she was advocating a bilingual
approach where these two languages would be used separately. Burke's
most important point is the need for two languages to coexist in deaf
education. Note, however, the emphasis in her combined method does
not equally balance the two languages. Instead, she advises to:

> emphatically urge the necessity of teaching by articulation
> [speech], so as to bring back the lost sense of speech by constantly
> and thoroughly exercising the vocal organs . . . . As a means
> of rapid and vivid communication, [presumably communica-
> tion between the deaf and the majority of members in society],
> nothing can supersede this judicious use [speech], and instead of
> impeding the deaf child's progress in language of the develop-
> ment of his mind, they help it on. I would, however, advise the
> gradual relinquishment of signs as the pupil advances, but their
> entire abandonment I could not counsel. (Burke, 1880, p. 173)

E. M. Gallaudet praised Burke's approach by commenting in front
of the members of the fourth National Conference of Principals of
American Institutions for the Deaf and Dumb:

> I desire to express my gratification with the line of thought
> presented in the paper which we have just heard. It is a happy

thing to us who are working in the interest of the deaf and dumb that in this country we do not witness that division of our teachers into parties where a greater or less degree of bitterness of feeling exists, and where rival systems are combatting each other with sometimes more earnestness than discretion, as has been the case in past years in many places on the other side of the globe; and it is a matter for which we cannot be too thankful that in this country we are working together, as is shown by the coming together on this occasion of the heads of institutions who represent the various systems and methods that are now pursued in the country.

This paper is upon the combined method, which aims to unite all that is good in every system that may be employed for the benefit of the deaf and dumb. Whether such combination in a single institution is possible or not, is a legitimate question for discussion. Some think it possible; others have a different opinion. If the presentation of this paper can draw out from those present to-day an expression of those different opinions, we shall all be benefited. (E. M. Gallaudet, 1880, pp. 174–175)

Despite Gallaudet's emphasis on the collaborative interest for the deaf rather than a division and despite his emphasis on Burke's call to develop a marriage between spoken English and sign language using the combined method, these two paradigms would clash historically only a few months later.

## Milan Revisited

A dramatic outcome of the paradigm wars secured its place in deaf history in September of 1880 during the Second International Congress on Education of the Deaf in Milan, Italy, planned by the Pereire Society, an oralist organization. Despite the fact that the Milan meeting was "conducted by hearing opponents of sign language" (Lane, 1999, p. 113) who openly advocated the oral method and proposed to ban sign language in all schools throughout the world (Gannon, 1981; Van Cleve & Crouch, 1989), it was still an open invitation to all stakeholders including principals. At the fourth National Conference of Principals of American Institutions for the Deaf and Dumb held on May 27, 1880 (nearly 5 months before the meeting in Milan), Edward Allen Fay, presiding officer of the conference and editor of the *American Annals for the Deaf and Dumb* offered:

> a resolution, which was adopted, empowering and request-ing President Gallaudet, Dr. Gillett, Mr. Denison, and any other principals who may find it convenient, to represent the Conference as delegates at the International Convention to be held in Milan, Italy, in September. (1880, p. 217)

Only two additional conference members (I. L. Peet and C. A. Stoddard) attended the Milan conference, joining delegates, E. M. Gallaudet, Thomas Gallaudet (who went in Gillett's place), and J. Denison, a total of five members. They represented the United States and were among the only delegates (along with one from England) to vote against the infamous resolution banning sign language, which would seriously impact many countries around the world, including the United States. To be sure, the delegates of the United States were in the minority; the rest of the delegates agreed with the president of the Milan meeting, who stated that "oral speech is the sole power that can rekindle the light God breathed into man, giving him a soul in a corporeal body" (Lane, 1999, 114). The resolutions that were passed at the meeting intensified interest in the oral method that had already begun to spread. According to Lane (1999), in hindsight, the Milan congress was the "single most critical event in driving the languages of deaf communities beneath the surface" (p. 113).

Before Milan 1880, documents published in the proceedings of the national Conferences of Principals of American Institutions for the Deaf and Dumb, proceedings of the Convention of American Instructors of the Deaf and Dumb, and other professional publications reflect careful and intense debates on education and language use. In fact, one educator concluded back in 1868 that:

> when we seek to make improvements on a system that has stood the test of a round century in the land of its birth

[France], and of a full half century on this side of the Atlantic, it is evident that we should be sure that we do not make rash innovations, and that what we do should be rather a development of principles well established, than an attempt at progress from a new starting point. (Peet, 1868, p. 171)

The system that Peet was referring to was the language of signs "the true basis of deaf-mute instruction . . . [and] we should not propose to disuse any signs that have been well established" (Peet, 1868, p. 171). Unfortunately, Milan 1880 did just that; the resolution not only denigrated signs but also supported banning sign language in all educational facilities.

One of the main advocates for banning sign language in America was Alexander Graham Bell, who established the School of Vocal Physiology and Mechanics of Speech in Boston, one of the first deaf oral schools in 1872 (Britannica Biographies, 2012). Bell and his supporters brilliantly lobbied for oral-based deaf education in day schools and within classes. General education specialists testified before state legislatures "advancing their arguments directly within the institutions of hearing society, rather than at residential schools or the associations of deaf adults" (Buchanan, 1999, p. 24), although Bell vigorously defended his position in various conferences and conventions within deaf education. Bell and other supporters of oral-only education sought to identify institutions that had the power and ability to make these constructive changes in deaf education. Like Itard did in front of the Society of the Faculty of Medicine in 1808, Bell addressed the National Academy of Sciences in 1883 and reported that there was a rise of a "defective variety" of the human race. He believed this trend was a result of deaf people's "isolation" from society because of their use of sign language, intermarriage rates, and segregated associations/educational institutions. During this same speech, Bell proposed that deaf schools convert from sign-language-based instruction to oral-only instruction and replace deaf teachers with hearing teachers (Buchanan, 1999).

Two years after Milan, documents in the Proceedings of the Tenth Convention of American Instructors of the Deaf and Dumb on August 26–30, 1882, indicate a tide of members supporting Bell. One notable presenter, Emma Garrett, an oral-based teacher for the deaf, made a plea that the deaf-mutes of America be taught to speak:

> It seems to me impossible to add to the weight of evidence that we already have in favor of speech for the deaf.
>
> Nevertheless, as the majority of those that teach them in America think that speech is not for the mass of the deaf, I cannot meet with these instructors without uniting my voice with those who claim that these deaf-born but not dumb-born children can be taught to use their voices. If the Milan convention failed to convince our American instructors, will not the fact of France acknowledging the superiority of the oral method at a recent national convention at Bordeaux convince them? Is it in the nature of things that France, the birth-place of the sign system, should accept the oral method, unless led to do so by an overpowering evidence in its favor? (Garrett, 1883, p. 16)

Her plea, interpreted in sign language by Thomas Gallaudet to the deaf members (teachers mostly), invokes Milan and France (birthplace of the manual method) converting to the oral method as a means to justify an oral-based pedagogy. Garrett adds that "if speech is better for hearing people than barbaric signs, it is better for the deaf . . . . [T]he power of speech and lipreading brings the deaf into general communication with mankind" (Garrett, 1883, p. 18). As a teacher, Garrett equates speaking with normalcy and sign language with being unnatural. This type of plea was also echoed by principals and superintendents from some deaf schools during this time to reinforce the oral-oriented approach as being of great importance in the instruction of deaf children.

During the proceedings of the Fifth National Conference of Principals of American Institutions for the Deaf and Dumb in 1884, Mr. Greenberger, then principal of the Institution for the Improved Instruction of Deaf-Mutes (New York), reinforced the importance of speech and that "*imperfect* [emphasis added] speech, is far more beautiful than the most beautiful expressions by signs" (Biennial Report, 1884, p. 173). To this principal of a deaf school, imperfect speech was superior to sign language; that is, impartial speech carried more value than a whole message in sign language. As the conference was about to adjourn for the day, E. M. Gallaudet felt the need to "beg the consideration of the Conference to the question before us [the value of speech]" and pressed that many deaf people who had no speech functioned perfectly well in business and in life (Biennial Report, 1884, pp. 174–175). Gallaudet hinted cautiously (so as not to be out of order) that the debate on whether speech should be a dominant criterion of humanity needs to be called into question:

> I may be allowed to so claim and not be considered out of order, that when we have the fact before us in this country, that now for a period of sixty or seventy years men and women, deaf from birth and dumb to death, have lived, have loved, have labored, have built homes, have paid taxes, have supported themselves, have helped to bear the burdens of society, have taken hold upon the grand prospects of the future life, have lived and walked and died as noble specimens of humanity, who have fulfilled their parts in society, who have prosecuted various sorts of business with eminent success,—who as a class, (this class of deaf and dumb people who have lived here in this country,) when I say they have done all this, we have a little different understanding of just what this question means. (Biennial Report, 1884, p. 176)

Gallaudet concluded his lengthy speech by reminding the Conference members that "it is the training of the mind, it is the training of the heart, it is the formation of character, it is the making of boys and girls into men and women for whom it is worth while to life, and for whom it is worth while, too, the country should live" (Biennial Report, 1884, p. 178).

Immediately, Bell, "pained to hear this discussion" (p. 179) rose to speak in response to Gallaudet's speech. Bell emphasized that the value of speech cannot be measured because it is inherently innate to what it means to be human. For Bell, to measure the value of speech is to measure the value of life; something that cannot be denied or intrinsically separated; in essence, to speak is human. Bell's goal for speech would bring "the deaf child closer into companionship with hearing people . . . [and] that the great aim of education of the deaf and dumb is to bring the deaf into more close contact with the hearing to *restore them to society* [emphasis added]" (Bell, 1884, p. 179). Bell used his wife, who was deaf, as a "success" story while Gallaudet used his mother, also deaf, as an alternative "success" story. Toward the end of the debate, one member suggested that nobody had the authority to measure speech, but it was the parents of the deaf child to decide the value of speech. Gallaudet responded immediately that he had met many parents who "would not have their children taught to speak under any consideration, after they had visited the school and heard the children attempt to speak" (Biennial Report, 1884, p. 180) and Mr. Tuton (superintendent at the Institution for the Deaf and Dumb of Kansas) added that he had "received letters from parents requesting me [Mr. Tuton] to take their children out of the articulation class and that they were not making the progress . . . and their speech was no benefit" (Biennial Report, 1884, p. 180).

The same Conference met again in 1888 with the same debates that Burke had forewarned. In the sixth National Conference proceedings, there were echoes to return to sign language and to question the validity of speech as an effective means for instructing deaf students. Bell did not defend whether or not spoken English was effective; it appeared that oral-oriented pedagogy was already dominating the deaf educational system. Instead, he expressed his concerns with the low percentage of students being taught articulation. A graph indicated that from 1884 to 1887, the number of students being taught articulation increased from 27.3% to 32%; Bell, among others, contended that there should have been a higher increase (Table 3.1).

Although in the 1850s, about "250 of the 550 teachers and administrators in the burgeoning national network of schools were themselves deaf" (Buchanan, 1999, p. 4), their numbers decreased radically between 1880 and the early 1970s (Janesick & Moores, 1992; Van Cleve & Crouch, 1989). Hearing teachers who taught spoken English as a leading pedagogical method for deaf students increased while teachers who were deaf declined within the overall teaching profession from 42.5% in 1870 to 14.5% in 1917 and then to 12% in 1960 (Buchanan, 1999; Lou, 1988). However, these numbers would rise slowly. A study conducted in the late 1990s found 15% of teachers in schools of the deaf were themselves deaf (Andrews & Franklin, 1997) and in 2008, 22% of the teachers were deaf (Simms, Rusher, Andrews, & Coryell, 2008, p. 384).

TABLE 3.1:    RATES OF INSTRUCTION IN ARTICULATION, 1884–1887

| Year | Total Number of Pupils | Taught Articula-tion | Not Taught Articulation | Per centage Taught Articulation | Per centage not Taught Articulation |
|------|------|------|------|------|------|
| 1884 | 7,485 | 2,041 | 5,444 | 27.8 | 72.7 |
| 1885 | 7,801 | 2,618 | 5,183 | 33.5 | 66.5 |
| 1886 | 8,050 | 2,484 | 5,566 | 30.8 | 69.2 |
| 1887 | 7,978 | 2,556 | 5,422 | 32.0 | 68.0 |

*Note:* A chart in Bell's possession at the Sixth National Conference of Superintendents and Principals of American Institutions for the Deaf and Dumb (National Conference, 1888, p. 135).

A. G. Bell, at the sixth National Conference of Superintendents and Principals of American Institutions of the Deaf and Dumb, demonstrated his frustration and "shame that any principal should put a speaking pupil under a deaf teacher" (Bell, 1888, p. 143). Subsequently, many principals proceeded to follow Bell's call, and deaf teachers were replaced by hearing educators trained in the oral method. The deaf teachers were excluded mainly because they obviously could not hear, but also because they "would not promote oralism" (Burch & Sutherland, 2006, p. 139). During this time, aural instruction was no longer an experiment; because of "the results and the benefits it confers on the class for whom it is designed, it has earned the right to a prominent place in every institution for the deaf" (Gillespie, 1888, pp. 137–138).

With aural instruction as the prominent mode of language pedagogy, scholars were ready to write deaf history. Indeed, Westervelt (1891) addresses the need to have a "History of the Education of the Deaf" and goes on to outline the "historical descriptions of the (a) Sign or 'combined' Method; (b) Manual Alphabet method; (c) Auricular [*sic*] method; (d) Oral method" (p. 223). In the same article, he advertises what his organization, the American Association to Promote the Teaching of Speech to the Deaf, can do:

It is only by experience and a full expression of views and opinions that the best method of carrying on our work and of conducting our meetings can be arrived at. For the afternoon work, from three until five o'clock, there will be given, in practice classes, practical exemplification of the methods of: (a) Oral teaching in 'combined' method schools; (b) Oral work in a manual-alphabet school; (c) Auricular training; (d) Pure oral schools. (p. 224)

Nowhere in the same article (or journal for that matter) is there any mention of providing sign-based language training. However, in this same volume, there is an article discussing the early stages in deaf education, which highlights sign language and includes a few comparative cases from other countries using sign-based approaches and a few in America (Kinsel, 1891, p. 211). Interestingly, the journal ends with "advertisements" such as the following:

Summer School of Oral Training School for Teachers of the Deaf, established 1881, will be at Forest City, Lackawanna Co., Pa. Eight students enrolled for summer. About thirty graduates teaching in Schools and private families in U. S.; several are Principals of Oral schools. (p. 236)

Milan 1880 and the immense pressure by A. G. Bell allowed oral-based philosophy to dominate the deaf education pedagogy in America from 1880 to the 1970s. This time frame has been considered by many deaf people in the community as the dark era in deaf history (Gannon, 1981). The Milan 1880 event and the charismatic efforts by Bell had a severe impact on the divisive languacultures in deaf education,[5] including school dynamics:

In America, there were 26 institutions for the education of deaf children in 1867, and ASL was the language of instruction in

---

5. The recent 2010 International Congress on Education of the Deaf, the very same Congress that met 130 years ago, recognized that the removal of sign languages from education programs for the Deaf "contributed detrimentally to the lives of Deaf citizens around the world" (Moores, 2010, p. 310). As a result, in a symbolic gesture, the members of the International Congress on Education of the Deaf formally rejected the 1880 resolution banning sign language.

all; by 1907, there were 139 schools for deaf children, and ASL was allowed in none. (Lane, 1999, p. 113)

Many members of the deaf community opposed the oral ideology established by hearing educators and emphasized the importance of sign language in education. In 1880, the same year as the Milan conference, one social movement in the United States established the National Association for the Deaf (NAD) with the mission of preserving sign language. This association would contribute to the paradigm wars that contested spoken English and sign language as contrasting languacultures in the debate to determine the criterion of a normal and deviant deaf individual in deaf education. Sign language would never be the same after Milan 1880 because of the rise of oralist movement, but in

> the larger sense, the oralist movement failed. Sign language continued to be used, and vigorously defended, by the deaf community. Deaf parents passed sign language on to their children, and those children who were deaf passed it on to their school mates. Indeed, even most schools that were trying to discourage the use of sign language found that they could not do it entirely, reserving it for the always substantial number of older "oral failures." Oral communication was too impractical for many deaf people, and sign language too cherished by the deaf community, for the latter to disappear completely. (Baynton, 1999, p. 94)

During this time, scholars and practitioners from the oral discipline continued to promote the oral method as the most effective pedagogy to "correct" the deaf-mute individual. In 1891, A. G. Bell funded the American Association to Promote the Teaching of Speech to the Deaf, which would later become the Alexander Graham Bell Association for the Deaf and Hard of Hearing. The 139 schools for the deaf, staffed with mainly (if not all) hearing teachers for the deaf, used the oral method and sign language was banned at all times. This situation would last until in the 1960s, when sign language reentered the academic debate of languacultures in deaf education.

## Contrasting Paradigms: Different Languacultures

Sign language was re-introduced in the deaf educational debate after 1965 after an English professor at Gallaudet University, William Stokoe, published the first ASL dictionary. Dr. Stokoe gained worldwide support that ASL was indeed a language for the deaf. Stokoe was extremely technical in his findings; he was able to deconstruct ASL linguistically to show that it had the same linguistic properties as a whole language. After Stokoe's pioneering work on ASL, Kathryn P. Meadow (1972) was one of the first to recognize the connection between ASL and deaf individuals' identity as part of a deaf community, a linguistic community with a subculture (Schein, 1968; Stokoe, Casterline, & Croneberg, 1965) that was also a minority group (Vernon & Makowsky, 1969). Meadow used ideas in Fishman (1968) and Hymes (1964, 1966) about understanding the "sociology of language" by means of "ethnographies of communication" to place language and deafness in the framework of languaculture. This effort led to a plethora of research, including studying deaf people as an ethnic group (Markowitz & Woodward, 1978) and deafness in a sociocultural context (Washabaugh, 1981). Carol J. Erting (1981, 1982, 1985, 1987 1988, 1994) then incorporated this work in her study of deaf children in education. Although Erting incorporated an anthropological perspective in her study on deaf education, her work changed the way deaf education was situated and gave rise to the importance of language and culture in education.

While a transformation of knowledge was occurring with respect to sign language and deaf education, practitioners who used the auditory/oral-based pedagogy continued to promote their pedagogy as the most effective way to prepare deaf students for a successful mainstreaming process,[6] especially into the realm of higher education, as a foundation for their "successful" future. To them, success was measured by an individual's ability to speak and hear. Today, practitioners of this approach advocate mainstreaming only after deaf students have been "trained" through the oral-based pedagogy to prepare them

---

6. The transition from the oral classification to the mainstream usually starts between third and fifth grades.

for mainstreaming. Therefore, mainstreaming programs tend to be aligned more toward the philosophy of oral-based institutions because by "functioning in a hearing environment, deaf children would absorb the language of the larger community [spoken English]" (Moores, 1992, p. 15). In addition, this type of program "often leads to an emphasis on oral communication" (Moores, 2010, p. 28). The goal for oral-based pedagogy is to prepare the deaf student for full assimilation into society by means of mainstreaming.

The goal of the sign-based pedagogy, however, is for the deaf child to engage in a process of cultural transmission that would preserve their sign language. For scholars who support this goal, sign language has historically been defended, beginning with Epée, as a "native" language for deaf people, and any eradication of sign language is comparable with the colonialization of the deaf community by means of linguistic annihilation (Lane, 1999; Lane & Grosjean, 1980). These scholars also defend that the "deaf community is the one language group that can never be totally assimilated and whose language can never be totally eradicated" (Lane, 1999, p. 172). Scholars have raised the concern that the current education of deaf children attempts to assimilate with the major goal of "hearizing" them (Lucas, 1995, p. 124). Some scholars claim that the mainstreaming system, formed in 1910 as a branch of the oral-based pedagogy, is ineffective and is neither a context nor a solution designed to improve the academic achievement and linguistic opportunities of deaf students (Kent, 2003; Kluwin, Moores, & Gaustad, 1992; Ramsey, 1997). For these scholars, deaf students who are mainstreamed in the hearing public schools "fail to meet two of the criteria for membership in the adult deaf community: linguistic differentiation and attitudinal deafness" (Kluwin, Moores, & Gaustad, 1992, p. 59). Scholars, including those who reject the mainstreaming and oral educational philosophies as an ineffective pedagogy, have extensively focused on the sign-based philosophy (Lane, 1995; Moores & Martin, 2006; Padden & Humphries, 1988; Ramsey, 1997; Wilbur, 2000).

Harlan Lane, a professor of psychology and scholar of deaf culture, goes on to add that for the last 25 years, there has been an educational assimilation, or rather, a dominance of spoken English, auditory/oral indoctrination, mainstreaming, and then surgery (cochlear implants).

This trend marks the long history of "medicalization" of the deaf community, including how these medical "experts" continue to dominate deaf education in terms of linguistics, identity, and academic achievement and "continues to prove to be a failure decade after decade" (Lane, 1999, p. 129). Lane (1999) contends that

> countless hours and a great deal of money are spent specifying these audiologic and psychometric differences, but they make little difference in what we do to or for the deaf people . . . . [T]here are no educational strategies that link up to various test outcomes. (p. 81)

Scholars who support sign-based pedagogy argue for a departure from the medical paradigm and acceptance of a sociocultural paradigm in which deaf people are a part of a linguistic minority and defend the position of the United Nations in 1987 that the deaf and hard of hearing populations "are to be recognized to have their native and indigenous sign language accepted as their first and official language and as the medium of conversation and instruction" (Wrigley, 1996, in Barnartt & Scotch, 2002, p. 50).

These scholars summarize their perspective on deaf education after decades of classroom teaching, heated debates at conferences, and publications by noting that "ASL and English-based signing are here to stay" (Stewart, 2006, p. 207). However, I would like to add that oral/auditory spoken English pedagogies for deaf children are also here to stay. As of 2012, there were 47 oral schools in the United States[7] and about 60–70 schools for the deaf that use a combination of both sign language and spoken English.[8] According to a 2003 statistic, out of these schools that use sign language, there are 19 ASL-based schools that recognize themselves as bilingual-bicultural—this represents the 36% to 40% of residential and day schools for deaf students (LaSasso & Lollis, 2003). In addition, there are countless programs

---

7. Schools listed at http://www.oraldeafed.org.
8. This approximate count was tallied from http://www.csdf.k12.ca.us/deaf-schools/site/main_site.htm and http://www.deafconnect.com/deaf/school.html

within the larger public school systems that serve both hearing and deaf students. A more comprehensive listing of both sign-based and oral-based schools can be found in the annual reference issue of the *American Annals of the Deaf* titled "Educational Programs for Deaf Students" and while it is comprehensive, it is not visibly entirely clear whether these programs are oral-based or sign-based. For example, Central Institute for the Deaf and Kendall Demonstration Elementary School are listed as Day-school(s), but the former uses the oral-based approach while Kendall incorporates ASL in their pedagogy. The most important point here is that both sign-language-based and oral-based schools are here to stay for the next century, just as they have been here for the last 250 years. An article dated July 26, 2011, from *New York Times* titled "Among Twists in Budget Woes, Tensions Over Teaching the Deaf" reinforces that point. In addition, numerous academic journals flourish in the debate: academic journals advocating oral-based pedagogy (e.g., *American Journal of Audiology, American Journal of Speech-Language Pathology, Journal of Speech, Language, and Hearing Research,* and *Volta Review*), academic journals advocating for sign-based pedagogy (e.g., *Sign Language Studies*), and journals that provide a platform for both pedagogies (e.g., *Journal of Deaf Studies and Deaf Education* and the *American Annals for the Deaf*). Similarly, annual conferences hosted by the Alexander Graham Bell Association for the Deaf and Hard of Hearing provide the latest training on aural/oral approaches that includes auditory and speech therapy and auditory/oral methods, and other conferences like the one hosted by the American Sign Language Teachers Association (ASLTA) provide the latest pedagogical approaches using sign language.

In this respect, scholars have used different professional perspectives by which to examine deaf education, and most of them have categorized these perspectives using these two opposing paradigms as a framework for analysis in their attempt to solidify ideology about what it means to be deaf and how deaf students should be taught in the deaf educational institution, including language pedagogy. There appears to be a paradigm clash on language choices, which in turn, affects the social constructions of culture for a deaf child. Even more alarming is that these two paradigms provide "evidence" supporting their language as the most effective language pedagogy for the deaf. Some of the scholarly work providing "evidence" for the sign-based paradigm includes the following:

- Deaf students in a bilingual school setting using ASL as a cultural tool (Bailes, 1999; Cummins, 2000; Kuntze, 2000)
- Identity formation among parents, teachers (both hearing/deaf), and deaf children through ASL (Erting, 1982, 1988, 1994)
- Families' involvement with their deaf children by means of ASL and its educational impact (Akamatsu & Andrews, 1993; Erting, 1987; Koester, Papousek, & Smith-Gray, 2000; Snow, Barnes, Chandler, Goodman, & Hemphill, 1991; Spencer, 2000; Spencer, Erting, & Marschark, 2000; Tabors, Roach, & Snow, 2001)
- Mother's communication methods with their deaf children by means of ASL (Erting, Prezioso, & Hynes, 1994; Jamieson & Pederson, 1993; Meadow, Greenberg, Erting, & Carmichael, 1981; Swisher, 2000)
- Studies of curricula for deaf students with ASL (Johnson, Liddell, & Erting, 1989; Strong, 1988)
- Teachers' positions in the classroom and the important implications of using ASL in the classroom context ASL value (Erting, 1985)
- ASL as a language and literacy in deaf children (Erting, 2003; Maxwell, 1984; Mayer & Akamatsu, 1999; Mayer & Wells, 1996; Nelson, 1998; Padden & Ramsey, 1998; Prinz & Strong, 1998; Schirmer, 2000; Strong & Prinz, 1997)
- Language policy in deaf education (Kuntze, 1993)
- Case studies of ASL-English bilingualism (Bailes, 2001)
- ASL as a native language for deaf people (Veditz, circa 1913, in Padden, 2004)

Scholarly work providing "evidence" for the oral paradigm include the following:

- Teaching "deaf-mutes" how to speak and write (Arnoldi, 1777, in Davis, 1995; Moeller, 1909)
- Oral-based instruction as a successful tool in deaf educational setting (Geers & Nicholas, 2003; Hart & Risley, 1995)

- Benchmarks to evaluate spoken language progress of children with cochlear implants (Nicholas & Geers, 2008)
- Oral education and shared book reading (DesJardin, Ambrose, & Eisenberg, 2008)
- Successful measurement of deaf children with cochlear implant using speech perception, speech production, spoken language, total language, and reading (Moog & Geers, 2003)
- Guidelines to raise a successful deaf child using auditory/oral-based pedagogy (Alexander Graham Bell Association For the Deaf and Hard of Hearing, 2009)
- Innovations in hearing aid technology to improve speaking capacities (Bentler, 2009; Guiberson, 2005)
- Speech as a necessary consequence of the functioning of hearing and as a whole (Itard in a speech to the *Society of the faculty of Medicine* circa 1808, in Davis, 1995)
- Cochlear implants providing a positive identity for children and their emotional functioning (Schorr, 2006)
- Sign language as an "intellectual prison" and emphasis on the success of speaking (Bell circa1800s in Lane & Grosjean, 1980)
- Speech as an advancement in deaf education (Amman, 1694)
- Speaking as an effective form for deaf students (Wallis, 1699)
- "Natural" hierarchal classifications of the features for speech and speech pathology (Amman, 1700)

These two pedagogies of language come armed with "evidence" to support their claim as to why each approach is more "effective." Each paradigm socially constructs ideas, values, norms, and criteria of language that play an important (and dangerous) role in the construction of the deaf student and contribute to the larger framework of what it means to be deaf and human. In 1913, George Veditz, a former president of the National Association for the Deaf, in the landmark film *Preservation of the Sign Language,* said that sign language was God's noblest gift to the deaf (Padden, 2004). For others, "talk is cheap, unless you're deaf, then it's priceless."[9]

---

9. Stated on the home page of the website for the Moog Center for Deaf Education, an oral-based program.

As previously said, most deaf children are born to hearing parents whose language is English and whose culture belongs in the dominant ideology. Deaf children become acculturated first in their homes, then in schools that will serve to reinforce meanings and values of their deafness, including languaculture and ideology. Thus, schools—as social control institutions—and languaculture become critical to the study of social constructions of deafness.

## REFLECTION ON THE ARCHAEOLOGY OF DEAFNESS

There is extensive literature covering the archaeology of deaf education. Scholarly work includes diverse perspectives on deaf education from numerous countries, including Great Britain (Branson & Miller, 2002), Australia (Komesaroff, 2008), Japan (Nakamura, 2006), and Ireland (LeMaster, 2002). Many of these scholarly works on deaf education have a recurring theme: the languacultural conflict of deaf education based on language pedagogy. The literature suggests that the placement (or nonplacement) of sign language in the school setting plays a powerful and exacting role in the development of socially constructed ideologies on what it means to be deaf. This chapter has presented a partial archaeology of American deaf education, specifically in terms of the role of language (both sign language and spoken English).

As the archaeology of deaf education and languaculture indicates, the sociohistory of deaf people reflects an ongoing struggle involving language choices to define and redefine the dominant ideology of deaf education. For the past 250 years, deaf students have been framed and reframed using readily identified epistemological properties to culturally and socially construct who they are as humans in the name of normalcy. Social control institutions construct social representations of deafness by constructing a specific type of "corpus of knowledge" or "archaeology of knowledge" by means of social control processes. These institutions continue to present their "evidence" in constructing certain types of knowledge that serve to reinforce their specific ideologies. Thus, this chapter has examined who defines this knowledge and how these properties are defined as types of knowledge, including the importance of hegemony and the impact of social control institutions as well as their processes (Lauderdale & Inverarity, 2003; Marx & Engels in Bunge, 1999).

These processes serve to maintain and solidify hegemony; more importantly, they define the historical place of deaf students in terms of normalcy and deviance (Horejes & Lauderdale, 2007). Thus, the literature review reflects an archaeology of deafness, including its "epistemic" space, the types of knowledge produced and reproduced, and the archival records of historical documents that slowly evolve into the types of examinations developed when discussing the sociohistory of deafness.

Stakeholders within each ideological domain consider themselves as the defenders of preserving the successful ways of deaf education and to cast the other as the "enemy." Role players in deaf education construct certain types of knowledge to craft what a "normal" deaf child ought to be and simultaneously construct specific parameters of a deaf child rooted in deviance (i.e., the use of sign language or placing the deaf child in mainstreaming programs). Unraveling the claims and related types of information constructed in these paradigm wars requires another level of analysis (Lauderdale, McLaughlin, & Oliverio, 1990). This deeper analysis includes an examination of two contesting ideologies and the ways they continue to shape the parameters of normalcy and deviance for the deaf. There is a need to implement a comparative literature base to reexamine how language modalities contribute to the social constructions of deaf students. Throughout the archaeology of deafness, these epistemological constructions of deafness use these epistemological properties to construct a specific type of "corpus of knowledge" or "archaeology of knowledge" by reinforcing which languaculture will reign supreme.

Exploring socially constructed deaf students is important, in part, because of the experiences that influence the development of one's identity and language acquisition especially in preschools (Nikolaraizi & Hadjikakou, 2006; Vygotsky, 1926/1997). Educational institutions as different ideological state apparatuses are able to "regulate" certain types of knowledge using their own claims and types of "evidence." Determining which knowledge is important may unintentionally construct stigmatizing definitions in deaf education practices by determining what is most "natural" and "privileged" (e.g., whether ASL or spoken English ought to be the most "natural" language or how culture in the classroom ought to be facilitated).

I suggest that stratifications also reproduce divisive ideologies and social inequality in the construction of deafness, deaf education, and best practices. These divisive factors may have forced a worldview and identity onto the deaf child, instead of providing choices that would be most advantageous to him or her. Highly divisive (and often problematic) constructions of normalcy and deviance suggest a cautionary note to role players in the educational social control institutions concerning what they feel is best for deaf students. A reexamination on deaf students' constructions through pedagogy of language, cultures in the classroom, and teacher knowledge may be a heuristic way to study some of the social constructions of normalcy and deviance in deafness.

In Chapter 4, examining the "life" and the constructions of two classrooms in two different kindergartens is important as crucial sites for this study, especially because these types of early childhood programs "are complex institutions serving children, parents, and indirectly, the wider society . . . and reflect and affect social change" (Tobin, Wu, & Davidson, 1989, p. 2). The study of two classrooms can offer insight into how these schools may construct what it means to be deaf. Understanding classroom life and its constructions "is too complex an affair to be viewed or talked about from any single perspective . . . . [W]e must not hesitate to use all of the ways of knowing at our disposal," including the different methodological orientations for studying classrooms (Jackson, 1968, p. vii). Chapter 4 examines these two different classrooms that include two different language pedagogies. The diverse physical ecologies of the classrooms, teacher facilitation, biographies of the students, uses of technology, and types of performativity in the classroom all contribute to the overall languaculture; these factors will be analyzed to compare the different educational institutions and their social constructs.

I use comparative theoretical frameworks and their connections to methodological orientations to uncover types of information that can be transformed into analytical information, which can build on relevant elements of a grounded theory of deafness (see Appendix A for a detailed explanation on methodology). These theoretical frameworks become opportunities to then analyze comparable theoretical ideas, including the constructions of normalcy and deviance within the larger structural dimensions of deafness and deaf educational institutions.

# CHAPTER FOUR

# A "Tale" of Two Classrooms

There is an extensive body of research and literature on deaf education, its pedagogies, "best practices," and "promises" toward a "better" education for the deaf, as documented in the previous chapter, but rarely are these works framed in a cross-comparative platform as sites of study. The limited cross-comparative ethnographic data have prompted this ethnographic research to compare diverse schools containing unique pedagogies and ideologies in the constructions of deaf education. Ethnographic research here involves making sense of language and culture occurring in these schools as sites of acculturation/enculturation (Erting, 2003b, p. 458).

The two schools in this study were selected based on their contrasting language pedagogy and languaculture. One school advocates sign-based practices that emphasize the development of the natural sign language as the primary language, then anchors that language to written and/or spoken English. The second school is oral-based and advocates spoken English as the primary choice of language pedagogy for deaf students. Although a large portion of deaf students are placed in public schools or in what scholars call "mainstreaming" programs, the two schools that were studied here represent—on a larger level—the ongoing cultural conflict that has lasted 250 years and continues to exist in solidifying social constructions on what it means to be deaf. Using these two diverse schools as cross-comparative sites of acculturation/enculturation for deaf students, specifically, a sign-based and oral-based kindergarten, I studied two nonrandom samples to improve conceptual models and contribute to understanding social change (Lareau, 1989, p. 228). The conceptual models here include pedagogy of language, culture in the classroom, and teacher knowledge as major contributors to the languaculture for the deaf. These conceptual models are explicated further in Chapter 5.

The process to become acculturated into culture and language is a complex process for deaf children. Because over 90% of deaf children have hearing parents and siblings, acculturation of deaf children into a deaf culture occurs largely outside the family. Thus, I chose students who were in kindergarten (ages 5–6 years) because, for many deaf children, kindergartens serve as one of the earliest and primary sites of enculturation into culture and language (Erting 1982, 1994). The results of the data collection were derived from more than 70 hours of classroom observations over the course of two full school years (2008 and 2009) that were documented using field notes, including a videotaped "day in the classroom" for each classroom (see Tobin, Wu, & Davidson, 1989, for a methodological comparison).

The ethnographic data offer a way to analyze some constructions of deafness, specifically, deaf education practices (i.e., languaculture) from a comparative and narrative analysis of the two schools. I also present a reflective analysis of my visual sense of the two classrooms. Reflectivity helps me in my role as an observer and researcher, because of the

> greater social and self-awareness/consciousness of the whole intellectual/research process: of a) subject of the research along with b) social spaces in which the research knowledge is produced as well as c) a much fuller sense of the spaces, locations—personal, cultural, academic, intellectual, historical of the researcher in actually building the research knowledge. (Plummer, 2001, p. 208)

I reflected on being able to position myself in different cultural boundaries, having been raised in the oral system, immersed in the deaf world with sign language, and seen as a member of both the deaf and hearing community. As an ethnographer, I participated in and observed cultural scenes in the classroom, which requires time interacting with members of the culture in different settings and fluency in the language of that culture. In this respect, I was able to translate my emic data into etic information that could be made explicit for the hearing audience. It is the ethnographer's job to conceptualize "writing as a version of one culture that will make it comprehensible to readers living in another" (Emerson, Fretz, & Shaw, 1995, p. 15). This process enabled me to switch my research identity (i.e., a speaker or signer, depending on what boundaries I was in) to maintain my insider status. Certain aspects of the data in the deaf classroom are "difficult, if not impossible, for a member of hearing populations to grasp empirically and formulate conceptually" (Zinn, 2001, p. 159). For example, my experiences as a former oral student allowed me to immediately recognize the rigorous and intensive one-on-one instruction with the teacher, the specific structure of the classroom, and the spatial relationships between the teacher and students. Similarly, certain traits in the ASL classroom are best understood as customary to its culture (e.g., tapping, grunting, and constant movement from the hands/arms of the student). My role allowed me to be more "cognizant and accepting of complexity and internal variation, better able to understand the nuances of language use," and able to access specific boundaries and then translate them to the "outside" hearing world (Zavella, 1993, p. 54). With my multiple roles as an observer/participant researcher in mind, I provide a unique "tale" of two classrooms based on my observations and interviews. My narrative findings of the two classrooms are organized and interrelated, in three parts: the classroom, the students, and the teachers. The dynamics of the classroom, the role of the students, and teachers are three important aspects that provide clues on the diverse language and educational pedagogies within deaf education.

## Narrative of the Oral School

For the oral school, the function of the classroom as an intermediating process, the facilitation of the teacher, and passiveness of students provide a narrative on what an oral-based pedagogy might look like and how these three aspects of the oral-based school prepare their deaf students for mainstreaming. I start with the classroom.

*Classroom*

Central School[1] was founded in the late 1990s and is a privately funded school with approximately 40–45 students and 11 teachers. The school is a single-story building with an annex specifically for children younger than 1 year old. The annex is a place used by school practitioners to screen and determine eligibility for enrollment. The school has 10 different classrooms, and each classroom consists of no more than three students to one teacher. The age ranges for students are between 1 and 9 years ("Kris," personal communication, October 8, 2008).

There are no obvious indications of the physical structure of the school such as playgrounds, sports fields, flag posts, and/or school buses that signal this place is an educational facility, except for a small street sign that says, "Central School," which can easily be missed if one were not looking for it. It is one of the only oral schools in the state of Arizona, and the enrollment policy is stringent. It is highly desirable at Central School for the child to be younger than age 1 or 2 years at the time of enrollment. The deaf child must exhibit an ability to hear through technological devices, cochlear implant, or hearing aids and must demonstrate the ability to speak. If the child does not meet those two requirements, he or she is not considered for enrollment and is often referred to the second school discussed in this chapter ("Kris," personal communication, October 8, 2008). The tuition rate varies with the child's age and the specialized program in which she/he enrolls. For a 1-year-old deaf student in this "early-intervention" program, the tuition is approximately $11,000 per year, although the school strives to find scholarships and/or private donations to help fund each deaf student, depending on the parental income.

Once entering the classroom, I was seated in the "back" of the room and would remain in this position throughout my observations while Kris, the head teacher, was in the "front" of the classroom. She

---

1. Names of both schools as well as teachers and students have been given pseudonyms. Indications of personal communications throughout provide only the teacher's pseudonym.

was seated at the center of the smaller side of a trapezoidal table, while two students (average age of 5 years) were seated at the two horizontally opposing sides of the trapezoidal table (Figure 4.1). The chair in Figure 4.1 represents where the teacher normally sat.

The visual outlook of the classroom is neatly organized—no clutter on the floor, books neatly arranged, and posters on the walls neatly aligned. The physical ecology of the classroom is very organized into three main areas: (a) the teacher's desk overlooking the entire classroom, (b) the mini-kitchen area with student toothbrushes and a sink, and (c) the trapezoid-shaped table for classroom instruction (see sociospatial spaces in Figure 4.2). The bookshelf acts as a visual divider in the classroom.

There is a technical "area" by the entrance of the door that resembles a battery charger and acts as the generator for the FM system and/or cochlear implant devices. All of the students wore a cochlear implant, and once entering the classroom, each student would obtain an FM system from the technical area before being seated. The purpose

FIGURE 4.1.   Trapezoid table in the oral classroom, with a chair showing where the teacher sits; students sit on opposite ends on either side of the teacher.

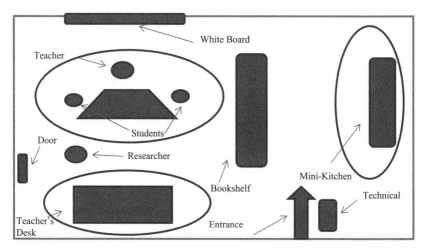

FIGURE. 4.2.    Physical ecology of oral classroom.

of the FM system was to increase their ability to hear the teacher, who would have a mini-microphone attached to her body.

The students almost always sat in a neat fashion, with their legs confined within their chair space and their arms folded, hands clasped and rested on the trapezoid table, and with heads angled toward the teacher. As the teacher instructed each student individually, the other students continued to gaze at the teacher and glance at their peers occasionally. There was little interaction between the students, but there was intense interaction between the teacher and each student, with the teacher acting as the dominant facilitator. When interactions occurred between the students, they were more one-dimensional, with one student talking to the other who typically gave no verbal response; however, the other student would indicate understanding by nodding, and this process was validated by post-observations and comments from the teacher. Each student patiently waited for their turn for most of the activities, and rarely did any student interrupt another student while he or she received individualized instruction.

Although rare, there were times when the teacher attempted to include both students in the same activity at the trapezoid table, and these situations were more of a "test" to see whether the other student was paying attention and to re-motivate the students to continue the speech therapy. For example, the teacher would quickly go to the "inactive" student and ask, "Did you hear what I said to the other student?" to "test" whether she/he was able to "hear" the teacher. Although the teacher was giving the individualized instruction to the other student, she wanted to encourage the inactive student to passively participate in the instruction by hearing other conversations. I followed up with the teacher to inquire when she "decides" to include the other student, and she said that speech therapy in the classroom is often an exhausting lesson plan for the students, and they often get tired very quickly, so she usually tries to maintain motivation at these points. This process was validated at points when I observed the students yawning and rubbing their eyes; at those times when the teacher observes she's losing her students' attention, she includes social interactions that appear to reenergize the students. They talk as a collective, momentarily feeding off of each other's energies, and then the teacher goes back to the one-on-one instructional mode.

Instruction in the classroom was highly structured and organized. The daily classroom schedule was rigorously broken up into 30-minute educational activities. Some of the activities included the following:

> conversational language where they learn new concepts and use their acquired language skills to converse, syntax—a structured period where they learn new linguistic structures and syntactic elements—and speech and auditory training (work to acquire new speech sounds and use their existing sounds in developing their speech and train their auditory channel in the cochlear implant/hearing aids to pick up sounds). ("Kris," personal communication, October 8, 2008)

The school schedules were organized to simulate a traditional public school program in which each student typically experienced different teachers and different classroom environments. To further prepare the deaf student to successfully mainstream into their hearing schools, the classroom was set up as a typical classroom with traditional props such as an ABC poster and United States map. I did not detect any props that resembled anything attributed to deafness, for example, an ASL alphabet poster or posters referring to sign language.

Although each student had one designated "homeroom" classroom where he/she could store personal items in a locker, throughout the day, students typically went from one classroom to another with different teachers (three to four daily) for different "subjects" such as math, science, and social studies. However, the oral school does not consider these topics as subjects; rather, their subjects are categorized as syntax, conversational language, vocabulary, and speech vocabulary. The categorization of classroom subjects as the curriculum is consistent with the interviews I had with the teacher, who would discuss how each "subject" benefits the students' educational pedagogy. I identified a bookshelf neatly organized with plastic bins for the teacher, and each was labeled according to these categories. The labels were for the teacher's use and included "syntax," "vocabulary," "auditory training," "conversational language," and "speech games." I would be able to identify which "subject" the teacher was incorporating by observing which plastic bin she pulled from the bookshelf for educational instruction.

The classrooms themselves were organized primarily for the teachers, not the students. For example, the classroom showed little indication of personalized student posters. The only personalized "space" for the students was their lockers, which they accessed once at the start of the day and once when leaving for home.

The teacher relied on speaking and hearing for all of her instruction. Each topic (i.e., math) was structured to embed speech therapy into the lesson plans, and no sign language was used. I was informed that once students are mainstreamed, they typically do not have a sign language interpreter and often rely on using their technological devices and their speaking/hearing abilities learned from the oral school to succeed in the classroom. Often, the school district contributes some financial funding for the child to attend the oral school in hopes that, once mainstreamed, the student will not need an interpreter, thus saving financial costs in the long run ("Kris," personal communication, March 12, 2009).

The classroom instructional pedagogy follows the Moog Curriculum. According to the website of the Moog Center in St. Louis, the

> focus of the curriculum is accelerating development of spoken language and, when the children are ready, to help them learn the same subjects as their hearing age-mates so they can catch up and be *full participants in the mainstream* [emphasis added].[2]

All of the textbooks and lesson plans follow the Moog Curriculum; instructional pedagogy is structured for speaking and hearing/listening in most classroom activities and conversations.

A main component of the oral school's curriculum is conversational analysis. This strategic lesson plan is tailored to encourage students to create sentences to which the teachers then add more words for the students to expand their vocabulary. Equally as important is the procedure to enable the student to effectively pronounce each word in the sentence. One example of conversational analysis focused on clothing and weather. The theme was the Arctic culture, and each large-sized page was filled with real photos and computer printed words. The photo book had various "chapters" along with flash cards showing various photos, including the building of the Arctic igloo, clothing (fur) not only in the winter but also in the summer, and the food (both in the winter and summer). One flash card displayed a photograph of an adult wearing fur with "fur," as a textual caption, and the teacher asked, "Is the guy wearing fur?" The student replied with a simple, "Yes." Then, the teacher encouraged the student to elaborate by saying, "Yes what?" In response, the student stated, "Yes, the guy is wearing fur." This lesson plan was repeated by the student several times, and then the teacher went to the next student and asked, "What color is the fur?" The other student replied, "Brown," and the teacher asked the student "What is brown?" which prompted the student to repeat in a complete sentence, "The guy is wearing brown fur." If a student mispronounced a word, the teacher would use speech

---

2. See http://www.moogcenter.org, website for The Moog Center for Deaf Education.

therapy, including repetition, to ensure that the student mastered the word. The student would then repeat the entire sentence before moving on to the next topic. After discussing clothing, weather was the next topic in this situation. The teacher incorporated the terms *hot* and *cold* and, at one point, brought the students outside (the classroom had an entrance to outside) and asked them, "Is it hot or cold outside?" The students responded, "It is hot outside." Then the teacher asked, "Is the weather like this in the Arctic?" The students responded, "No, it is not like this in the Arctic. It is cold."

During these conversational exercises, there were visual cues such as flash cards with words and drawings of objects to help students identify words with the objects. The students were prompted to pronounce the object and connect the vocabulary word with the object, often repeating several times to "get it right." Use of speech superseded the importance of reading the text, as the teacher would make the student elaborate on words and sentences that were not included on the flashcards.

Another classroom exercise related to conversational language used the "never, sometimes, always" terminology and applied it to real-life activities. The concentration was on the ability to conduct speech and hearing within this exercise. The activity was developed as a type of board game in which every time the students completed a speech lesson, they would roll the die and move their pieces toward the "finish" line. The game consisted of flash cards with two photos that also had a noun and an action verb on it along with a "never/sometimes/always" label. Each student looked at the noun/verb words and pictures and formed them into a sentence using *never, sometimes,* or *always*. After the student formed a sentence, the teacher added more words to make the sentence longer and more structured. Then, the teacher asked the other student the same question. By the end, each student would have gotten several chances to roll the die and move the game pieces. The following exchange is an example of a 5-minute exercise with the two students and one teacher using flash cards that showed a pool and an image of a cochlear implant.

Student:  Pool! (*gets excited*)
Teacher:  What else do you see in the flashcard?

Student: My cochlear implant (*points to his cochlear implant*).

Teacher: That's right! So, do you never, sometimes, or always wear a cochlear implant in the pool?

Student: (*laughing*) Never!

Teacher: Say it in a sentence.

Student: Never wear cochlear implant in pool.

Teacher: Whose cochlear implant? (*makes facial gestures to indicate the student*)

Student: Mine!

Teacher: Okay, say that again in a sentence.

Student: I never wear mine cochlear implant in pool.

Teacher: Mine or my?

Student: My.

Teacher: OK, say the whole sentence again.

Student: I never wear my (*with emphasis by tilting his head*) cochlear implant in the pool.

Teacher: Say cochlear one more time with two syllables (*emphasizes each syllable by using her hands to indicate when to speak and when to stop with a pause, as if she was the conductor of a band*) Coak <.5 second pause>

Student: Coak <.5 second pause> Lear.

Teacher: Very good! Now say the whole thing one more time.

Student: I never wear my <.5 second pause> Coak <.5 second pause> Lear implant.

Teacher: In the pool? Say it again.

Student: I never wear my <.5 second pause> Coak <.5 second pause> Lear implant in the pool.

Teacher: Very good! (*goes to the other student*) Do you wear your cochlear implant in the pool?

The other student repeated the same exercise by saying "I never wear my cochlear implant in the pool"; however, she repeated the exercise twice. The teacher elaborated by asking the student what she does with her cochlear implant before she goes in the pool, thereby ensuring that she properly pronounced each word in her sentences. Other flash cards indicated outdoor activities such as sports. In lessons on other days, the flash cards focused on daily activities such as brushing one's teeth or going to bed. It appeared that these flash cards were clustered into themes to make it easier for the students to connect the same types of thematic concepts while being able to focus on their speech in conversation.

Instruction relied heavily on one-on-one individualized teaching; the teachers were the dominant facilitators of instruction, and the students followed a strict process to follow the teacher's instructional pedagogy. Students limited their social interactions with each other because the "rules" of the classroom demanded that the teacher have maximum attention from each student during his or her turn to receive instruction.

On different days, I observed instruction of students of the same age with different subjects. Activities varied, depending on the times of day. During the mornings, the teacher engaged in "calendar" time, asking the students to point out on the calendar what today, yesterday, and tomorrow were as well as what the weather is like today, will be like tomorrow, and was like yesterday. Activities also varied, depending on the days of the week; for example, every time I observed the classroom on Monday at the very beginning of the day, the teacher usually started with what the students did last weekend. During this time, the teacher allocated nearly 15 minutes for each student to allow them to talk as much as they wanted. This moment was one of the very few times that the teacher did not interrupt the students while they discussed their weekend. She encouraged the kids to speak by nodding her head and expressing interest. Often, she had to direct the other students to pay attention. After the students were finished, the teacher discussed her own weekend. However, as soon as she was finished discussing her weekend, it was clear that the atmosphere of the classroom switched into a more formalized approach. This transition was noticeable when the teacher's demeanor changed from playful to more serious. She quickly would also lay out various flash cards and photos on the table to signal that it was time to go back to work.

On Fridays, the teacher typically asked the students what they planned on doing during the upcoming weekend and used a teaching approach (conversation analysis) similar to what she did on Mondays. Classroom observations revealed that the teacher was the facilitator of classroom activities, and the students followed the pace and information established by the teacher. With the teacher as facilitator, the students served a passive role, but played an equally different, yet important contribution in the oral-based ideology of deaf education.

## Students

The deaf students in the oral classroom ranged from ages 5 to 6 years and were in kindergarten. Many of them had traditional first names (i.e., Joe, John, Ashley), and the teacher confirmed that they were predominately "White." All of them had some technological device in their ears at all times; many students in the school had two cochlear implants or two hearing aids. A follow-up with the teacher revealed that more than 90% of the deaf students at the school had at least one cochlear implant.

Although the students simulated gestures at times, they did not exhibit any form of ASL since most of the gestures consisted of pointing at objects. The students relied solely on speaking as the primary communication mode for educational activities and instruction. They exhibited little willingness to interact with other students; they knew that their purpose in the classroom was to interact with the teacher. Students would ask questions and/or provide feedback directly to the teacher about the information that the teacher was teaching and not to his/her classmates. The students' behaviors were extremely disciplined and patient, and they reflected obedience to the teacher by speaking only when asked. This dynamic was reflected through the classroom activities when the teacher would prompt one student to engage in a process of instruction while the other student waited patiently for her turn. The following is a summary of a 5-minute go-fish drill with two students and one teacher. Student 1 held a card with a picture of a bear while Kris, the teacher, had a book open with an image of a penguin.

> Kris: Do you have a penguin?
> Student 1: (*appears to be mumbling and speaking fast*) No, I do not have a penguin.
> Kris: (*rests her left hand on the student's clasped hands*) Say that one more time, (*points right hand to her mouth*) slowly (*Kris removes her left hand from the student's hands*).

Student 1: (*slowly*) No . . . <*.5 second pause*> I do not have a "punguin."

Kris: Try saying "peng" (*Kris points one finger to own closed set of lips tucked in mouth for emphasis on "p"*).

Student 1: Pung.

Kris: No, "Peng." (*repeats 'Peng' four times motioning the closed set of lips in mouth for "p" then slowly reveals the lips with heightened cheekbones for "eng"*)

Student 1: Peng.

Kris: Very good. Now say "guin" (*points to mouth and indicates tongue work is required*).

Student 1: Guin.

Kris: Now say the whole word again, peng (*one second delay*) guin.

Student 1: Peng (*one second delay*) guin.

Kris: Very good, so do you have a penguin?

Student 1: No, I do not have a penguin.

Kris: Very good! (*She proceeds to work with Student 2, who had not been paying attention to the exercise and was fixed on the book, mumbling to herself as she looked at pictures of different animals.*)

In this activity, the student attempted to pronounce *penguin* in the 5-minute drill while the other student waited for her turn. Throughout the observations of teacher facilitation, this type of individualized speech exercise for nearly all subjects was a reflection of the classroom philosophy, which required tremendous reliance on hearing the teacher voice the textual words while focusing on the lip movement to embed the voice and the speechreading of textual words into spoken meaning. The majority of the classroom activities/instruction is based on the capacity to speak textual words and connect them orally into grammatical structures. The primary focus is on the student's ability to speak these vocabulary words with effectiveness rather than on the context and the meaning of these words. The teacher did not neglect the importance of context, but based on observations, the teacher tended to divide certain words that had no significant meaning once divided, for example, the teacher focusing on "peng" and then "guin" on separate occasions. This observation is not to claim that the contexts of the words were unimportant in the instruction, but simply that a great amount of time and energy was spent on making sure that the students pronounced the words correctly.

My interaction with the students was extremely limited. As a participant/observer, I felt more like an observer than a participant. When I first started observing the classroom, the teacher introduced me to the students and indicated that I was a "successful" deaf person who was in college. I introduced myself verbally and was hesitant to use sign language with the students since I was contained in an environment where sign language was forbidden. Most of the time, the students did not look at me or attempt to make conversation with me; their focus was directly on the teacher. The teacher also did not start any conversations with me or look at me during my classroom observations.

Being a researcher who is deaf, it is obvious that I could not "hear" the effectiveness of their speaking ability, but through my observations reading the students' lips and through information I got from the teacher by means of interviews, the students were able to speak effectively (at least according to the teacher's standards) by converting the textual words into spoken English. Also, the students' ability to understand the teacher by reading the teacher's speech and, at times, looking at the book or an educational tool reflected their ability to listen and comprehend educational instruction. Their speaking and listening ability in the classroom confirmed accomplishment of the teacher's objective and the school's pedagogy of learning. For example, during one book reading exercise, the teacher opened a book to read the words out loud without pointing at the words. The students appeared to understand what the teacher was saying because she would quiz them by asking a question as to where a specific planet was in the book. The students' eyes were focused on the book itself when being asked their questions, and immediately, the student would point to the exact planet that the teacher inquired about. Other times, the teacher would ask something about the planet's characteristics and the students would confirm the teacher's statements while continuing to be fixed on the book, which indicated that the students heard the teacher.

Another example was the discussion comparing the size of Saturn and Earth. The teacher asked a student, who was gazing at the photos in the book, whether Saturn was bigger than Earth. The student replied "Yes," and the teacher encouraged the student to repeat that answer again in a full sentence. According to the responses from the teacher, it was apparent that the student did not pronounce Saturn correctly, so the teacher highlighted Saturn, repeated the word herself, especially focusing on the first syllable, in particular the *S*, by pointing her finger at her mouth to instruct the student how to pronounce Saturn by stressing the *S*. Once the student accomplished the pronunciation of the word, she was made to repeat it in the entire sentence, "Yes, Saturn is bigger than Earth."

Other questions asked about the color and temperature of Earth, and students were then asked yet again to repeat their answers in full-sentence form to ensure that the students were able to develop their speaking capacity. For example, when the teacher inquired why there was no life on Mercury, the students replied that there was no life because it was too hot. The teacher then asked the students whether there was any oxygen and water on Mercury, and they replied "No, there is no oxygen and water on Mercury." Then, when Earth was being discussed, the teacher reminded the students why Earth has life and compared Earth with the other planets. While this dialogue was occurring, the students appeared to be able to comprehend the teacher by responding accurately. However, there were times when the student would say the sentence and use facial expressions as if he or she was uncertain, looking to the teacher for her confirmation.

Other times, the student clearly did not understand the teacher. One example that recurred in various forms throughout my observations occurred when the teacher was explaining rules for a game. She stopped and went over to a student, asking, "Did you hear what I said?" The student nodded in affirmation, but when the teacher asked her what she had said, the student could not reply. The teacher responded by saying the rules again and looking at the same student to make sure she was paying attention, but did not "lecture" her to look at the teacher. It appeared that the student knew to pay extra attention after the teacher caught her off guard.

Students relied on their technological devices to "hear" instructions along with speechreading. As a result, some classroom time was devoted to ensuring that these modes for comprehension were working properly. Every morning, the students were instructed to "test" their device with the teacher to make sure that it was working properly. Sometimes, the student would tell the teacher that his or her device was "acting funny," and the teacher would take the device and "test" it herself, including placing the hearing aid in her own ear to "hear" the sounds being emitted. She was able to determine the cause of most of the problems, including whether the battery was low or whether there was a hole in the tube. Immediately, she would fix the problem in front of the students. Almost all of the students' hearing aids/cochlear implants were decorated with personalized symbols. One cochlear implant had a symbol of Batman while another implant had flowers painted on it. The technological device played an important role in the classroom instruction by being able to connect the hearing sounds with the spoken words, which was facilitated by the teacher.

Students were strictly trained to speechread, identify sounds making up the words, pronounce these words, and then connect the words into a sentence. Often during this process, students would have to repeat words to achieve the correct phonetic sound, which reflects the oral-based pedagogy for the deaf. This pedagogy relies heavily on the teacher's ability to clearly speak words and foster an environment where the deaf child incorporates outside culture into his or her own language development and acquisition of words. Thus, the teacher's pedagogical strategies and facilitation/maintenance of information by means of language plays an influential role in the social construction of the deaf child.

## Teacher

Kris is a hearing teacher in her early 30s, who graduated with a bachelor's degree in Education and a master's of science in Education with a focus on Deaf Education, from a university that specializes in speech pathology/therapy ("Kris," personal communication, September 15, 2008). She has taught deaf children for 9 years. She knows very little ASL and does not intend to incorporate ASL in the classroom, saying often that it is not the school's objective to inject ASL into the classroom. This perspective was reflected by her heavy reliance on the oral method and speech therapy at all times.

Kris defends the oral method for a deaf child at an early age and goes so far as to say that if her child were deaf, she would place her in the oral classroom setting. She believes that the younger the child is indoctrinated with the oral method, the greater the "window of opportunity." Kris said that the cut-off age to determine whether a child is able to succeed in using the oral method is the age of 3–4 years because the school thinks that to teach a child spoken English coupled with auditory/oral instruction after that age would be too challenging and too risky to the school's reputation. When asked how she measures children's ability to succeed under the oral method, she contended that "you just know when they will be able to speak, because those who make no effort in speaking and use gestures are obviously in the wrong educational modality" ("Kris," personal communication, September 9, 2008).

While Kris argued it was important that the oral method be instilled at an early age for selected deaf children to benefit from the limited window of opportunity for success, she also agreed that instilling ASL at an early age also provided the same window of opportunity in mastering the ASL language; however, she claimed that the oral method was more effective in helping the deaf child to achieve success. She stated that if the child learned ASL, the child would not want to learn how to speak, and therefore, it would be more difficult for that child to be able to grasp the opportunity to ever speak in the future. She reasoned that if the child was able to master the oral method, then she/he could always learn how to use ASL in later years because learning ASL was much easier than learning how to talk.

She defended the oral method as the superior approach in teaching deaf children on the basis that they would be able to function with their hearing counterparts and especially with their families. It was the ability to communicate with their families (Kris reminded me that 90%–95% of the deaf children had hearing parents) that would enable them to foster a positive identity and establish firm communication skills necessary for the hearing world. She claimed that the population of deaf people was limited when compared with the larger world; thus, the oral method ought to be the most important language acquisition choice for the child. To instill the ASL method in the deaf child rather than the oral method was to defeat the purpose of trying to prepare the deaf child for interaction with the majority of the community.

Kris contended that a major setback in using the oral method with a deaf child was the opinion of the deaf community. She stated that the deaf community had rejected the oral method and that it was viewed as a "hearing cultural tool." When I asked Kris to clarify what she meant, she claimed that deaf people would not welcome oral deaf people into the deaf community because of their inability to "understand deaf culture"; that is, they spoke the hearing language "as a tool" and had no knowledge of ASL. Kris also said that she lost some friends who were former oral-based teachers after they decided to reject the oral pedagogy in favor of ASL. Kris purported that although a deaf child may not develop "deaf" cultural skills defined as important in the deaf community, it was really the identity of the deaf child that was more important. She maintained that the best way to develop a deaf child's identity lay within the family, and the best way to interact with family was to be able to speak the same language as them.

Kris remarked that the unique location of Central School made it a challenge for deaf students to be bused from public schools to the oral school because the school had students from all over the valley, and busing would interfere with their learning experience because of missed time. The student would have to wake up at 5:00 a.m. to arrive at school by 8:00 a.m. and then finally get home at 7:00 p.m. Kris advocated the mainstreaming process where deaf students would eventually be able to be mainstreamed into their local school communities and be able to go to school with their neighborhood friends and siblings.

When asked about the "least-restrictive environment," Kris supported the "restrictive" environment for the child, where the deaf child is placed in a restricted oral setting to maximize his/her learning ability to speak and to accelerate his/her educational skills, as opposed to placing the child into a classroom with 30+ students and one teacher. That least-restrictive environment would place a burden on the deaf student because he/she would not be getting the appropriate pedagogy necessary to develop his/her linguistic skills. Kris supported an environment where there would be 15 hearing students and one deaf student to one teacher; however, she realistically contended that the state's public schools did not have that capability; the ratio for students to teacher was usually 20–30 students to one teacher in an elementary mainstreamed setting (usually about third to fifth grade). Nonetheless, she felt that the deaf child's best chance to maximize his/her education and foster linguistic skills is to be placed in a restrictive environment like Central School to better prepare for assimilation in the long run.

Kris also valued parental involvement with the deaf child. She warned that teaching the deaf child to integrate his or her education with speaking was a 24/7 process and not an 8:00 a.m. to 3:00 p.m. process, as some parents assumed. It is the parents who determine the overall success of the deaf child. Kris indicated that most parents play an active role in the student's learning process. Many of them attend not only parent-teacher conferences but also various workshops to better learn how to incorporate speech therapy at home.

She also contended that No Child Left Behind (NCLB) and the Individuals with Disabilities Education Act (IDEA) failed to emphasize the importance of family involvement for the deaf child. Kris said that both pieces of legislation had generally been ineffective, and the reason for the huge division between the educational quality for deaf students and hearing students was due to the unrealistic goals that those acts set for deaf children. However, Kris affirmed that the best is yet to come; she confidently stated that in the next 5–10 years, the overall success of the deaf child in the oral school, especially those with a cochlear implant, will improve drastically and that the NCLB and IDEA need to start measuring the success of deaf children with consideration of the cochlear implant. Kris mentioned that most of the students in oral schools had a cochlear implant (almost 90% of the students) and many are still too young to be included in the current measurements. Therefore, we will need to wait until they are adolescents to determine their overall success.

Kris was very open and informative and was not afraid to express her opinions. Before I concluded one of my several interviews with her, she clarified a specific episode that transpired during my visits. A deaf child was amazed to see me, a deaf adult, with hearing aids. I thought the reaction was just one of amazement when I said, "Yes, I too, am deaf just like you" because I assumed the students had little, if no exposure to the deaf community. Discussing this episode with Kris to elicit her perspective, Kris corrected me and informed me that the deaf student was more amazed at the fact that I would classify myself as deaf. Kris explained:

> The deaf kid thinks that he will grow up to be [quote] hearing [unquote] and no longer be [quote] deaf. [unquote] They think that being deaf at their point of their lives [is] just a temporary transition into being hearing, and that the only way to [quote] function [unquote] in a hearing world is to learn and master the ability to speak. Once mastering the ability to speak, they think that they will transcend themselves into a level amongst hearing people and will finally no longer consider themselves deaf, and *that is unfortunate* [emphasis added]. ("Kris," personal communication, March 12, 2009)

Surprised at Kris's remark, I asked what, then, can she as a teacher for the deaf do to remind the deaf child that it is okay to be deaf? She said that it is not really up to her but, rather, the parents. She was disappointed that most of the parents of the deaf children make impossible demands for their child to transform radically from being deaf to being "normal." It is these parents who foster the kind of environment that provides the child with the notion that the only way to be successful is to be hearing and, thus, neglect the celebrated diversity of being deaf. In this conversation, Kris acknowledged that the school tailored the deaf child to be prepared for mainstreaming in a "hearing" environment as the final step to become a "hearing" person, although Kris personally thought that it was unfortunate. She also pointed out that many teachers in the public school system also fostered that kind of thinking. At one point, Kris stated that she remembers one teacher at a public school calling her and telling her about the wonderful success the teacher had with "Sean" (a former student at Central School). The teacher had remarked that she couldn't even tell that he was deaf! ("Kris," personal communication, March 12, 2009).

As conversations between Kris and me became more in depth, I brought up several cochlear implant issues to explore what unique data I could elicit from her. Kris expressed concerns that the oral school might "confuse" the deaf child in thinking that the oral school is a "temporary" phase the deaf child will have to undergo before being transformed into being "normal." I asked whether the cochlear implant encouraged similar thinking. She reluctantly answered that it was an inevitable process that the deaf child would have to go through if he/ she wanted to be successful in the future. Both the cochlear implant and the doctrine of the oral pedagogy were windows of opportunities that became smaller as the years went by. She contended that it was unfortunate that there were no alternative approaches in fostering success for a deaf child. Kris was aware that the kids would not be able to make a decision whether to get a cochlear implant, but that it was one of those unavoidable kinds of issues.

The data gathered from the oral classroom reflect a unique perception of how certain constructions are formed in an oral classroom, which is a small reflection on the larger ideology of oral-based pedagogies. More analytical findings are discussed in Chapter 5. This section now turns to the narrative description of the ASL classroom.

## NARRATIVE OF THE SIGN-BASED CLASSROOM

For the ASL-based school, the daily use of the same classroom, the lax moderation of the teacher, and the highly socialized students provide a narrative as a site where students usually spend most of their time and the interactive role of the teacher with the students provide an idea of what an ASL-based classroom might look like. Like the narratives with the oral-based school, I start with the classroom.

### Classroom

Magnet School is a public institution founded in the late 1960s, which requires no financial cost for enrollment. There are approximately 65–75 teachers who instruct students at the elementary, middle school, and high school levels. The student-to-teacher ratio varies depending on the level of education. The elementary school averages 6 students to 1 teacher (who sometimes has the assistance of a teacher's aide), while the high school has a ratio of 20 students to 1 teacher ("Jan," personal communication, September 29, 2008).

The school currently has between 270 and 300 students ranging from the ages of 2 to 22, with no enrollment limit. Because the school is funded mostly by the state and/or the specific school district from which the student is referred, it is public; thus, the school is unable to systematically exclude any student ("Jan," personal communication, September 29, 2008). According to Jan, an ASL-based teacher at Magnet School, there have been students who enter the school showing little linguistic structure, even at a later age, and they cannot be excluded, unlike other schools where these students are often excluded from enrolling. The only major requirement at Magnet School is that the student exhibit the physical ability to learn ASL (i.e., must have at least basic use of his/her hands), even if the student does not know any sign language initially. One teacher jokingly stated that "we [the school] accept the rejects," including students who do not qualify for Central School (oral school) and the public school system.

This newly remodeled school has several annexes, with one main building that serves as the administrative offices and the high school. The structure of the school is very large, sprawled out, with each annex representing a specialized program (i.e., elementary school branch, gymnasium, evaluations department, multidisability program, and so on). There is a very large digital sign outside of the school next to a major road that reads "Magnet School for the Deaf," below which are LED lights that display the dates of the different recreational activities and athletic events at the school.

The main building contains numerous 13-inch flat-screen televisions in the hallways—to replace public address systems that are customary in hearing-based schools—and televisions in all classrooms and administrative offices. These televisions show different students and administrators signing various educational, social, and cultural announcements regarding student news, weather, and sports. One televised announcement was made by a teenage student in middle school, who signed that "if you see a teacher talking to another teacher without signing, it is your job to inform the teacher to sign at all times." Immediately, I made sure that I signed at all times to maintain my membership, since every administrator knows sign language, including the secretary, janitor, physical education teacher, audiologists, principals, and obviously, teachers.

The students I observed were in kindergarten and ranged in age from 5 to 6 years. That classroom was rectangular and was arranged in five main areas: (a) an area consisting of a crescent-shaped table for the class, which faced a white board (Figure 4.3); (b) an area with a cluttered desk for the teacher, which faces the wall; (c) an area with a large rectangular table; (d) an open area for unstructured play and storytelling; and (e) a mini-kitchen area with a sink with student toothbrushes visible by the sink.

As Figure 4.3 shows, a signed alphabet poster hangs on the wall, and on the right of the image, there are whale shapes, each of which has a student's name on it. Also included in the photo is a smaller desk that is cluttered with various lesson plans, markers, and educational objects that the teacher uses for instruction. This photo was taken in 2008, and in 2009, the white board was replaced with a SmartBoard®. The classroom shares a bathroom with an adjoining classroom. Figure 4.4 represents the ecology of the ASL classroom.

The classroom was a busy and disorganized sight, cluttered with student-made posters in sign language and visual educational displays, including a map of the United States and an ABC poster in ASL. Many of the physical features of the classroom were labeled in ASL, for example, the alphabet and a label for towel in ASL (Figure 4.5).

There was no "technical" station visually present with which to test hearing aids or cochlear implants. Toys, beanbags, pencils, and crayons were sprawled across the floor, while the teacher's desk was piled with paper and books. There was a "wall of awards," where each student had stars to serve as positive reinforcement for good performance. The classroom seemed personalized, and I later received confirmation that the students remain in the same classroom all day, with

FIGURE 4.3.    Semicircular table in the ASL classroom.

the same teacher for all of their main subjects, with an exception for Physical Education, Computers, and Library, for which they go to specialized classrooms. Other personalized features of the class included pictures of each student with his/her name spelled in sign language

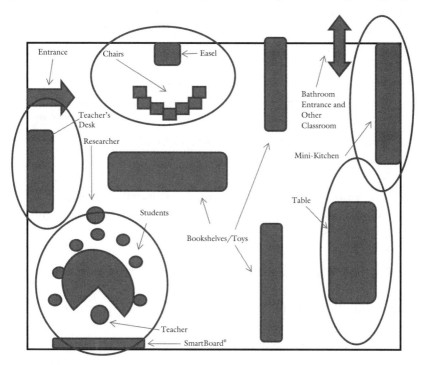

FIGURE 4.4.    Physical ecology of ASL classroom.

FIGURE 4.5.    The English alphabet with ASL next to each letter (left), sign for towel next to the textual word (middle), and rules of the classroom with both English and sign language.

attached and several previous projects that students had done. The students usually sat in an "open spaced" position, where their body language and position frequently shifted, depending on who they were talking to. The design of the crescent-shaped table allowed students to sit around the curve, facing the teacher and equidistant to all students.

When I asked the teacher about a typical day for a kindergarten–Grade 1 student, she indicated that it was usually

> an 8:00 school arrival; 8:15 breakfast; 8:40–9:15 outside recess; 9:15–9:45 calendar and group time daily events; 9:30–10:30 communication (on Tuesdays and Thursdays); 9:45–11:00 alphabet, vocabulary, and stories; 11:00–11:10 lunch preparation; 11:15–12:00 recess and lunch; 12:00–12:30 journals and brushing teeth; 12:30–1:00 math; 1:00–1:30 handwriting; 1:30–2:25 specials (such as ASL storytelling, computers, gym, and so on); and 2:30–3:00 snack and wrap up. ("Jan," personal communication, September 29, 2008)

The teacher remarked to me that the daily classroom routine often changed, that each day was a "new" day, and that she felt it was important to be flexible in accordance with the progress that the students were making educationally.

The ASL school did not divide its curriculum into traditional subjects like math, science, computers, and English. However, there were elements of each subject incorporated into lessons. These elements were not neatly divided into time frames or formalized neatly into each subject but, rather, determined by the flow of the classroom. The teacher explained that this approach was more efficient because there was no "one lesson that fits all" when discussing the uniqueness of her students, which makes it very difficult to try to create consistency. The high student/teacher ratio made teaching more challenging. The lesson plans were flexible and were taught at a flexible pace. Many of the subjects were often embedded, and the various lesson plans that I observed on different days were a combination of various subjects. For one exercise, the teacher used a PowerPoint presentation on the SmartBoard® (computers) to teach a numbers game (math). These numbers (1–10) would be counted using groups of animals (science) displayed on the SmartBoard®. Each student would identify a certain number of the same animals, and then once they counted the animals by means of sign language, they would click on the screen to be given feedback. If there was time and the students were progressing, the teacher would add more lessons using the same system. For example, the teacher might ask the student what color (art) that specific animal was and in what types of environment (science) the animals were usually found (e.g., water, land, or air). In this exercise, the students signed the animal, the color, and how many of the same animals were present on the SmartBoard®.

The classroom's first lesson (9:15 a.m. to 9:45 a.m.), or what the teacher calls daily calendar and group activities, was conducted routinely every morning. It was a combination of a calendar exercise and an expression of the students' mood for that morning. First, a student was picked to determine what today was. He or she faced a calendar on the wall that already had *Xs* on the past days. The student then identified the next unmarked *X* on the calendar and connected that space with the columns for the word for that day (e.g., "Tuesday"). After signing Tuesday, the student got up and "instructed" each student by walking around signing "Tuesday" and expecting each student to respond with "Tuesday." This type of exercise went on to include what day was yesterday, what day would be tomorrow, what the weather was today, and how many days was the weather hot, cold, rainy, or windy. Then, the teacher asked each student what their "mood" was for the day. Next to the calendar was a poster indicating facial expressions of happy, sad, angry, scared, excited, nervous, tired, or some combination. All but one student chose happy. One student selected an angry face but did so with a smile on his face. The teacher sarcastically signed back to the student imitating the student's facial expressions (smiling) while signing "angry" and suggested that the student was being silly. All the students laughed and sided with the teacher. The student continued to say that he was angry by signing it with a smile. The teacher explained that to be angry, the student needed to express the anger. The student then expressed anger facially and signed at the same time, but the teacher immediately signed that the student was being silly and put down on the poster that all of her students were happy.

Throughout the observations, the role of the teacher often switched, first leading a series of brief individualized instructions for several students and then leading group instruction. Most of the "fast-paced" students were able to proceed without any individualized instruction but were involved in the group instruction. During one exercise, the teacher was assisting the students with drawing, cutting, and providing some academic context (i.e., colors, their names). Then immediately thereafter, the teacher went to assist one student who was brushing his teeth, helping him to put toothpaste on the brush. Another day, a student spilled some water on the floor and the teacher had to clean up the mess while the students went on with their exercise. Every time the teacher left the table to assist in unexpected situations, the students were left occupied with their drawing or making small talk with one another.

Going back to the pace of the classroom, one exercise is relevant. All students were gathered at the rectangular table to engage in making a turkey from different colors of cardboard. At this time, the teacher and her aide had their hands full trying to help each student complete a different step. The students were moving at their own pace in various steps of the exercise, and the teacher and her aide were multitasking. In this particular exercise, there were two students sitting next to each other with the sketch of a turkey that they needed to draw. One student carefully drew one section of the turkey by tracing its lines while the other student frantically and hurriedly used one color to draw the entire turkey. When time ran out for any particular exercise, the teacher would collect the work and either save it to complete the next day or ask the aide to provide one-on-one assistance to those who were not finished while the teacher would go on to the next exercise.

Throughout my observations, there were several instances in which particular students needed more attention and/or guidance. One student went as far as to call the teacher Mama or NaNa; when I asked for clarification during my interviews with the teacher, she explained that the student used NaNa as an indication for needing attention and would often equate the teacher as her mother. At another time, I observed one student wearing one hearing aid while the other was dangling from his body, tied to a string attached to his shirt to ensure it would not get lost. After a few minutes, the student requested assistance from the teacher to put the dangling hearing aid back in. Immediately after tending to that student, she turned to another student to assist him with the current exercise.

Overall, the mood of the classroom for me was frenzied, over-stimulating, loud, and with constant visual interaction in ASL between the students and teacher as well as between the students. Although everything being discussed was educational in one way or another, there were a lot of "conversations" that included humor and off-the-wall topics and that at times switched from formal to informal education. It was clear that the students were the main facilitators of the many classroom activities and that they determined the overall pace of the classroom. The teacher's instruction and moderation of the class depended on the progress made by the students.

## Students

The deaf students in the ASL kindergarten classroom were ethnically diverse, which is consistent with the population of students at Magnet School. The majority of the students had names reflective of their Hispanic culture, for example, Jose, Maria, and Miguel. Most students had either hearing aids or one cochlear implant, which were sometimes used together; students rarely had two cochlear implants (in contrast to the oral school, where many students had two). All students had some technological device present in their ears at all times. Because the school is public, the socioeconomic status among these students varied, and I was informed by the teacher (with confirmation from the principal) that many students came from a lower socioeconomic background, which was also reflected in the worn quality of their clothing. The school also relied heavily on funding from the state for free and reduced lunches for students; the principal indicated that many of them could not afford to purchase lunch on their own.

As a participant researcher in this ASL setting, I actively engaged in many activities with the deaf students. Most of the students were fully aware that I was deaf (by detecting my hearing aids) and would often tap or wave at me to get my attention, as if they were equipped with a cultural sense of how to "communicate" with me. At one point early on in my continuing observations, a student completed his exercise and was dismissed for unstructured play, the student talked into my ear, but I did not recognize the boy's attempt to get my attention because the classroom was already so loud with all the students talking, stomping their feet under the table, and making humming noises. The student must have spoken louder in my ear to the point that I could feel the air coming from his mouth. It was then I finally realized that the student was trying to get my attention by speaking so I turned to the boy. I then immediately ignored the boy by turning my head back to observe other students. The boy then tapped me on my shoulder requesting my attention for a toy that he was interested in using. It appeared that maybe the student was trying to "test" whether I was hearing or deaf. Many of the students in the ASL classroom often looked at me and attempted to converse with me. I would either tell them to pay attention to the teacher by pointing at the teacher or I would quickly acknowledge the conversation with a nod, depending on the classroom activity. The teacher did not mind, but I sensed that she felt pressured to tell the students to "leave me alone" so I could focus on my work. I got the sense that she was more concerned with ensuring that I could do my research than with whether it was "wrong" for the students to engage in a conversation with me.

Early on in my observations, there was a specific episode in which a student came up to me during structured play, wanting me to read her a story. The teacher saw the student make this inquiry and told me, "Go ahead, if you don't mind. That would help greatly." This situation became a sticky ethical point for me. In one respect, her invitation confirmed the teacher's trust in me and that my presence served as a benefit and encouragement to these students because I was "one of them." But in another respect, I wanted to maintain my role as a researcher. I went ahead and read that story and would continue to interact from time to time, but then would revert back to my researcher role. I could not count how many times I switched my role from participant to observer because I was constantly switching.

The dynamics of the ASL classroom was hectic. Students exhibited high levels of physical energy and energetic socialization with other students and the teacher. Students generated vivid physical and vocal actions toward other students, including a lot of touching and tapping, loud grunting, banging on tables, and stomping on the floor. During classroom activities, students were constantly asked to "lower" their level of physical energy and pay attention. The teacher would channel the influx of energies being displayed in the classroom; often, she would allow the students to exhibit high levels of energy and maximum social interaction with the other students.

For example, consider this 5-minute exercise, conducted in ASL, between Jan, the teacher, and several students in which they discuss a book placed on an easel.

> Jan: Where is the fish?
> Student 1: (*stands up and signs*) Over there fish![3] (*points to the fish*)
> Jan: Very good! What color fish have what?
> Student 1: (*continues to stand up*) Red colors fish have red red red fish. (*repeats sign of "red" in excitement to point toward his shirt, which also has red colors, as other students point to her shirt and say, red color me have too!*)
> Jan: What other colors fish have? (*She looks around the students to welcome other student involvement; at this point, some students are standing up signing different colors. Jan picks one student and other students pause momentarily to pay attention and wait for their turn.*)
> Student 2: (*stands up and signs*) Fish face has purple on face purple!
> Jan: Yes, that's right! (*calls another student to come up next to the easel and asks Student 3*) Does the fish have yellow colors?
> Student 3: (*points to the section where the fish has yellow colors and then to the teacher and students for confirmation*)
> Jan: (*Three students standing up excitedly respond with a flurry of signs to the location of the colors and the*

---

3. The ASL structure is different from standard English. In ASL, the context (e.g. the environment, the time, and the setting) is established first and then the noun is introduced into the ASL syntax. The ASL provides a rich linguistic structure that is "difficult to represent in written English" (Johnson & Erting, 1989, p. 71).

*teacher suddenly stops the activity and settles the three by telling them to sit down with a stern facial expression.*) Yes, please tell the other students what you mean.

Student 3: (*sits and signs*) Yellow colors fish have.

Jan: Very good. (*turns page, revealing an illustration of an octopus and expresses excitement by widening her eyes and opening her mouth in amazement*)

Jan: What is that?! (*At this point, most of the students are standing up and telling each other, using a flurry of signs; some shout unintelligible words/signs, gesturing "big in size," while others sign "octopus" and others emphasize the number of "arms" the octopus has. It is clear that other students are sharing expressions and gestures to come up with their own conclusions.*)

Jan: (*calms the students down and tells them to sit down*) What is that? (*points to the octopus and signs a student's name and looks at her*)

Student 4: Octopus that! (*shows the sign for "octopus" by using her fingers to indicate the arms*)

Jan: That's right, arms how many it have arms?

Student 4: (*The child starts counting the number of arms using sign language while other students watch her. Others are counting from the photo, and although others display the sign for eight, the teacher ignores them and tells them to pay attention to Student 4.*) Eight!

Jan: Very good! (*shows the correct sign for "octopus," emphasizing her hands as the arms of the octopus, and each of the six students sign "octopus" and start laughing with each other*)

Jan: Octopus same colors fish same? (*All students stand up again and sign "No!" One signs that the octopus has a gray color, and another signs that the octopus does not have red colors!*)

Throughout this exercise, students demonstrated constant face-to-face interaction with their peers, conveying their thoughts, feelings, messages, and ideas through sign language, babbling, gestures, and incoherent yelling/grunting/humming. They waved their hands, pounded on the table, and tapped other students—often interrupting the students and the teacher—which is reflective of deaf cultural traits ("Jan," personal communication, March 20, 2009). Their positioning when using ASL was very open and assertive. Their hands flew everywhere as the teacher "listened" vigilantly to what they were saying.

This exercise exhibited the students' overt and aggressive displays of their thought processes, in contrast to the demeanor of students in the oral classroom. The teacher displayed minimal resistance, allowing the students to express their thought process. The activity elicited maximum creativity from the ASL students through a high level of interaction that allowed them to search for meaning within these texts and its metacognitive application to real-life situations.

Students also engaged in other activities such as handwriting and drawing at their own unique pace. The teacher interacted with each student according to his/her own pace while, at the same time, trying to incorporate students into a larger instructional process (for example, by asking one student what color the other student was drawing). This process was a reflection of the diverse levels and types of knowledge each student had. The teacher tried to continue to stimulate those who were already "highly functional" while, at the same time, investing equal time in those who were still lagging in certain exercises. Also, students could share information with not just the teacher but also other students, who in turn shared multiple identities, meanings, and knowledge. In this sense, the teacher maintained and facilitated information in the classroom, which in turn, constructed a unique type of knowledge during the acculturation/enculturation of the deaf students within the classroom.

### Teacher

"Jan" is a hearing woman in her 50s, who graduated with an associate degree in Early Childhood Education and a bachelor's degree in Special Education and who then decided seven years later to get her masters in Deaf Education "to get a little more money." She also has another job as an ASL instructor at a local community college. She has been teaching at Magnet for more than 20 years and uses ASL and certain variations of the oral method simultaneously.

Jan is firm in her position that Magnet provides the most superior education possible for all of the students. The ability to use ASL as a "broad and flexible" language for deaf people allows the flexibility for the majority—if not all—of the students to have a superior education without communication barriers. ASL, in Jan's view, allows a huge opportunity for students to be more stimulated in the classroom setting by enabling them to communicate with the teacher and other students.

Although Jan promotes any type of communication modality that best fits the deaf child, she admits that Magnet strongly advocates the philosophy of using the ASL method because it provides the student the maximum potential to obtain a good education. She makes it clear that each child is very different and that she has to carry the large burden of treating each child individually while, at the same time, trying to moderate the classroom, which she reminds me is a 6:1 student-to-teacher ratio (sometimes with the addition of a teacher aide). She also points out that Magnet has a large Hispanic deaf student population, whose parents speak only Spanish. She adds that many parents use the school as a "dump and flight" mechanism, where the parents expect the school to "babysit" the children.

Although she admits that she does not formally use the oral method, she does use her lips and voice because it will benefit some deaf children, especially those who are hard of hearing but not fully deaf. She views her use of the oral method as a way to expose the children to the different ways they can express themselves and emphasizes that ASL is the most effective means by which to teach the whole classroom. The oral method, according to Jan, is not practiced in a formal approach, but teachers are encouraged to use their voice and their lips while signing to expose the oral method to certain students, who then have the option to speechread and watch ASL simultaneously. She stresses that Magnet has struggled to find an "affordable professional speech therapist" for any student who wishes to have a few hours of speech therapy and acknowledges that the job position would be challenging. Jan says that the cochlear implant does work for the majority of students, but she warns that it will be effective only after years and years of speech therapy; so, it may be ineffective when trying to apply speech into the child's communication modality at an early age.

Jan points out that the children use ASL with one another because it provides more stimulation than the oral method and because ASL includes emotive meanings by means of facial expressions and the person's tone of emphasis. She contends that the oral method, as a "one-dimensional language," does not offer this important cultural tool in a classroom setting. She stated that the communication modality is fairly flexible and that she is willing to adapt to each student, but she uses ASL at all times. When asked about the IEP and its effectiveness for providing a "fair" education for the deaf child, Jan expressed frustration and called it "political mumbo jumbo." She contends that

> the IEP actually pulls down the student's capacity to achieve their educational abilities, because we [Magnet] set the goals for each child to more of a realistic level, without setting the goals higher where they can challenge themselves further. They may not reach to that goal, but they have progressed enough to almost accomplish it. To me, that is progress, but to the IEP's standards, it would say that the child failed . . . This is why we have to set each educational goal in the IEP one grade lower so that they will "pass" in the eyes of the educational administration . . . [which is] especially important since we're talking about funding. ("Jan," personal communication, February 22, 2007)

The IEP, to her, is a waste of time because it sets unrealistic and detrimental expectations for the students. She maintained that it (a) is unrealistic because it is not tailored for each child individually, but rather, sets a uniform standard unless the parent decides otherwise and (b) lowers the goals and standards for the student. Jan thinks that the parents need to become better advocates to challenge their child's IEP but states that the teacher cannot promote that type of advocacy because it would actually cost the school "more money." She contends that the special school system and its heavy usage of the IEP required under the IDEA and NCLB legislation is a gross misinterpretation of the actual quality of education that Magnet provides. The IEP, according to Jan, has "too much red tape and too much bureaucracy and it does little to deal with the actualities of these students."

The "least-restrictive environment" is not, according to Jan, a feasible criterion for the child's ability to obtain a fair education. She argues that, "of course, the deaf child will be restricted in some way from their hearing counterpart" and that there is no logical way to make sure that the deaf child will not be restricted. Jan remarks that the child will be restricted not only from their hearing counterpart but also from their deaf counterpart, and to determine what is the "least restrictive environment" is absurd.

When discussing the future goals for the children, the teacher praised my efforts to draw data from my observations to be made "public." She felt that the "rest of society" looks down on them and considers them a poorly qualified educational school that handles the already failed students and that my work would be a good thing for the students.

## REFLECTION OF THE ETHNOGRAPHIC DATA

A major goal of my research was to uncover the different ways that languaculture plays an influential role in the acculturation/enculturation of deaf students. As I used a cross-comparative approach, I sought to find similar and different ways within these two diverse schools that languaculture's role plays out. As a result, there is an abundant amount of information to be drawn from the data in these two different classrooms, and this situation is where grounded theory is useful as a methodological orientation. The grounded theory becomes a design to examine language and cultural development in the educational setting, including in deaf education. (More on grounded theory is detailed in Appendix A.) Identifying the various cultural displays of knowledge constructed specifically in these two classrooms will help provide the "implications of this research for the design of curriculum and learning environments" and will show how certain themes have an impact on the student's learning, identity, and meanings (Lee, 2007, p. 16).

My analysis of the ethnographic data collected in Chapter 4 began with "concepts that are grounded in and reflect intimate familiarity with the setting or events under study. From close, systematic attention to the field notes as data, the ethnographer seeks to generate as many ideas, issues, topics and themes as possible" (Emerson, Fretz, & Shaw, 1995, p. 166). As I gathered the data and then organized them using qualitative software (NUD*IST), I was able to build on three major themes occurring from my observations that I believed had a strong impact on the child's languaculture. The three theoretical themes to build on languaculture as a core concept included (a) the pedagogy of language in the classroom, (b) the "culture" in the classroom, and (c) the teaching techniques by means of language facilitation used within the two classrooms. As an ethnographer, there is a need to "to recognize and make explicit their [my] core theoretical interests and commitments as they [I] determine what is looked at and what is treated as significant in the process of data collection" (Emerson, 2001, p. 305). Thus, it is important to realize that these themes are not the only themes that influence languaculture for a deaf child. Rather I believe these three themes, as theoretical blocks for facilitating what it means to be normal/deviant for deafness, not only hold powerful "epistemological stances toward problem solving that are fundamental to the discipline" of educational pedagogy but also hold the ingredients to possibly foster a positive environment for these deaf students when shaping beliefs, ideologies, and the larger meaning of the social world (Lee, 2007, p. 33). Like Bahktin's notion of discourse, everyday and classroom discourses are continuously dialogic in nature, and the incorporation of these theoretical themes within the educational setting "establishes cultural inquiry, of argumentation with evidence, of hypothesizing, of intellectual risk taking as norms for participation in class," and of constructing norms in their cultural society (Lee, 2007, p. 61).

With the three themes that contribute to languaculture for the deaf, I now turn to a deeper analysis of the different ways that these three theoretical themes frame and reframe the dimensions of positive/negative constructions of deafness. These themes contribute to understanding languaculture of the deaf and offer a larger glimpse of some social constructions of deaf education at these schools. Chapter 5 reveals the ways that these three themes serve as possible issues and contributions to the broader social implications for reevaluating the educational pedagogy in deaf educational practice. These examinations may also offer a way to explain how normalcy and deviance are formed and constructed in the larger notions of deafness.

# CHAPTER FIVE

# CONSTRUCTIONS OF DEAF LANGUACULTURES

My narrative descriptions of two diverse classrooms in the previous chapter show diverse pedagogies of languaculture that may have possible implications for the students' acculturation/enculturation. Also, the narrative suggests that schools, as sites of cultural and linguistic capital, may play a role in constructing certain identities of students and the types of knowledge that the teacher mediates in the classroom as major contributors to the overall languaculture for the deaf. From these observations, three critical themes become important conceptual ideas with which to examine languaculture for deaf people and the larger social constructions of deafness in education. These themes, which have become more crystallized as I analyzed my data, include (1) the pedagogy of language, including the language usage and maintenance in the classroom; (2) the "culture" in the classroom; and (3) teacher knowledge and the capacity of teachers to facilitate "academic knowledge" within their two classrooms through specific language usage. Studying constructions of languaculture using these three themes offers ways to examine certain ideological assumptions about which language ought to be the norm, determined by how languaculture occurs within deaf educational practices, and the larger implications of deafness. Figure 5.1 is one way to look at these themes as they contribute to the construction of languaculture for deaf people.

To be sure, there are other possible (and equally important) themes that play a role in the languaculture for deaf children in the realm of education, including family involvement, role of the community, demographic location, and socioeconomic status to name a few; my research did not build sufficient data to develop these emerging themes for this book, but they are critical and useful for future research. Instead, my data reflected the pedagogy of language that was

FIGURE 5.1.    Organization of data into three themes in determining constructions of languaculture.

used, the varying "culture" in the classroom, and the powerful role of teacher's knowledge and how it helps shed light on the importance of languaculture and the social constructions of deafness.

Because deaf education is not homogenous, every deaf classroom contains a variation of these three themes, and they will have different effects in different schools because each classroom contains specific cultural constraints within the three themes to construct what it means to be deaf. It is not the goal to objectify the data that build on these three themes or to represent generalizations of deaf education; it is the goal to show the ways that these three themes contribute to some elements of a nascent theory of deafness, specifically, deaf languacultures. All deaf schools contain a unique pedagogy of language, all deaf schools possess a certain "culture" in the classroom, and teachers in all deaf schools embody a particular teacher knowledge that plays an instrumental role in the classroom. Taken together in one level of analysis, they become a corpus of epistemological production in the social construction of deaf education. In essence, these three themes contribute to the larger constructions of languaculture for deaf people, and I suggest that these themes, as theoretical orientations, can also be used in future research for comparative analysis and toward a nascent theory of deafness and deaf languacultures.

Studying the constructions of languaculture, by using these three themes as a guiding point, holds powerful "epistemological stances toward problem solving that are fundamental to the discipline" of not just educational pedagogy. This effort may also possibly foster a positive environment for these deaf students as they shape beliefs, ideologies, and their larger meaning of the social world (Lee, 2007, p. 33). To be clear, these three themes are not viewed as static and isolated, rather, they influence the interwoven construct of the classroom, deaf student, and the teacher. For example, I examine the ways that the academic knowledge of the teacher (teacher knowledge), including their language use (pedagogy of language), impacts deaf students' education in the classroom (classroom culture). These themes act as theoretical orientations and become important sites of analysis in examining language, culture, and teacher "knowledge," including the ways they contribute to the formations of normalcy and deviance as constructions.

Social constructions of deaf educational practices are shaped by the importance (or neglect) of the culture in everyday practices and how they connect to the classroom culture, the specific languages used in instructional discourse, the understanding of teacher knowledge, and student learning. Deaf students are examined as linguistic minorities when examining the school as a site of cultural practice and knowledge construction. These inquiries show diverse ways that these themes may play a larger role in implications for the students' human values, ideology, and notions of deviance and normalcy.

## Socially Constructed Formations of Languaculture of Deaf People

Studying social constructions of languaculture for deaf people becomes a way to examine various factors that may potentially influence the classroom, deaf students, and teachers. Some factors include educational strategies, different cultural displays of knowledge, and different approaches to "best practice[s]" for language and cultural development in the deaf educational setting. Carol D. Lee (2007), in *Culture, Literacy, and Learning*, emphasizes the importance of understanding cultural displays of knowledge

> constructed in the everyday routine practices of children and adolescents and the relationship of such displays to targets of academic knowledge . . . [including] curriculum and instruction in a way that helps kids make connections between what they already know and what we want them to learn. (p. 25)

Identifying the diverse social constructions of deafness—specifically in these two classrooms—not only will help explain the "implications of this research for the design of curriculum and learning environments" but also will show how these themes have an impact on the student's learning, identity, and meanings (Lee, 2007, p. 16). These three theoretical themes reveal cultural displays of knowledge constructed within the two diverse ideologies of deaf educational practice and the larger understanding of deafness (Lee, 2007). I now turn to a deeper analysis of the different ways that these three theoretical themes frame and reframe the dimensions of languaculture of deaf people, starting with the pedagogy of language.

## Pedagogy of Language

The language for any group is the "vehicle for transmission of cultural patrimony through the generations; it expresses traditions, rituals, *norms* [emphasis added], and values" (Lane, Pillard, & Hedberg, 2011, p. 41). The transmission of culture by means of a language is languaculture. Spoken English and ASL are identified as languages. They are a form of discourse in social situations that "actively construct and display . . . roles and identities" and, in turn, mediate the fluidity of social interaction to produce cultural meaning (van Dijk, 1997, p. 3). These discourses, as a form of action, mediate the knowledge and relationships between specific groups and society, including the social power to mediate such relationships. Van Dijk (1997) offers an explanation of social power: "one group has power over another group if it has some form of control over the other group" to maintain their ideological position in society (p. 17). This socially constructed process enables certain groups to have access to mediating language as constructions to make it "natural" and "normal" in the pedagogy of language as the most "effective" instruction for deaf education. Classrooms mediate unique and diverse pedagogies of language, in turn these pedagogies of language are constructed to include the larger structure of educational and instructional curricula and philosophies. These philosophies contain very diverse social meanings for their deaf students, including the constructions of deafness and its criterion of normalcy and deviance.

The classroom descriptions show the contexts in which different languacultures exist and the relationship of these contexts to the literacy practices that constitute and structure both oral and signed language environments (See Bagga-Gupta, 2000). The relationship between the pedagogy of language and communication modalities is critical because they are both "the foundation of literacy," and effective communication is critical for the deaf child to function cognitively, linguistically, and socially (Meadow-Orlans, 2003, p. 40).

One of the greatest challenges facing a deaf student is the acquisition of language (see Chapter 3), and deaf education has struggled to find successful solutions to this challenge. One strategy includes a re-focus on literacy and a reexamination of it as the highest priority. Literacy and language development is one of the most important areas (if not *the* most important area) that needs to be reexamined in deaf education in order for deaf children to succeed. There are many educational activities, such as guided or shared reading, that incorporate new cultural practices as potential tools for literacy and language development. The oral and sign language schools obviously tend to disagree on certain culturally responsive design rationales necessary to encourage children to gain metacognitive skills and achieve literacy, such as through these seemingly simple educational activities that incorporate tools for literacy (Lee, 2007, p. 20). Reviewing and comparing oral classroom activities (the peng/guin exercise) and the ASL classroom activities (the fish/octopus exercise) suggests that there are opposing pedagogies of language that are applied to the deaf education.

To scholars advocating the use of sign language, deaf children are "seeing people" and "visual human beings" who rely on visual cues to make sense of the world (Erting, 2003a, p. 376) and deafness is a "visual experience" (Erting, 1985, p. 226). Other scholars add that acquiring ASL provides a "gain" for the deaf person (Bauman & Murray, 2010). Visual cues [aides] can be found throughout the ASL classroom (e.g. ASL posters) and the teacher uses the visual cues to create enriched visual spaces. According to these scholars, the oral pedagogy of language minimizes the use of the children's visual skills. These scholars contend that "for many deaf children, sign communication is the only efficient way to express their needs, desires, curiosity, and creativity" for literacy development, and this development is reinforced through conversations with the ASL-based teacher (Marschark et al., 2002, p. 102). There is evidence that deaf children who sign at a young age "tend to be better adjusted emotionally . . . do better in school and have better social relationships . . . in comparison to children with similar hearing losses raised only with spoken language" (Marschark et al., 2002, p. 74). Mason and Ewoldt (1996) emphasize that "deaf children who communicate naturally with their peers, teachers, parents, and Deaf adults in ASL can feel empowered and can progress both academically and socially" (p. 294). Conversely, DesJardin et al. (2008) claim that the ability to identify and manipulate various sounds (i.e., *peng* and *guin*) develops phonological awareness and becomes a strong predicator for success in literacy. According to this alternative view, by the deaf child's inability to hear and to manipulate sounds through voice, the deaf child lags in most aspects of education, including literacy and phonological awareness.

In the sign-based school, the visual components of ASL that enable literacy activities to be successful include rhythmic movements, exaggerated facial expressions, increased sign space, and exaggerated sign size. Whereas the components that enable literacy activities to be successful at the oral school include vocal rhyming, alliteration, word awareness, syllable awareness, and phoneme awareness (DesJardin et al., 2008). These two different constructions of language pedagogy, one that uses visual aspects and the other that uses listening and speaking aspects, will have a strong influence on how the deaf student uses his or her own diverse skills, whether it will be done visually with signing or by listening and speaking. These different constructions of languaculture also influence how the deaf child will incorporate his or her unique skills to make sense of the world. For example, those with sign language often enter the world relying on ASL interpreters for communication assistance, while those who rely on spoken language rely on technology (e.g., assistive listening devices like cochlear implants and hearing aids) for phonic comprehension or speechreading for word comprehension.

Through my observations, using ASL in reading activities builds a connection between the signed meanings of the word and the language of the texts (written English) and connects the two languages, enabling greater contextual comprehension for literacy (Erting & Pfau, 1997). For example, in the ASL exercise with the fish and octopus, the teacher connected the signed number of eight (referring to the arms of the octopus) to the printed word *octopus* in the book (wherein a picture showed its eight arms). This exercise also connected the visual/pictorial colors of the fish to the ASL signs for those corresponding colors. However, the oral method uses precise phonological representations to display sublexical connections between written and spoken forms of the language, increasing the children's knowledge of the letters and phonemes that connect the two forms of the language, thus enabling greater vocabulary comprehension and increased literacy (Hermans, Knoors, Ormel, & Verhoeven, 2008; Lederberg & Spencer, 2009). While both approaches use written English as a dependent variable in their pedagogy, they connect the written English to two contrasting variables: one connects the written English to the signed ASL meaning of the word, and the other connects the written English to the connection of the spoken English word. These different connections to the written English word may have a major influence on how the deaf student will construct meanings and may be applied toward teaching and learning practices, as well as socialization practices, in the future.

The divergent pedagogy of language observed in the two classroom types reflects these diverse languacultures as divergent ideologies which are presented by the two educational institutions for the deaf (see Chapter 3, archaeology of deaf education). In connection with the archaeology of deaf education, some scholars contend that while use of ASL in the classroom will enable deaf students to learn the meanings of written words, it is not enough. According to them, deaf children must be able to develop a written lexicon, which requires capturing the syntactic and morphological specifications of each word into constructed vocabularies. This method can be achieved only by using the spoken language in individual auditory/oral instruction, which develops the mental lexicon of written words, including the syntactic and semantic properties (Carlisle & Stone, 2005; Hermans et al., 2008; Windsor, 2000). Through the oral method, words are better developed by extensive one-on-one instruction with a teacher, whereby the teacher has the maximum agency to provide the lexical and syntactic model of the words to connect them to the acoustic and articulatory aspects of the word. Some deaf education scholars like Donald Moores and David Martin (2006) disagree with that view, contending instead that "words need to appear in contexts that define their meanings . . . [and] are best learned when students experience them in a meaningful manner including classroom discourse and incidental conversations in and outside of the classroom . . . includ[ing] opportunities for self expression" (p. 209). For them, words are better developed when the deaf student is given the opportunity to express their meanings using ASL, including the use of signed gestures and facial expressions, in formal and informal conversations with their peers and teachers.

The presence of technology is another important implication for constructing the pedagogy of language. The oral school relies on cochlear implants and hearing aids as important artifacts for successful speech repetitions which are mandatory in order to maintain the oralist pedagogy. Some scholars contend that this reliance represents oppression in which "the dominant culture creates borders saturated in . . . inequality, and forced exclusions" that include suppressing the use of cultural tools like ASL (Giroux, 1992, p. 174; see also Ohnma, 2003). The maximum use of technology for a deaf student at an early age minimizes any possibility of his or her needing to be exposed to ASL, instilling the principle that "speaking" and "listening" are the necessary components to achieving "normalcy," as well as the enforcing the notion that ASL is subordinate to speech because of "the demands of a technocratic and specialized literacy" (Giroux & Simon, 1989, p. 236; see also Goffman, 1968; Haraway, 2003; Maudin, 2007).

The ASL classroom emphasizes the importance of social interactions in combination with sign language as the pedagogy of language instead of relying on speech and sound reception as the primary channel for teaching language. Conversely, the oral classroom relies on the importance of speaking and hearing by means of technology to facilitate the student's learning process and relies heavily on the combination of technology and speech therapy to achieve its pedagogy. This method was apparent when the oral teacher would "test" the students' hearing aids and cochlear implants at the beginning of class every day. Also, the teacher would request that a child repeat words more than twice to achieve phonological comprehension and accuracy, without emphasis on meaning or relating the recited words to other areas of knowledge. This mode of instruction divided the word *penguin* into parts that are visually incomprehensible to the deaf students. This approach indicated that the meaning of the word *penguin* was not the priority, but the main focus was on the child's ability to pronounce *peng* and *guin* accurately.

Through observations in the ASL classroom, the emphasis was visibly different. The students were able to identify the written English word for the animal (here, an octopus) and express their thoughts about the animal through sign. Then, the teacher was able to provide instruction about the personality of the animal, what it eats, its color, how many arms it has, and its daily activities/habits, all through the use of ASL and gesture. Finally, the students were able to look at the English word again for scaffolding. Simultaneously, the ASL-based teacher was able to make explicit the connection between the different linguistic representations (ASL, written English, image, gesture, and spoken English) of an octopus by means of chaining (Humphries & MacDougall, 1999).

Scholars advocating oral-based pedagogies contend that almost 75% of deaf students are (or will be) mainstreamed before they enter secondary education; thus, the most common classroom environment for the majority of deaf students is in the hearing school (Leigh, Maxwell-McCaw, Bat-Chava, & Christiansen, 2009). The deaf environment is natural only when self-contained, but once the deaf student is placed in the hearing environment, the situation changes. Languaculture becomes negotiable when prioritizing which cultural boundaries shall be more important. Deaf students who learn to speak and use cochlear implants or hearing aids to communicate form better relationships with their hearing peers and allowing them to progress better socially, and thereby being better able to become "normal" (Bat-Chava & Deignan, 2001). Advantages of learning how to speak and being prepared for a mainstream setting include

(1) promotion of social interaction with the hearing world, (2) availability of normal linguistic and behavioral models provided by peers, (3) a stimulating and highly oral environment with rich linguistic input, (4) increased opportunity for learning and socialization opportunities. (Eriks-Brophy et al., 2007, p. 6)

The different types and claims of relevant evidence reflect the conflicting and often contrastive ideologies made by practitioners in deaf education as to what they believe are the most "natural" forms of language pedagogy as well as what types of environments deaf students ought to be immersed in and what boundaries they should have. This idea of "natural" has serious implications when the deaf child is indoctrinated with a certain ideology of what is "natural" for him or her, and the schools play a major role in constructing what the students think "natural" pedagogy of language ought to be, that is, into what type of languaculture they ought to be acculturated.

At the oral school, the teacher's pedagogical instruction relied heavily on the use of English language syntax and lexicon; English is considered the "master status" criterion in language use. By relying strictly on the oral method, the teacher prioritized the capacity for the students to express their meaning of the animal using phonemics. The main priority was to ensure that the deaf student made the phonemic connection by hearing and speaking the word. This priority was accomplished by the deaf student looking at the textual word, hearing the teacher say the word, studying its lexicon and syllables, then speaking and repeating the word. For many educational activities, ASL scholars insist that it is important for the child to "gaze" first at the word, then at the teacher for critical feedback through sign language to make sense of the word, then allow the child time to conjure a visual message, and then gaze back at the word. The word, whether through spoken English or ASL, becomes a "conversational object" (Meadow-Orlans, 2003, p. 40) and a coding scheme (Goodwin, 1994) from different approaches whereby the meaning of the word becomes negotiable. How the deaf students view the conversational object becomes the focus of their cognitive analysis; based upon their educational setting, the deaf students are indoctrinated to view the object, including its meaning, quite differently (Gee, 1993).

Going back to Gee's (1993) analysis on the social construction of color and Goodwin's (1994) usage of coding schemes, the meaning of certain words becomes socially constructed through use and is much like a language "game" that can be manipulated (Wittgenstein, 1953), which in turn molds the child's cultural knowledge. Language and culture produce and permeate ideology; simultaneously, ideologies "monitor how language users engage in discourse as members of (dominant, dominated, or competing) groups or organizations and, thus, also try to realize social interest and manage social conflict" (van Dijk, 1997, p. 7). In both classrooms, the construction of a deaf child's own languaculture is "valued as the most important social, cultural, and economic capital which produces a status degradation ceremony for the other languages," whether the other languaculture is sign language or spoken English (Harry & Klingner, 2006, pp. 120–121).

Both teachers, in my interviews and observations, defended their pedagogy of language as the most effective for the deaf student's academic achievement. The oral-based teacher stated that ASL was much easier to learn, but only as a justification for learning orally first, since the deaf students would be able to learn ASL "later on," as if spoken English was more complex and more important than ASL. The ASL-based teacher simply said that the oral method was a "one-dimensional language" that does not include the important cultural aspects of learning. For the ASL classroom, the two languages (i.e., textual English and ASL) "are kept separate and a comparative perspective on language learning is deemed significant," which provides a powerful symbol to the students that ASL is a respected language in its own right (Bagga-Gupta, 2000, p. 100). ASL has been able to provide the students empowerment through their own language; there was little or no resistance from the students in expressing themselves through signs during both structured play (octopus story) and unstructured play (informal storytelling). The ASL-based teacher encouraged the students to use signs critically as often as possible and gave them a choice (and the authority) whether they wanted to use their technology to hear the teacher, speechread, or sign. In the oral classroom, the combination of spoken English and written English conditions the deaf student to view English as the "master" language. The use of spoken English in the oral classroom is authorized and maintained by the teacher, which in turn gives the impression to the students that it is the teachers who are in control of the language, including what to say and when to say it.

The state of being inherently deaf does not influence which pedagogy of language will be effective, nor does deafness have an effect on the acquisition of literacy skills. Instead, it is how these languacultures are constructed around and within each child that critically affects their linguistic, cognitive, and literary development (Schirmer, 2000, p. 45). ASL students learn that to sign is human, while oral students learn that to speak and hear is human. These constructions of languaculture also influence the types of culture the student understands in the classroom.

## Culture in the Classroom

Classrooms are a site of complex ecologies filled with cultural systems: what the student brings to the classroom, what the teacher brings to the classroom, and finally, the cultures that emerge within the classroom, all of which contribute to the overall complexities of the culture of the classroom. Complexities of culture, in this respect, refer to the embodiment of various features, including

> patterns, explicit and implicit, of and for behavior acquired and transmitted by symbols, constituting the distinctive achievement of human groups, including their embodiment in artifacts; the essential core of culture consists of traditional (i.e., historically derived and selected) ideas and especially their attached values; cultural systems may, on one hand, be considered as products of action, and on the other as conditioning elements of further action. (Kroeber & Kluckhohn, 1952, p. 357)

Some scholars argue that the classroom environment ought to allow as much individual and group agency as possible to encourage and foster the transmission and diffusion of cultural knowledge in the classroom (Lee, 2007). Some scholars feel that a one-on-one, individualized approach enhances and maximizes the types of knowledge transmitted to the students (DesJardin et al., 2008). For other scholars, fostering positive attitudes about "cultures in the classroom" maximizes student participation, so cultural knowledge is explicit and mediated to make positive connections between everyday knowledge and school-based knowledge, to develop students' cultural identities as individuals, and to understand their larger role in the socially constructed world (Lee, 2007, p. 143).

A day in an ASL classroom seems flexible and is dependent on the students' pace of learning. The priority is to ensure that the students are maximizing their learning capacity; thus, some activities take longer than planned to accomplish some of these learning objectives. Conversely, the oral classroom has a rigorous set of different types of sessions mandated by a time-schedule to which students are required to conform. The daily schedules and views expressed in interviews with the teachers (shown in the narratives in Chapter 4) are indicative of this assessment.

The ecology of the oral classroom's trapezoid-shaped table indicates that the teacher is the primary focus of the class, with the two students sitting on the opposite sides of the table (see Gallego et al., 2001, for classroom ecology). The table, as a product of human social and cultural activity, provides resistance to social interaction, as opposed to the crescent-shaped table in the ASL classroom that allows more student to have face-to-face interactions (Fig. 5.2).

ASL scholars contend that crescent-shaped table setup increases students' socialization and collaboration, as well as stimulates various levels of metacognition and conceptualization (Bagga-Gupta, 2000; La Bue, 1995).

From my observations, the trapezoid-shaped table in the oral classroom effectively and purposely minimizes individual agency, allowing the teacher to construct a unique languaculture through which he/she can apply speech instruction with complete authority and without individual resistance, the effect of which creates less socialization practices among students (Aronowitz & Giroux, 1991; Gallego et al., 2001, Harry & Klingner, 2006; Rogoff, 2003; Swanson, 2007). In contrast, the crescent-shaped and oval organization of the seating arrangement in an ASL classroom enables the students to see their classmate's talk clearly and "be in a position to give visual feedback" to maintain communication in the classroom, which constructs a different languaculture for deaf students (Bagga-Gupta, 2000, p. 99).

FIGURE 5.2.  Comparison of two types of classroom tables (the table on the left is from the oral classroom, and the table on the right is from the ASL classroom).

There were situations in the ASL classroom where the deaf student would roam freely, choosing to engage in his or her own learning process, whether it was reading a book or playing on the computer. The deaf students in the oral classroom, on the other hand, were strictly confined to their social space, and once seated to begin classroom instruction they rarely left their space. This confined space allowed the teacher to have the maximum attention of the students, while in the ASL classroom the students enhanced their individual agency by developing their own ways of learning. One popular exercise for the ASL students was to go to the bookshelves, open a book, and "tell a story," often signing to themselves, which drew attention from other students, and they would share the story with one another. This process reinforces the findings of a recent study by deaf education scholars that reported that deaf students in the oral classroom were often excluded from participating in storytelling events, while ASL students were encouraged to provide maximum participation in their own storytelling (Kim, King, & Veno, 2009).

The "technological" and "audiological" labels on the shelves in the oral classroom (i.e., "syntax," "auditory training," "speech games") focus on the ears and mouth as the center of analysis, a form of "medico-pedagogy." This pedagogy reflects the type of instructional curriculum used, which is heavily rooted in speech therapy or auditory training. The ASL classroom, with its ASL posters, the ABCs in sign language, and the myriad of books on the shelves that contain ASL vocabulary, focused more on cultural pedagogy.

The ASL school carefully ensured that its environment is as natural as possible, with barrier-free communication, and that accessibility revolved around the deaf students. The unique environment strongly indicated that hearing individuals had to conform to the deaf culture, exemplified by the rule of signing at all times. This school's effort was intended to eliminate any possibilities of the hearing social world creating barriers to the deaf cultural arena. This practice of creating a barrier-free communication environment was reflected in the mandatory use of sign language by all staff members (including hearing) and in the fact that all announcements in the hallways were presented in sign language on flat-screen televisions. Both of these practices enhance deaf cultural transmission.

Conversely, the oral school's goal was to create an environment that prepared the oral student for hearing assimilation. For some scholars, this type of objective is to "replace the native (deficient) culture [ASL] with American cultural knowledge" (Gallego et al., 2001, p. 976). However, the oral school felt that the deaf child's native culture ought to be acquired by immersion in hearing society, thereby creating a "natural" atmosphere that resembles a mainstreaming environment, using the tools of hearing and speaking as "proper" American cultural practices. The very definition of "native" becomes socially constructed and negotiated. The ultimate goal of the oral classroom is to prepare students for assimilation and mainstreaming, preferably when they are in first grade (approximately age 5–6). The curriculum in the oral classroom is modeled to enable the students to adapt and apply their abilities in order to meet the hearing public school system's expectations (i.e., mainstreaming in public schools). It was evident that the students were trained in hearing and speaking as a fundamental criterion of being a "complete" student and to be "normal" in the larger scheme of the educational institution. They were trained to be successfully mainstreamed into hearing society and equipped to use their hearing and speaking tools to be accepted in the hearing public school system. This was one step toward the students becoming part of the normal social and cultural world, thus, reinforcing this form of languaculture. This kind of thinking was clearly illustrated by an interaction in the oral classroom when I told one deaf student that I was deaf like she and her classmates were and she was shocked because, as the teacher told me, most of the deaf students think they will become "hearing" adults. The ASL students, in contrast, have interacted with many other adults who are also deaf, like teachers, janitors, and principals, who all use sign language. These children are acculturated/enculturated through the transmission of ASL as their native languaculture as a part of their cultural world, and what they understand as being "normal."

The visual presence of accomplishment recognitions in the ASL classroom, like the star stickers on the students' wall, compared to the lack of these visual positive reinforcements being displayed in the oral classroom, emphasize the differences between these two disciplines. Both classrooms used various methods of instruction to teach students obedience to authority and to create self-discipline in the students. For example, during the fish exercise in the ASL classroom, the students exhibited their own way of following the rules by navigating their train of thought in a metacognitive approach. In contrast, the students in the oral classroom performed speech repetition to master certain types of pronunciations in order to maintain a successful representation of one's self as constructed by the teacher.

The diverse range of ethnicities and socioeconomic statuses within the two classrooms also plays an important role in the classroom culture. The oral classroom contained predominantly homogenous students, mostly middle to upper class, since the oral school is private and the cost of entering the school was approximately $11,000 per year. The oral students' designer labels reflected the materiality of their families' economic wealth—a powerful reflection of their economic and cultural capital, which shapes this pedagogy and establishes "privilege" over subordinated populations. For example, having deaf students learn spoken English and identify sounds are critical steps to prepare them for assimilation in hearing society, and the student may attain an advantage over the ASL students. One scholar indicates that examples of educational pedagogy that reflect "coercive relations of power are . . . teacher education programs that prepare teachers for a mythical monolingual monoculture white middle-class student population" (Cummins, 2000, p. 46).

Extensive research indicates that family background profoundly influences children's schooling outcomes, in addition to those who have higher socioeconomic statuses (Buchmann & Hannum, 2001; Chudgar & Luschei, 2009) and receive more education (Geers, Moog, Biedenstein, Brenner, & Hayes, 2009). The parents of the oral students at Central School had higher socioeconomic statuses and were more highly educated compared to the parents at Magnet School.

The family background and the child's schooling also affect the discipline in the classroom. The oral-based teacher did not have to exert control over the classroom because the students were very obedient; the teacher was able to maximize instruction and not be sidetracked by dealing with disruptive students. However, the ASL-based teacher often felt that she switched from being a teacher to a parent because many of the deaf students were not disciplined at home. The teacher contended that many of the deaf students in the ASL program were often neglected at home and not given attention. Communication between parents and these deaf children was frequently problematic. It was often up to the teacher to take on a maternal role in addition to her teacher role. One example given by the same teacher was an incident that occurred during a parent-teacher conference. The teacher was told by the parent to "scold" the child for something that had happened at home. Since the parents could not communicate with their child, they relied on the teacher to discipline their child because she *could* communicate with him. Consequently, the students seemed to look up to their ASL-based teachers as mother/father figures. The ASL-based teacher felt she held more responsibility to "teach" the children manners and discipline, which is usually a task reserved for parents. In a way, students rely on the teachers to help them gain a better sense of what is right and wrong, including what types of behavior are considered appropriate or inappropriate.

With respect to ethnicity, it seems clear that in the ASL classroom the students have had more experience with contesting memberships and constructing their identity, since some students had more than one minority membership (i.e., deaf and Hispanic). It is important to note that the number of children from Hispanic backgrounds enrolled in ASL programs "increased from 9% to 18%" from 1977 – 1997 (Meadow-Orlans, 2003, p. 44) and about 23% of deaf and hard of hearing students are Latino/a, in which 10.8% of all d/hh students are from Spanish-speaking homes (Gallaudet Research Institute, 2011). Most recently the Gallaudet Research Institute reported that there were about 30% deaf and hard of hearing students who are Latino/a from 2009–2010. During my observations, I found that most of the students who were Hispanic have parents who speak very little English, let alone know ASL; thus, communication is a major issue at home for these students. The flexibility of contesting membership and identities in the ASL classroom may provide agency to the students for developing their own sense of identity. However, at least one publication has indicated that the combination of cochlear implants and oral speech may benefit students whose first language is Spanish. Moore, Prath, and Arrieta's study (2007) found that at least one deaf student they tested had "substantially greater word accuracy compared to English-speaking CI [cochlear implant] peers with the same age of implantation and device" (p. 321). These researchers concluded that "knowledge concerning verbal productions of Spanish-speaking CI children will greatly aid the professional populations that serve Spanish-speaking children by providing norms or guidelines for development" (Moore et al., 2007, p. 338). Their findings require further research, but it is clear that the parent's native language plays a powerful role in the deaf child's developing languaculture—which in itself is another theme to consider for future research.

For example, the oral-based teacher commented that many of her students' parents are active participants in the student's learning process through their involvement in parent-teacher conferences and workshops. Most of these workshops educate the parents on how to provide speech therapy for their child at home, which would further reinforce the importance of speech and hearing as effective pedagogy for the deaf child. In contrast, the ASL school has struggled to get the parents of their students to attend school-based conferences and workshops. Teachers and administrators have often tried to encourage the parents to visit the school, and the classroom is "always open" for parent observation so they can learn how to better reinforce the teaching strategies at home. The school also offers free sign language classes to parents; unfortunately, not many parents have attended. The ASL-based teacher reasoned that the class is either too far from these parents' home, parents have no means of transportation, there is a communication barrier between the parents and the school (i.e., Spanish-speaking parents), or the parents are still in denial that their child is deaf.

The culture in the two classrooms is very diverse in terms of the physical layout of the tables, the types of knowledge facilitated by the students and teacher, the biographies of the students, and the types of individual or group agency exhibited. These differences lead to diverse constructions of languacultures and what the students and teachers view as natural and normal. Like the pedagogy of language, the culture in the classroom has important critical implications for the deaf students and their constructed meanings of culture and identity, as well as how those elements fit into the larger scheme of their everyday world. Their culture in the classroom relies heavily on teacher facilitation and the types of knowledge that the teacher uses in the classroom.

## Teacher Knowledge

Teachers are assumed to be the facilitators in the student's academic achievement, facilitators of their language construction, and managers of knowledge construction. Teachers also play a role in

> actively observing and looking for patterns in details observed [that] will lead students to search their existing knowledge base, to attend to connections between their existing knowledge base and the target problem, and be metacognitive by describing their own reasoning process. (Lee, 2007, p. 134)

Teachers are responsible for providing their unique pedagogy of language to shape diverse types of knowledge and languaculture "through the cultural resources and codes that anchor and organize experience and subjectivity" (Aronowitz & Giroux, 1991, p. 100).

Teachers who are trained in ASL/English bilingual pedagogy use ASL to build a bridge between the language of delivery (ASL) and the language of the texts (written English) and connect the two languages, enabling greater contextual comprehension for literacy (Erting & Pfau, 1997). The ASL-based teacher, Jan, whose parents and husband are deaf, is fluent in ASL and used some speech therapy techniques in the classroom, although she contended (in interviews) that she did not formally use speech therapy as the primary form of instruction. She had no formal academic training in speech therapy and she used ASL for every text, which is necessary for the students to connect these texts to conceptual thought processes. She used her prior knowledge of ASL and ways of knowing to include the deaf child's language in the classroom and expose them to the enculturation experience of deaf culture (Cummins, 1986). She allowed them to develop their own language skills and connect the sign to the printed word and their shared meaning. The ASL-based teacher mediated the text in a certain way to construct meaning in the books, which gave her students the opportunity to elicit a unique understanding of the text.

Teachers who are trained in speech pedagogy use precise phonological representations to exploit sublexical correspondences of English (written and spoken) to increase the children's knowledge of the letters, graphemes, and phonemes for connecting the two forms of the language, enabling greater vocabulary comprehension and literacy (Hermans et al., 2008; Lederberg & Spencer, 2009). Kris, the oral-based teacher, used her prior knowledge of auditory and speech therapy to include the phonetic sounds of the English words in the classroom (see peng/guin story in Chapter 4) to expose the deaf child to the values of spoken and written English. The oral-based teacher allowed the deaf students to develop one whole language rather than two languages (ASL and written English) as a part of the child's academic development.

The knowledge of their language base(s) that both teachers, Kris and Jan, brought to various classroom exercises allowed the students to transform unique and diverse information into conceptual meanings and make sense of that information. The teacher using ASL stresses the importance of allowing deaf students to express themselves freely (individual agency), even if it means violating the traditional student role (i.e., sitting down and not interrupting other students). By using her teacher knowledge, she enabled the students to share their metacognitive creativity (i.e., student incorporating red as a color from the fish to the real-life red shirt that another student wore). After allowing one student to count the arms of the octopus while their classmates paid attention, the teacher also provided the sign for octopus, emphasizing the reason for that specific sign (i.e., indicating the importance of the arms in the sign). This connection between the octopus's number of arms with the sign allowed the students to visually see the sign and to connect it to the real meaning of octopus. This ASL connection of the sign to the word transformed the guided reading experience visually, which enabled students to access this new knowledge and apply it to "real-life" situations.

In the oral school, the teacher is trained in speech pathology with a master's degree in speech therapy, and she demonstrated limited linguistic knowledge and skill in ASL ("Kris," personal communication, September 15, 2008). The use of voice as a cultural and educational tool in the most effective manner requires the embeddedness of a teacher who is professionally trained with an academic background in both science and medicine. This suggests that the oral-based teachers are more pathologically trained—rather than culturally trained—when it comes to deaf pedagogy (Hoffmeister, 1996). Voice becomes the most important cultural tool. The oral-based teacher used her prior knowledge from science-driven fields of deaf education to provide educational instruction. For example, the oral-based teachers are trained in speech pathology and know how to maximize the child's ability to speak and hear through technological devices such as the cochlear implant, which will benefit them once they transfer to a mainstream school. Some scholars contend that children with cochlear implants, given the proper teaching instruction and speech pedagogy, have been able to catch up with their hearing-age mates in spoken language (Geers, et al. 2009).

ASL scholars contend that oral-based teachers lack the cultural "ways of knowing," including common cultural practices of deaf people that deaf students cannot understand without someone from the deaf community explaining it to them (Erting, 1988; 1985). For example, the oral-based teacher at Central School was unsure how to educate her deaf students on the issue that it was okay to be deaf. Although she felt that it was unfortunate, she claimed that most students in oral programs maintain the notion that they can become "hearing." The main goal, however, of the oral-based teacher is to prepare the deaf students for assimilation, including providing the necessary cultural capital required for them to be successful and achieve age-appropriate spoken-language levels in order to be mainstreamed in kindergarten or later grade levels (Geers & Nicholas, 2003). In this respect, the oral-based teacher felt that she had the capacity to train and prepare deaf students in common cultural practices of the hearing society as alternative "ways of knowing."

An effective teacher is responsible for what transpires in the classroom, including the "interplay of thoughts that occur when teacher and student draw from their individual portfolios of language and communication skills to negotiate an understanding of one another" (Moores & Martin, 2006, p. 207). The teacher is placed in a unique position to facilitate reading and literacy development as a "social and cultural activity . . . to establish meaningful contexts to help the students construct understanding" in the environment (Marschark et al., 2002, p. 6). In the oral classroom environment, this facilitation is established with the trapezoid-shaped table to maximize total attention from the student, coupled with the teacher's pedagogical approach of demanding one-on-one attention from each student. This arrangement is designed to minimize group agency, including social interaction. Instead, the table shape and seating arrangement is designed to achieve the maximum capacity for speech instruction, including the detailed lexicon of words and their pronunciations.

The ASL-based teacher at Magnet School looks for opportunities to increase stimulation and social interaction to maximize creativity and cooperative learning as a part of direct instruction and whole language pedagogy. The use of whole language provides children with "access to complete, natural language (through-the-air and in print) . . . and many and varied opportunities to experiment and choose their own strategies and their own learning goals" (Mason & Ewoldt, 1996, p. 294). This ASL-based teacher, using her prior teaching knowledge, elicits information from the students, which fosters classroom discourses on various symbols, figurative concepts, and literary meanings (Marschark et al., 2002).

During the several educational exercises, the oral-based teacher did not stress the importance of facial expressions and body language. Rather, she emphasized the importance of the English cultural symbol, printed word, and connects it to voice. Voice becomes a cultural symbol of the student's learning process, which is significant because "symbols are emergent and appearing to the child to elicit knowledge" (Shirmer, 1994, p. 146). The oral-based teacher, using a monotonic approach, asked the student whether he had a penguin on his card and focused solely on his ability to pronounce the names of and respond to questions about the animals in the book. The use of repetition and the breaking down of the word into syllables was noteworthy because the teacher emphasized the speech aspect of the word rather than the meaning of the word.

The ASL-based teacher taught signs as important symbols and did not stress the pronunciation of the English words, this "reduced [verbal] communication so the child recognizes [that the topic] is important . . . meaningful, and worth watching" (Marschark et al., 2002, p. 70). This type of instruction in either classroom, however, serves to construct what the teacher thinks is important. The oral-based teacher's emphasis and repetition of the vocal cues suggested that pronunciation of certain words is a critical type of information, which likewise constructs what the teachers think is worthwhile to learn. The ASL-based teacher "organize[d] face-to-face interactions in ways that position students as sources of authority and [made] the structure of complex problem-solving explicit" (Lee, 2007, p. 27), which was seen during the octopus story exercise. The oral-based teacher used her authority to construct a direct instructional routine that elicited pre-scribed responses from the students, including rhyming, lexicons, and pronouncing various divisible terms.

Each teacher demonstrated a unique way of scaffolding new information to connect it to existing knowledge. The ASL-based teacher stressed the importance of distinguishing the animal (fish/octopus) from other animals in the book by enabling the students to discuss the colors, shape, and characteristics of the animal, a process that would distinguish important and unimportant information via a problem-solving task. To some scholars, this metacognitive exercise, incorporating the students' multiple intelligences (visual-spatial, body-kinesthetic), would enhance language development and develop emergent literacy concepts, and would construct meanings for future dialogue (Marschark et al., 2002). The oral-based teacher emphasized the importance of first distinguishing the lexicon, vocal structure, and syntax of the animal (penguin) from other words by enabling the student to identify each syllable. A process that distinguishes important vocal phonemic sounds from unimportant sounds when learning a vocabulary word, and then connecting the individual sounds within that word to the full English word.

The two teachers' opinions of educational policies such as NCLB and IDEA and the ideology of the least-restrictive environment were different. The oral-based teacher supported the restrictive environment (opposing IDEA's mandate for the least-restrictive environment) as the greatest opportunity for the students to capitalize on their oral and "hearing" training through extensive one-on-one time with the teacher to prepare them for mainstreaming. Her ideal mainstreaming classroom would be 15 hearing students to 1 teacher, but she admitted that the public school systems do not foster that type of arrangement. The oral-based teacher contended that the oral school will ultimately be able to better prepare its students for the most successful "least-restrictive" environment, seeming to imply that deaf students are better off when assimilated with hearing students. Conversely, the ASL-based teacher said that whether the school ought to provide the "least-restrictive environment" possible is "missing the point." Students, whether they are mainstreamed or remain in the deaf school, will be restricted in some ways; she emphasized that it is important to provide as many choices (i.e., using sign, gesture, technology, speech, or speechreading) for the students to feel less restricted. The oral-based teacher's goal was to prepare the deaf student for assimilation into the least restrictive environment, while the ASL-based teacher's goal was to prepare the deaf student for his or her own unique cultural transmission into an environment that would be deemed less restrictive.

## SUMMARY AND CONCLUSION

The three themes—pedagogy of language, culture in the classroom, and teacher knowledge—are critical to understanding the positive and negative formations of the educational environment, including its critical impact on the deaf student. These themes contribute to some constructions of the diverse languacultures in deaf education and may play a critical role in the successful, positive construction of the deaf child's literacy, language development, and identity formation. My research suggests that a reexamination of these themes may contribute to the larger implications of languaculture, deaf education, and deafness. Table 5.1 provides one way of organizing the data.

The first theme, pedagogy of language (whether spoken or signed), is the foundation of literacy as well as communication practice and plays an important role in the deaf child's cognitive, linguistic, and social life (Meadow-Orlans, 2003). My research uncovers evidence indicating that both the ASL classroom and the oral classroom were able to foster what they claim is a positive educational environment that provides healthy and constructive ways of knowing. By using ASL in the classroom as a form of pedagogy of language, advocates say that the environment becomes "natural" for the child's cognitive, linguistic, and social development. In contrast, other advocates recognize using the auditory/oral pedagogy as a critical factor in developing the deaf child's vocabulary by means of phonemics, which they claim leads toward literacy. According to these advocates, those literacy skills

Table 5.1:   A Breakdown of the Data that Contribute to the Three Themes

| Oral Classification | ASL Classification |
|---|---|
| **Pedagogy of Language** | |
| Use of the ear and mouth | Use of eyes, hands, and facial expressions |
| Voice/Speech | American Sign Language (ASL) |
| Emphasis and maintenance of speech to the text | Emphasis and maintenance of ASL to the text |
| More agency of language between student and teacher | More agency of language between student and student |
| Connection of English with spoken meaning | Connection of English with ASL meaning |
| English is the master status | ASL is the master status |
| **Culture in the Classroom** | |
| Privately funded classroom | Publicly funded classroom |
| Small classroom ratio (3:1) | Large classroom ratio (6:1) |
| High resistance to social interaction between students | Low resistance to social interaction between students |
| Linguistic and cultural capital from hearing "culture" | Linguistic and cultural capital from deaf "culture" |
| Schools as a transitional site | Schools as a cultural site |
| Goal: Assimilation into hearing cultural society by means of speaking/hearing | Goal: Cultural transmission in deaf culture by means of ASL |
| **Teacher Knowledge** | |
| Trained in Deaf Education with emphasis on speech therapy | Trained in Deaf Education with emphasis on ASL |
| Background in Science/Audiology | Background in Liberal Arts/Deaf Studies |

coupled with maximized speaking and hearing skills, result in preparation for hearing society by minimizing communication barriers in the mainstreamed setting. My research identifies these two contrasting languacultures as constructed ostensible "natural" outcomes of their respective ideologies; one is visual and the other is rooted in speech/ hearing. Both schools of thought rely differently on English; ASL-based connects English with the signed meaning of the word while spoken English-based connects English with the phonetics of the word. Regardless, my research suggests that both diverse pedagogies of language play a critical role in shaping the deaf child's linguistic and cognitive skills. This research may have greater implications when discussing how these pedagogies of language play a larger role in constructions of normalcy and deafness, including the ways deaf students communicate not only in the realm of education but also in society at large.

My research describes the culture in the classroom, the second theme, as a complex ecology of cultural systems where values and norms are constructed. The ASL classroom modifies its practices to fit the students' learning process by using ASL as "effective" language pedagogy. Students are encouraged to express their creativity and socialization with other students as a form of group agency. The goal of the ASL classroom is cultural transmission where the students' culture is priority. Examples from my research include the visual televisions where announcements are shown in ASL, the staff members and teachers using ASL as the primary form of communication, the semicircular table, and the props in the classroom in the form of fingerspelled and signed ASL. The culture in the oral classroom requires the student to adjust to the teacher's process, and the student adapts to the school's culture to better prepare him- or herself for assimilation in the hearing public school and society. Examples include the one-on-one individualized instruction facilitated by the teacher, the "natural" learning center used to stimulate a hearing classroom, the minimal socialization between students, and the reliance on hearing and speaking through technology to prepare students for communication access as necessary for "success" in the hearing public school.

The diverse range of languacultures described by my research in both classrooms is important to consider when discussing the constructions of normalcy and how certain indicators in the classroom may play a critical role in the child's understanding of his or her world as well as what it means to be deaf. The child becomes acculturated to what is considered normal in his or her everyday action in the classroom by means of socialization practices (whether with other students or individually with the teacher) embedded in the school's educational practices. This approach may also contribute to a deaf child's socialization skills in society (deaf and hearing) and to the types of cultures in which they are immersed.

The third theme in my research, teacher knowledge, is the corpus of information maintained to facilitate and present unique educational data to the students. The teacher's knowledge of language shapes and maintains the types of languaculture transmitted in the classroom, including the interplay of thoughts through educational activities and exercises as "best" practice. The ASL-based teacher's knowledge optimizes group agency by enabling the students to express themselves creatively and by finding ways for the classroom to adapt to the students' culture to create a positive "classroom culture." ASL storytelling is conducted as a group, wherein the teacher's ASL skills allow her to comprehend the student's social interactions with one another and to facilitate knowledge throughout this educational exercise. Conversely, the oral-based teacher's knowledge in speech therapy, pathology, and audiology enables her to translate educational information into phonological representations to master speech. Her knowledge is primarily facilitated through one-on-one instruction where she maximizes her teacher knowledge through technological devices to develop the child's capacity to hear and connect spoken words. My research suggests that the divergent facilitation and maintenance of teacher knowledge in the two classrooms plays an important role in how the student receives certain educational information and what types of information are embedded into their educational exercises. Both teachers claim that their unique teacher knowledge provides an advantage for the deaf child through their own unique educational pedagogies, which they view as the "best" practice.

The constructions of these two educational practices indicate two different environments with diverse types of knowledge (both academic and everyday)—in essence, two different languacultures—which have implications for the research of deaf education. My research suggests that the goal of the ASL classroom is cultural transmission whereby deaf culture and its types of knowledge become a high priority. The goal of the oral classroom is ultimate assimilation to the hearing society, using the culture of the dominant majority (i.e., hearing and speaking).

The examinations of the three themes that contribute toward languaculture of deaf education present a small analysis within the larger structural issues of deaf education and deafness and indicate that a simple cultural tool (such as the pedagogy of language, type of culture, or teacher knowledge) plays a pivotal role in the over-all educational setting and what it means to be deaf (Nikolaraizi & Hadjikakou, 2006). The research here suggests that the two deaf educational settings are very heterogeneous. It also supports the need in deaf education research that calls for "all forms of research, comparison group, correlational, descriptive, and ethnographic. . . . in different settings" (Luckner, 2006, p. 51). These forms of research address the implications of languaculture for deaf students in each environment.

More important, on a larger scale the two schools may have neglected the importance of recognizing the cultural practices within complex and divergent critical exercises within the two classrooms, as well as their potential impact on determining best educational strate-gies for deaf students and addressing deafness. My research describes the different types of "evidence" provided by each school that fur-ther strengthens their divergent ideologies regarding "best" practices in deaf education. This construction may reinforce each paradigm as one being the more "effective" and one more privileged than the other. My research indicates that this type of privilege exists when one form of language (e.g., ASL or spoken English), the dynamics the classroom, and "effective" teacher knowledge become constructed and contested in deaf education. I suggest that this construction may promote one camp contending to having more "privilege" than the other, which may further stigmatize the other camp as being devi-ant (Johnson, 2000). Ignoring the potential stigma and struggles that may exist in these two schools on one level of analysis may serve to reinforce a "rationale for not examining teachers and students in concrete school settings" (Aronowitz & Giroux, 1993). Thus, lan-guaculture becomes an important way to examine the contested con-structions of normalcy, deviance, and stigma within these schools and within deafness.

Considering the critical concerns of the various social constructions of languaculture in deaf education as "best practices," Chapter 6
summarizes the major findings of this research for future discussions
on deaf education and deafness. Additionally, Chapter 6 sets the stage
for developing constructive and positive strategic changes in deaf education and in the larger issues of deafness.

# CHAPTER SIX

# Coming Full Circle

This book started out with my emic journey to examine my deaf identity and its meanings in the social world as a critical contribution to the research on deafness. Languaculture was introduced as a gravitating theme to indicate the ways that language and culture are inextricable and critical to the understanding of the social constructions of deafness. Social constructions were introduced as a theoretical framework, and normalcy/deviance were used as concepts to help understand how and in what ways social constructions are developed, framed, and maintained to strengthen ideology. Using social constructions as a theoretical framework, the archaeology of deafness and deaf education, including languaculture, revealed ways that ideological positions on deaf education have shifted throughout sociohistory, mainly as a result of the varying social constructions of what it means to be deaf.

With the help of social constructions and concepts of normalcy/ deviance (Chapter 2) as tools of analysis, this book provided an archaeology of deafness and deaf education (Chapter 3), then made the connection to microlevel social processes occurring in two diverse types of deaf education (Chapter 4). This micro-examination of two classrooms in two different schools contributes to the larger scope of diverse social constructions that continue to permeate ideas and definitions about deafness and what deaf education ought to mean.

This analysis would not be complete without examining my positionality as a writer and as an individual (Chapter 1). There were many intersections between my personal narrative in Chapter 1 and my narrative findings on two educational institutions with vastly different ideologies, as well as my explanation of how these institutions became important and powerful sites to maintain and regulate certain types of knowledge (Chapter 4). As an ethnographer, I cannot be a "completely neutral detached observer, outside and independent of the observed phenomena" (Emerson, Fretz, & Shaw, 1995, p. 3)—in this case, these two classrooms. If someone had never attended an oral school and instead had attended a sign-based K–12 school, he or she would have written an entirely different Chapter 4 with different sets of knowledge construction. However, despite the differences between that person's positionality and my own, our approaches would converge when considering languacultures and the powerful social constructs that drive language perception and, in turn, the type of culture in which one lives. We both would be able to use the three themes (pedagogy of language, culture in the classroom, teacher knowledge) as theoretical frameworks to develop a knowledge construction of deaf languacultures. It is these types of knowledge that construct diverse languacultures, producing conflicting notions of what it means to identify as deaf. However, it is important to keep in mind the major quandary that "the case of the deaf and deaf identity is not the tension, but rather, the fundamental incommensurability of the emic and etic constructions" (Reagan, 2002, p. 44). I do want to contend that the "fundamental incommensurability" and the "clash in paradigms" of these languacultures are what create tension and continue to plague visions of a positive view of deaf education and what being deaf ought to look like.

Both emic and etic constructions are important; emic constructions (my personal knowledge and my narratives of the two classrooms) enable the ways (using social constructions, normalcy/ deviance, an archaeology of deafness as tools of analysis) to make explicit etic constructions of knowledge on deaf languacultures. My personal emic experiences throughout education and my narratives of the two classrooms become connected to the larger macrolevel etic analysis on schools. Using both emic and etic frameworks, one can begin to see how these educational institutions serve as very powerful forces in shaping identity, deafness, and the types of knowledge that come with the construction of deafness. I show, for example in Chapter 3, an archaeology of deaf education, specifically, the two paradigms that provide diverse "types of knowledge" in shaping what it means to be a deaf child in the name of normalcy. Too often, etic foundations on deafness have become detrimental because they are rooted in a narrow social construction of what it means to be deaf. This book attempts to reframe traditional etic foundations of deafness using emic processes, such as my personal journey and the micro-examination of two schools to locate alternative ways to make etic determinations in deaf education. In this sense, "an educational program grounded in an emic construction of deafness would actively encourage deaf children to be exposed to a wide variety" of educational opportunities and to offer different etic ways through which to look at deafness (Reagan, 2002, p. 59).

The findings suggest that discussions of the contrasting ideologies of languacultures and normalcy in deaf education may have important implications when examining the diverse ways that deafness and deaf students' identities are constructed. Included in these constructions are the different ways that the boundaries are maintained and permeated. Possible strategies will be presented in this chapter to develop a positive construction of deafness and ways to discuss the diverse ideologies of deaf education through careful, yet collaborative, inquiry toward a critical pedagogy for deaf students.

Larger critical justice issues related to deafness have important implications not only for influencing the types of knowledge and identities produced for deaf students but also for a greater understanding of humankind and our connections to the world. Instead of generating a narrow and static view on knowledge construction, languaculture, and social constructions, formulating a critical theory on justice would enable educators for the deaf to "link a theory of ethics and morality to a politics in which community, difference, remembrance, and historical consciousness become foundational" (Giroux in Moraes, 1996, p. 109). This link can be made possible only by understanding and respecting the relevance of social constructions and discussions through critical and collaborative inquiry. This task of collaborative inquiry must include discussions that are discursive and that follow two conceptual principles governing ethical human discourse stated by James Gee:

> (1) First conceptual principle governing ethical human discourse: That something would *harm* someone else (deprive them of what they or the society they are in view as "goods")

is *always* a good reason (although perhaps not a sufficient reason) to *not* do it.

(2) Second conceptual principle governing ethical human discourse: One always has the ethical obligation to try to expli-cate (render overt and conscious) any social practice that there is reason to believe advantages oneself or one's group over other people or other groups. (1990, p. 22)

For many people, their belief system about what is normal is based on experiences, assumptions, education, socialization, organizations, and family. This foundation is what makes Gee's two conceptual principles problematic at first glance because harm, advantages, and "ethical obligation" mean different things to different people. Some may argue that to withhold sign language from a deaf child is considered harm, while others assert that learning ASL instead of learning how to speak is considered harm. Choices about whether to provide a deaf child with a cochlear implant is another controversial debate that centers on the issue of harm (Brusky, 1995). In 2010, an Idaho deaf father was held in contempt for refusing to "force" his 8-year-old deaf daughter to wear cochlear implants ordered by Judge Stow. Clearly, Judge Stow and the father have two different viewpoints with respect to the "ethical obligation" of the deaf girl's care; whose ethical obligation shall reign supreme?

People also seek to validate certain choices stemming from their belief systems and to be a part of certain ideologies, including what ought to be the norm. However, it is important to examine these per-ceived notions and the motivation behind them. This examination includes affiliating these predisposed sets of beliefs and values with the types of organizations that advocate their belief system as a form of ideology. For example, when I was born deaf my parents attributed my hearing loss to the physical inability to hear and felt the need to correct my impairment. This predisposed belief system, including an "ethical obligation," led them to the ideological apparatus of the oral school to train me for a specific mode of normalcy, including the immersion in a specific type of language and knowledge construction.

The archaeology of deaf education and the study of the two classrooms suggest that certain organizations such as educational institutions play an important role in constructing perceptions of normalcy for deaf students, including languaculture. The two monolithic frameworks of languaculture supporting the two classrooms in this study present "evidence" to make a case for the most normal avenues to a child's education. For instance, views of normalcy are constructed that include whether or not the students are instructed by sign language, the culture in the classroom, and the teacher's knowledge. The diverse use of language (e.g., ASL or spoken English) may have implications for the child's linguistic and cognitive construction and for which language he or she feels is most natural or helpful. Some differences in the classroom culture (e.g., the level of social interaction with other students and the types of knowledge facilitation) contribute to the child's perception of his or her social world. Based on my descriptions of the two schools and on the archaeology of deaf education, I suggest that the childhoods and the future livelihoods of the deaf children are directly predicted by these children's placement in either school setting. Thus, deaf schools as sites of enculturation, socialization, and education have the ability to be the vanguard for positive versus negative constructions of deafness (Berger, 2005).

This book has two major summaries that will serve to organize my findings for future study:

1. Discussion of the contrasting ideologies of normalcy, which may have important implications when examining the diverse ways that deaf students and deafness are constructed through languaculture, specifically, the pedagogy of language, cultures in the classroom, and teacher knowledge.
2. Discussion that recognizes divisive paradigmatic camps of languaculture in deaf education as being monolithic and that proposes collaborative critical inquiry as one way to discuss the diverse ideologies of deaf education.

These summaries reflect important issues that stakeholders within deaf education must undertake if we are to move forward in positive social constructions of deafness and healthier aspects of defining what it means to be deaf human beings. After discussing these two summaries,

I then suggest the need for continued research on bilingualism as multi-languacultures and on what Marcia Moraes (1996, p. 1) has suggested as critical bilingualism, specifically because this book focuses both on bilingualism in the name of diversity and simultaneously places a greater emphasis on "interrogating" the social construction of difference and diversity. Revisiting the important contributions of bilingualism critically may serve as important starting points for redefining languacultures for deaf people and for addressing the concerns that I have raised throughout this book.

## Summary #1: The Critical Importance of Revealing Contrasting Ideologies of Normalcy

Adrienne Asch, a blind individual, reflects how the notion of "normal"—learned through her parents, professionals, and relationships to society—played a powerful and exacting role on her childhood and on her view of life. She notes that

> had they [her parents] not believed in my inherent normality and potential, and had they not had the good fortune to meet professionals who also believed in the inherent normality of blind children . . . my view of myself as a person who is among other things blind, my life would be totally different. (Hehir, 2005, p. 41)

Howard, a deaf member of his deaf community and child of deaf parents, reflected on his childhood experiences. It was not until he went to school that he realized he was being defined and treated as deaf. His perception of deafness shifted, and his perception of what it meant to be normal in the social world also shifted. He describes that

> he had spent his early childhood among Deaf people, but that when he was six his world changed: his parents took him to a school for Deaf children. "Would you believe," he said, pausing expertly for effect, "I never knew I was deaf until I first entered school?" (Padden & Humphries, 1988, in Berger, 2005, p. 153)

In my own experience, I thought I was going to be hearing just the same way the deaf child at the oral school assumed in Chapter 4; it was an uneasy feeling when realizing, slowly over time, that I was never going to be hearing. I struggled through a series of revelations to realize that I was deaf, then realize that I was not as deaf as some of the individuals I met, including some hearing people (Codas). My (re) categorization to the margins of neither being fully hearing or deaf at times contributed to my understanding of my place in society and what it means for me to be deaf.

In a PBS documentary about deafness, *Through Deaf Eyes* (Hott & Garey, 2007), Ted Supalla, a deaf child of deaf parents, narrates his childhood experiences as a deaf person thinking that everyone in his world was deaf—until he asked his deaf parents why his neighbors, not knowing that they were hearing, were "moving their mouths" in a weird foreign manner and why they "spoke funny." His parents clarified that the neighbors were "everywhere" and that he—like his parents—were indeed the minority. His perception of his hearing neighbors being "weird" suddenly shifted to one in which he and his family were possibly the weirder subjects, since they were the minority.

These experiences of deafness, my personal narrative, the archaeology of deaf education, and my descriptions of the two schools are reminders of how the guise of normalcy may lead to dangerous constructions of deafness for deaf students. Such constructions and perceptions may reflect the reproduction of social stratification, privilege, the roles of languaculture, pedagogy, culture in the classroom, and types of teacher knowledge (Becker, 1961; Horejes & Lauderdale, 2007). Throughout my observations, I have determined that curricula choices and language placement in these schools may have unintentionally constructed stigmatizing definitions in deaf educational practices by determining what is most "natural" and "privileged" (e.g., whether ASL or spoken English ought to be the most "natural" language or how culture in the classroom ought to be facilitated). I found that stratifications have also reproduced divisive ideologies in the construction of deafness, deaf education, and best practices. These divisive factors may have forced a worldview identity onto the deaf child, instead of providing choices that would be most advantageous to him or her.

One scholar warns that "in a [ politically] charged climate, it is easier to lose sight of the whole child" (Bailes in Johnson, 2011, p. 81).

Highly divisive (and often problematic) constructions of normalcy and deviance provide a cautionary note to players in the education field regarding what they believe is best for deaf students. With respect to constructions of normalcy, the current field of deaf education is divided into divergent ideologies as to how "positive change" should occur (Moores & Martin, 2006, p. 3). A reexamination of deaf students' constructions through languaculture, specifically, the pedagogy of language, cultures in the classroom, and teacher knowledge, may be a heuristic way to study some of the social constructions of normalcy and deviance in deafness.

The microlevel examination in my research of these two schools reveals a small aspect of deaf schools as institutions that continues to play a major role in constructing normalcy in deaf students' social fabric by shaping and forming specific identities, attitudes, opinions, behaviors, and knowledge. The constructions in the two classrooms, on a small scale, simultaneously construct "the symbols, representations, and practices of social life in a way that the basis of social authority and the unequal relations of power and privilege remains hidden" (McLaren, 1989, p. 174; Artiles, 2003, p. 184; see also Horejes & Lauderdale, 2007). This book has uncovered these "hidden" unequal relations of power and privilege in order to examine deafness, using deaf education as one site of study. Some examples in this research include diverse teacher knowledge and backgrounds, the impact of some instructional practices (both ASL and oral), and the strengths/ weaknesses of certain language pedagogies (e.g., phonetics versus signs). These examples offer a way to examine the importance of languaculture, its potential impact on deafness, and how the ideology of normalcy shapes and/or hides these cultural and social values.

The human experiences of Adrienne Asch, Howard, and Ted Supalla resonate strongly with my own social problems as a disabled/ deaf individual. Our stories and those of others, however, are rarely documented formally or taken seriously (Baynton, 2001, p. 52). It is possible that some social institutions have defined normalcy for the wrong ends. It has helped reassure their own normalcy by means of privilege and best practices, which simultaneously has reproduced stigma and labeled others as deviant (Longmore, 2003). Specifically, these two educational camps examined here may have constructed normalcy by means of maintaining their languacultures according to the way "social power . . . and inequality are enacted, reproduced, and resisted by text and talk in the social and political context" (van Dijk, 2003, p. 352). The issue of deaf languacultures is not about

> signing or speaking, it is about the development of con-nections in the child's brain that provide the framework for lifelong learning . . . there are benefits to acquiring signed lan-guages . . . [and] some d/Deaf children are able to learn and communicate through oral/aural modes, and thus it makes sense that they receive support for this in a holistic environ-ment allowing for *both visual and aural success* [emphasis added]. (Bailes in Johnson, 2011, p. 81)

In my research, once children enter either type of school for the deaf, they are defined by predetermined criteria of normalcy, which simultaneously also creates inequality and perpetuates divisions with the other school (Waldschmidt, 2005). For example, auditory-based schools believe that the only way for the child to become effectively immersed in a language is through the oral method, by means of hearing/speaking, to become a functioning and normal individual in society. Emphasizing speech and hearing, the oral school may have simultaneously imposed their values of spoken English through auditory/oral-based pedagogy as *the* language for deaf people, thus creating a sense of privilege. Conversely, ASL scholars and teachers contend that ASL is the normal and natural way for deaf people to communicate. In turn, these scholars and teachers reject auditory/oral-based pedagogy and, in some ways, reject the dominant language of our society.

George Veditz, a deaf charismatic leader for the deaf commu-nity, once said that sign language is God's noblest gift to deaf people (Veditz, 1913, in Padden, 2004, p. 245). This statement reflects the ideology of many who advocate ASL. In contrast, the mission of the Moog curriculum, used by the oral school in this study and many other oral schools in the United States, is "Talk is cheap, unless you're deaf. Then it's priceless" (see http://www.moogcenter.org). In other words, talking is already a fundamental basic for hearing individuals, but if you are deaf, talking becomes a priceless skill and privilege that would allow deaf people to be equal with hearing individuals and approach normalcy. According to the constructions of the oral school, to talk is human; according to the constructions of ASL school, to sign is human. This dichotomy indicates two highly divisive languacultures at work, and "not getting beyond the ideology . . . results in too many young deaf children experiencing varying states of linguistic and cognitive deprivation" (Bailes in Johnson, 2011, p. 81).

The attribution of these predetermined language choices for deaf people may possibly contribute to the narrow social constructions that surround deafness as a form of stigma and that neglect its possible contribution to humankind (Emens, 2008). For ASL scholars to claim that to sign is human and oral scholars to claim that to speak and hear is human leads to division and stigma, each against the other. I suggest that this dichotomy needs to be revisited and examined in terms of how it further constructs the "normal" deaf child, with its simultaneous constructs of deviancy (e.g., by dismissing one language for another). Viewing the deaf child as diverse might enable the schools to consider which diverse language placement and/or curricula choices would best help a particular deaf child, without limiting his or her potential. One way is to enable schools to ask questions such as "How will providing these accommodations benefit this person who is diverse?", rather than questions like "How will these accommodations 'fix' this person to make [him or her] human?" (Emens, 2008, p. 896). Departing from the parameters of normalcy when asking questions or constructing disability, deafness, or sign language, may make it possible to view deafness as part of human diversity, as it was viewed during the eighteenth-century European Enlightenment. This may enable us to find ways to "ameliorate discriminatory attitudes" that have evolved slowly over time regarding deafness and disability (Emens, 2008, p. 840).

In my research, oral practitioners contend that having access to the oral method gives a deaf student an advantage over a deaf student who signs. Conversely, ASL practitioners contend that the use of sign language is more advantageous for the deaf child than the oral method. Favoring one method's language pedagogy as a form of privilege may have designated language as a social tool that measures normalcy, deviance, ability and disability and is used to construct deafness (Derrida, 1974). My research suggests that parameters of normalcy become socially negotiable, including arguments of whether or not to incorporate sign language in the classroom, which has an impact, not only on the type of culture, but also the teacher's knowledge in the deaf classroom (Lee, 2007).

My research also addresses the importance of languaculture, specifically, pedagogy of language, the cultural implications in the classroom, and the types of knowledge, all of which are facilitated by the teachers who define and redefine constructions of deafness. This analysis includes why certain theoretical ideas—whether they relate to the use of signs or speaking—continue to frame deafness in a certain connotation of humankind, whether a deaf person's "hearing loss" is something that needs to be fixed or why sign language ought to be the native language for the deaf. I suggest that it is critical to examine why theoretical themes on languaculture continue to be contested, themes such as using sign language to prepare the deaf child for cultural transmission in society or teaching spoken English to prepare the deaf child for mainstreaming in society (Erevelles, 2002, p. 31).

Renegotiating deafness as an "impairment" has included deciding whether to educate a deaf child in sign language or spoken English in the name of normalcy. I suggest this kind of misnomer needs to be revisited; my research shows that when schools determine language placement—whether it be sign language or spoken English—it limits the possible educational tools for the child and further confines the deaf child to a specific set of ideological values. Instead, I suggest that one way to decide the language pedagogy for deaf children without considering the parameters of normalcy is to view the deaf child first and foremost as a human being, a priori in the name of diversity.

Some scholars have suggested that deaf people no longer be identified through the disability model as having a deficit and instead be identified as a linguistic minority (Charrow & Wilbur, 1975) or as an ethnic group (Lane, 2005; Lane, Pillard, & Hedberg, 2011). This move from the medical/disability model of deafness toward a model of difference by means of selfhood that is equivalent to what our society considers as a "normal" human may help society to avoid defining deafness as an impairment and as a negative ontology of defining normalcy.

However, there are some perceptions of "impairments" that are undeniable a priori (i.e., in terms of biology); yes, the attitudinal "impairments" associated with deafness have shifted over time, and "impairments" are social constructs, but the variation of "hearing" ability between a deaf human and the rest of the world is very real. The real question is: What do we do with this variation? This situation is a tricky puzzle. Imagine a society in which deafness no longer is measured by the variation of "hearing" but, rather, becomes a linguistic minority comparable with immigrants in America who know little English. After all, in a social model, there is nothing inherently wrong with deaf people except the communication that impedes their success. But, then, whose responsibility is it to provide this communication access? Under the traditional linguistic minority or ethnicity model, it would be the individual's responsibility (as it is for those who are linguistic minorities in America); however, under the disability model, it is the government's job to ensure this access through the Americans with Disabilities Act (ADA). To qualify for accommodations under the ADA, one would have to be regarded as disabled. However, this position is dangerous, because

> of the disability misrepresentation, Deaf people are more vulnerable to measures aimed at reducing Deaf births, to surgery where the risks and costs outweigh the benefits, to delayed language acquisition, to monolingual education in an oral language, to social isolation in the local school, and to marginalization when lacking both the dominant ethnicity of their parents and the minority ethnicity of their Deaf peers. (Lane et al., 2011, p. 55)

Harlan Lane, Richard Pillard, and Ulf Hedberg (2011) contend that moving the model of deafness toward an ethnicity model and away from the disability model is the most effective approach, although it would require a redefinition of ethnicity. This approach is a possibility. However, if the deaf community is adamant to support such a move, I warn that one must understand the dangers of social constructions surrounding the redefinition of ethnicity and how notions of normalcy/deviance may still influence attitudes on deafness as a deficit. People who are part of a traditional ethnic group have historically been viewed as having a deficit (Johnson, 2000), so redefining deaf people as an ethnic group would not necessarily eliminate the possibility that deaf people would continue to experience the stigma of having a "deficit." Regardless of wanting to redefine deaf people as an ethnic group or to maintain a definition of deaf people in the disability model, viewing deafness as a deficit needs to be included and understood as functioning within "axes of oppression," and we need to "enrich the discussion of the intersections of the axes of class, race, gender, and sexual orientation, and disability" (Linton, 2006, p. 171).

Toward that end, schools for the deaf need to lay down a foundation that viewing deaf people as deficient is discrimination, or a form of audism,[1] and is "on par with concepts like sexism, racism, and homophobia" (Thomas, 2004, pp. 572, 579). This challenge is a public issue. Deafness is a public matter (e.g., audism) while impairment is a private matter (e.g., stigma). Impairment does not cause deafness; impairment causes social oppression by causing the restricted activity that constitutes deafness as a deficit. Schools for the deaf need to avoid classifying deaf students within a framework of what it means to be normal and using impairment in its definition. It is possible that individuals may discuss their own impairment, but it should always be a private matter; however, on a social level, schools for the deaf need to address how restrictions to everyday activities are unethical as espoused by James Gee. Going back to Gee's two conceptual principles governing ethical human discourse, schools need to find ways to talk about the deaf child, regardless of proclaimed impairment or "severity" of hearing loss, in a way that will not harm the deaf child. Schools need to locate ways that will carefully discuss how the deaf child may be at a disadvantage if placed in a certain educational pedagogy, program, and/or curriculum and, at the same time, consciously avoid framing the child in a normalcy/deviance spectrum, but rather, as a child with

---

1. Audism is "the notion that one is superior based on one's ability to hear or behave in the manner of one who hears" (Humphries, 1977, p. 12).

possible choices that will be most advantageous to him/her and only him/her.

I suggest that to redirect what it means to be deaf, one needs to be open to all of the possible advantages for the deaf child rather than restrict language options, curricula choices, and the types of information that are facilitated. It may be useful to develop collaborative efforts with other social institutions that play a role in deaf education (Johnson, 2011), including a reevaluation of their pedagogies and social processes, when discussing diverse constructions of normalcy or deviance.

## Summary #2: The Need for Collaborative Critical Inquiry

Much of the work on collaborative critical inquiry in this section is derived from two major scholars. First, Jim Cummins's (2000) *Language, Power, and Pedagogy* is a book that makes a strong case for collaborative critical inquiry to discuss the importance of language and power formations and construct pedagogies collectively. In *Pedagogies of Choice: Challenging Cocercive Relations of Power in Classrooms and Communities,* Cummins (2009) asks several important questions, such as "How can coercive relations of power be transformed into collaborative relations of power? Second, Marcela Moraes's (1996) *Bilingual Education: A Dialogue with the Bakhtin Circle* provides theoretical analysis to understand the power of the oppressor/ oppressed through a dialogic-critical pedagogy. Moraes asks equally important questions such as "What are ways to build dialogue between oppressed and oppressors from which both groups can understand the social constraints that impede an emancipatory democracy, experience different levels of oppression, and comprehend their shared responsibility?" (Moraes, 1996, p. 113). Although Cummins criticizes Moraes for being too theoretical, they both agree on the importance of a collaborative critical inquiry, and I make the case that using both of their ideas is important in proceeding on a path of collaborative critical inquiry, and it is necessary to place deaf education in a social justice framework where contrasting paradigms could then be able to coexist in pursuit of a successful future for the deaf child.

My research on deaf education and languaculture is reflective of the larger issues within the monolithic deaf education field and is in line with Cummins's analysis of power, language, and pedagogy in linguistic and cultural minority students. Cummins's analysis includes case examples from Spanish and Korean students that show how these populations struggle under coercive power relations in the name of normalcy. Cummins presents a position that collaborative critical inquiry is necessary for transformative and positive pedagogies for these populations. Cummins not only presents a theoretical analysis of power, language, and pedagogy, but also offers a "set of guidelines" essential to accomplishing a successful collaboration between parties whose ideologies clash. These ideological frameworks need to agree to disagree; by doing so, collaboration would enable

> conditions for oppressors to critically analyze their own situation: to critically analyze the levels in which they are also oppressed because they live under various forms of social control. . . . [B]ut awareness of the oppressor is crucial in the sense that the oppressor can understand that he or she must collaborate for a better society. (Moraes in Cummins, 2000, p. 236)

Moraes (1996, p. 113) calls for a dialogic-critical pedagogy in which both groups can acknowledge the various social constraints that continue to fuel oppressive action and result in the inability to collaborate toward social transformation. Unfortunately, for deaf people, these divisive educational institutions believe that they are moral defenders of deaf children and that the "other" is the enemy (and oppressor) without realizing in another level of analysis that they themselves might be the oppressor. As a result, these camps have failed to provide an effective education for deaf students (see statistics in Chapter 3). This situation is reflective of Moraes's concern that "our definitions are always ideological" (1996, p. 113).

Both of these camps genuinely believe that they are providing the most "effective" pedagogy and the most positive social construct of languaculture for the deaf child. Therefore, before I can consider a transformative pedagogy, these highly divisive ideological positions on languaculture for deaf people must exist within the current dialogue because one "does not exist outside of a dialogue . . . the existence of self and other is a simultaneous experience; a dialogical existence" (Cummins, 2000, p. 237). Only then can we hope to "challenge and change this 'ready-made' ideological world" (Moraes, 1996, p. 113). These ideological perspectives are contributors (both good and bad) to the archaeology of deaf education and will continue to play a major role in the reconstruction of deaf education. Strength comes in numbers, therefore, a collaboration would open channels and avenues to a transformative pedagogy that would manage the issues that have continued to thwart success in deaf education. To be sure, these ideological perspectives (i.e., auditory-based and sign-based language pedagogies) are not dichotomous, even though sometimes these perspectives clash within these larger ideological frameworks.[2] Instead, here the focus is on the clash in languaculture, which is dominated by two major paradigms: auditory/oral-based spoken English and sign-based forms of language.

As indicated in earlier chapters, the languaculture for the deaf has been defined and redefined for the last 250 years by "experts" using a framework of normalcy or deviance, including not only what the culture of the deaf is but also how deaf and deafness are perceived and defined. Also evidenced in earlier chapters, positions on sign language and spoken English for deaf people are almost intractable; both camps feel that they are oppressed and that the other side is the enemy (Cummins, 2000, p. 3; see also comparisons of the interviews with the two teachers in Chapter 5). Research on these languacultures, including the formulation of knowledge and culture based on language, is primarily conducted by "several disparate disciplines whose discourses rarely 'speak' to each other" (Ladd, 2003, p. 267). In addition to these

---

2. Deaf Bilingual Coalition (DBC) was founded in 2008 with the goals of advocating for ASL as the primary language choice for deaf children, but some key members of DBC formed their own organizations after disagreements on certain deaf issues, including cochlear implants. Currently, DBC and these splinter organizations have a history of resisting collaboration despite agreeing on the importance of ASL to the deaf child.

pedagogies for the deaf being divisive, both are unwilling to collaborate, and reinforce the long-standing attitudes in education toward those who are culturally and linguistic minorities. Cummins (2000) indicates that

> [e]ducational debates on school effectiveness for culturally and linguistically diverse students have been enacted in parallel discourses that have rarely been brought together (mainstream schools that focus on effective schools versus theoretical and ethnographic research deriving from perspectives of multicultural education and critical pedagogy that highlights a very different set of practices and interventions). (p. 247)

A part of the challenge that culturally and linguistically diverse students (including deaf students) confront is that their curriculum choices and pedagogy are driven strongly by a narrow etic framework that focuses on "effectiveness" of the program. As such, these approaches are rooted on the notion that these students enter the classroom with a deficit and not on a notion that acknowledges their potential strengths. This framework is especially true when the deaf child is mainstreamed into a public school's system whose curriculum is based on society's values and not the sociocultural values of the deaf student (Johnson, Liddell, & Erting, 1989). These etic frameworks do not seriously consider theoretical and ethnographic emic research on multiculturalism. Rarely do educational reforms directed at mainstreaming these deaf students into the larger hearing public school system take into account the historical, sociopolitical, and languaculture roots of student failure (Cummins, 2000). What is needed is collaborative critical inquiry.

I suggest that both camps sit at the same table and discuss ways to work together for constructive collaborative inquiry to elevate dialogues on some of the issues within the current state deaf education. This effort would be one small step to discuss not just language pedagogy, culture, and curriculum choices but also the economic, institutional, and social implications for deaf education and deafness in future actions. At times, each camp has divulged information in journals (e.g., *Journal of Deaf Studies and Deaf Education, American Annals of the Deaf*) and at conferences (American Educational Research Association); however, too often each camp has used these platforms to pit itself against the other, armed with "evidence."

Necessary for constructive collective inquiry from both sides is discussion of the dialogic notions of oppressor and oppressed. By acknowledging these issues, these two camps would be able to

> critically analyze their own situation [and] to critically ana-lyze the levels in which they are also oppressed [and are the oppressor] because they live under various forms of social con-trol and are discursively positioned in contradictory ways that blind them to their own situatedness in relations to power and privilege. (Cummins, 2000, p. 236)

Moraes adds that "[w]e have to make the oppressor aware that everybody is oppressed at some level" by engaging in a dialogic language of awareness by means of multivoicedness in which power is given to these voices that rarely speak to each other. This process is what Moraes refers to as the emergence of the dialogic-critical pedagogy, which enables voices to be recognized; the "voice of the oppressed reaches the oppressor who is another oppressed—and both agents must be engaged toward a reciprocal social freedom" (Moraes, 1996, p. 116). However, Cummins warns that there is "no opponent of bilingual or multilingual education who is likely be convinced by the argument that 'our dialogic existence is something that cannot be denied'" (2000, p. 238). Nevertheless, by acknowledging that both play a role as oppressor and oppressed, they would begin to realize the power they possess in creating knowledge constructs on deafness and what it means to be human.

Understanding the power structures and the changes to consoli-date power within these two paradigms is critical for different bureau-cratic organizations, especially as society becomes more complex. For example, where power is increasingly concentrated, the hegemonic forces that prescribe privilege, rules, and laws and that proscribe cer-tain conduct as deviant play a greater role in the promotion, revision, and maintenance of demonizing categories and labels. Where power is more diffuse, deviance may still persist, but it is more likely to be construed positively as political deviance, as with the work of certain geniuses, artists, musicians, scientists, or leaders. Where power approaches complete diffusion, political deviance might be seen as "diverse" and not as abnormal, immoral, or unlawful. Thus, the consolidation of power and the persistence of categories of deviance correspond in a manner that highlights the utility of an approach that incorporates analyses of both power and deviance (Lauderdale & Amster, 1998).

The consolidation of power constructs rigid homogeneity in these deaf schools as the dominant system of values and ideology. There needs to be a

> recognition that dominant groups are no more homogenous than subordinated groups and to dismiss all of those who enjoy privileged status in our society as "oppressors" amounts to essentialization that will curtail rather than promote the dialogic process; there is a need to identify and reach out to those within dominant groups who are prepared to engage in meaningful dialogue. (Cummins, 2000, p. 239)

Here, I summarize Cummins's critical components to the process of collaborative critical inquiry to move from theory to praxis. First, in establishing a dialogic process, there needs to be acknowledgment that both languages—sign language and spoken language—are not homogenous; more important, one does not supersede the other in terms of power and privilege (Meadow-Orlans, 2003). Second, in making collaboration possible, these two educational and ideological social constructs—both ASL- and oral-based pedagogies—must identify important goals and values that transcend the "us vs. them" ideology and focus on a shared and critical ideology of diversity. This type of horizontal participation, or what Paulo Freire calls "participatory action research," would possibly

> empower those without a voice or the power to change prevailing hegemonies. The silenced are not just incidental to the curiosity of the investigator but are the masters of inquiry into the underlying causes of the events in their world. In this

context research becomes a means of moving them beyond silence into a quest to proclaim the world. (Freire, 1992/2004, pp. 30–31)

The two different academic pedagogies, each with its own curricula, traditional knowledge, and languacultures, could become embedded in transformative academic knowledge within the larger critical pedagogy of deafness and deaf education. Transformative academic knowledge could be defined as

> the facts, concepts, paradigms, themes, and explanations that challenge mainstream academic knowledge and expand and substantially revise established canons, paradigms, theories, explanations, and research methods. (Banks, 1993, p. 7)

It is this transformative knowledge that would provide a starting point for a critical pedagogy for teachers and practitioners of deaf education, to better understand their contributions to the larger social constructions of deafness (Freire, 1992/2004; Smith, 1990). I join "scholars signaling the need for new directions . . . a more expansive, nuanced, and interdisciplinary approach that encompasses the many ways deaf people live today" (Fernandes & Myers, 2009, p. 1). Everyday discourse is continuously dialogic in nature, and the incorporation of these diverse theoretical themes, including languaculture within the educational setting, "establishes cultural inquiry" (Lee, 2007, p. 61). Finally, the possible inconsistencies and conflicts about "best practices" in deaf education, its pedagogy, and languaculture need to be exposed. By revealing these inconsistencies, which may have been hidden by certain ideological positions, to prevent themselves from appearing to be "weak" or "unsuccessful," we could then be able to acknowledge the real possible strengths and weakness in curriculum and language choices for deaf students. I echo a concern from a teacher in 1891:

> Always bear in mind that questioning has a value for you and also for your pupil: that it draws out information, but that it may also give information; and that a lack of ability to express clearly any knowledge the pupil is supposed to have needs

> careful investigation by the teacher to ascertain if the matter
> has been presented in such a manner as to be plain to the
> pupil. (Steinke, 1891, p. 210)

More important, this acknowledgment of careful investigation through collaboration of shared knowledge would promote the importance of these differences and the idea that deaf children should be entitled to access various types of programs and language choices in their education.

Some scholars have warned that to promote difference in the name of diversity might produce more resistance and further consolidate power structures, including redefining what it means to be normal and deviant (Giroux, 1992, p. 171). This possibility is a considerable risk; however, it is a risk that would enable students to engage in

> cultural remapping as a form of resistance. That is, students
> should be given the opportunity to engage in systematic analy-
> ses of the ways in which the dominant culture creates borders
> saturated in terror, inequality, and forced exclusions. Similarly,
> students should be allowed to rewrite difference through the
> process of crossing over into cultural borders that offer narra-
> tives, languages, and experiences that provide a resource for
> rethinking the relationship between the center and the mar-
> gins of power as between themselves and others. (Aronowitz
> & Giroux, 1991, p. 174)

Obviously, the students I refer to in this ethnographic study do not have these opportunities initially because they are in kindergarten, but at least this approach would enable the students to become acculturated/enculturated to the point where they would eventually conceptualize learning as a cultural process (Lee, 2007) and be provided agency for self-determination on their identity, languaculture, and selfhood. Burchardt (2004, p. 743) recognizes that each group asserting its right to self-determination and formulating certain social justice issues "requires setting priorities . . . to promote human capabilities . . . to identify which capabilities are the most important," including which group should be more deserving than others. Being able to acknowledge and respect the diversity of the deaf world might offer opportunities to uncover hidden histories, knowledge, cultural values, and unnecessary prejudices. What is needed is an active community-based position that diffuses these power positions so they become voices of reason rather than voices of another oppressor to address these concerns.

Colorado, New Mexico, Arkansas, Washington, and California are some of the states that have a deaf education task force to specifically address such concerns. Currently, the state of Colorado has a collaborative project with the University of Arizona, Arizona State Schools for the Deaf and Blind, University of Northern Colorado, and Colorado Department of Education. While the projects do not include the comparative method (used in this research) to map out the possible differences between deaf schools in terms of the oral pedagogy and the sign language pedagogy, this book contributes to their endeavors, adding valuable resources for these task forces, as well as other states and universities undertaking similar projects.

It is important to note that while these states have established deaf education task forces, these states are also involved in grassroots organizations such as Hands & Voices. The name of the organization reflects the importance of both hands and voices in the deaf child's educational pedagogy and social experiences. The organization now has 26 approved chapters, 11 provisional chapters, and 6 start-up chapters (DeafMom, 2011). Their mission is to

> improve the social and academic experiences of our children, students, and mentees who are deaf or hard of hearing (d/hh). Whether we're talking, cueing, signing, or combining . . . this approach has exposed us to many families using a wide variety of communication choices—all that have resulted in really successful kids. Conversely, we've seen many other kids and their families not reaching their goals via a particular mode or method. (Seaver, 2004)

As one mom points out in her recent blog about Hands & Voices, "What I love most about Hands & Voices is that over the years, I've had the opportunity to meet such a diverse group of parents, professionals and deaf/hard of hearing adults from all over"

(DeafMom, 2011). The philosophy of the organization reflects some of the implications presented in this book: that it may not be effective for schools to focus on narrow aspects and pedagogies in a child's education and that a broader and more diverse approach may be more effective. In August 2011, on a flyer distributed by Hands & Voices, the organization announced hosting a special event involving two presentations: "Language Acquisition and Children Who are Deaf and Hard of Hearing: Why Early Intervention Needs to Be Early" by a professor from the Department of Speech, Language, and Hearing Sciences at the University of Arizona and "Raising Children in a Language-Rich Home" presented by two deaf parents of a deaf child. The write-up for the special event is central to languaculture because it outlines that

> [t]he critical time for learning language is the first months and years of a child's life. Thanks to early identification of hearing loss, we can provide early intervention that promotes language learning. Dr. Smith will discuss ways to enhance language acquisition for children who are deaf and hard of hearing in both English and non-English speaking families. John is the parent. He and his wife, Jane, who is profoundly deaf, are raising their two young children in a bilingual (English/ASL) family. He brings his practical experience and wisdom in creating a positive environment for language learning.[3]

Finally, at the end of the blurb, the organization informs that "All are welcome. Parents, Caregivers, Family Members, Early Intervention providers, Speech Language Pathologists, Teachers, Students."[4]

Recently in 2011–2012, there has been contention by members of the deaf community toward some Hands & Voices state chapters, claiming them to be biased and advocating only for the voices rather than the hands. In addition, deaf community members point out that

---

3. Taken from a Hands & Voices flyer in 2011. The names of these presenters are pseudonyms.
4. Taken from a Hands & Voices flyer in 2011.

there are certain people who are involved in chairing these Hands & Voices chapters, while at the same time affiliated with oral-based agencies, like Alexander Graham Bell, rather than taking an unbiased and neutral stance. The lack of collaboration with diverse agencies representing both sides of the continuum (both hands and voices) is detrimental to the search for collaborative critical inquiry and instead promotes dangerous constructions of deafness with neglect to diversity. If the chairmembers of Hands & Voices chapters want to affiliate themselves with agencies that provide a strong ideological stance supporting oral/aural approaches such as Alexander Graham Bell, then they ought to also be affiliated with agencies that provide alternative and equally as strong ideological stances supporting ASL and the deaf community. A great proactive approach by a Hands & Voices chapter in Arizona began in September 2012, and involves the coordination of a literacy event with a two-part session. The first session in the morning is hosted by an individual representing the oral/aural approach, specifically a speech pathologist specializing in spoken language who trains parents and professionals how to use sound in literacy training. The second session in the afternoon is hosted by another individual representing the sign-based approach, a literacy specialist from the Laurent Clerc National Deaf Education Center, Gallaudet University, who has nearly 20 years of experience teaching ASL. This kind of collaboration may lead to acknowledging the different strengths and weaknesses of each mode or pedagogy and respecting diverse contributions in deaf education (Luckner & Muir, 2002). More important, this collaboration may provide opportunities to address the need for more deaf education task forces and grassroots organizations to include critical factors like the pedagogy of language as a powerful social construct, and to contribute in the national effort to advance the lives of deaf students. However important it is that deaf education be collaborative on a national stage, I suggest that deaf education also needs to be studied on an international scale to see how other countries are maintaining the langua-cultures within their own deaf education programs. Moreover, this larger comparative study needs to be conducted using emic models that open lines of inquiries for discourse and do not claim one specific framework is more dominant or advantageous than others, but accept that some are a better fit for certain countries, cultures, and individuals.

I am collaborating with two other scholars (Dr. Joseph Tobin of University of Georgia and Dr. Joseph Valente of Pennsylvania State University) on an international-scale project, funded by the Spencer Foundation, studying kindergarten classes in schools for the deaf in three countries—United States, Japan, and France. Each country has its own deaf cultural traditions, early childhood educational approaches, forms of sign language, and deaf political struggles (Fischer, 2007; Hyde, 2009; Lane, 1994; Monaghan, 2003; Nakamura, 2006). By conducting the study in three nations, each of which has a rich and complex history of deaf education and deaf culture, we intend to disentangle the various pressures and cultural forces that are impacting and shaping contemporary deaf early education. Very much like the schools in this book, the schools for the deaf in these three countries compete to define and control not just pedagogy but also the meaning of deafness, languaculture, and identity. These stakeholders take strong positions, despite (or perhaps because of) the fact that no method of education has been shown to be effective for all deaf people. No method provides deaf children with native competence in the national spoken language. No method reliably teaches the majority of deaf children to speak intelligibly or to read above the fifth-grade level, as measured by standardized tests. The lack of empirical evidence in these methodological instructions in deaf education is reflected in the archaeology of deafness in America (Chapter 3). This new study (and similarly, this book) does not attempt to determine which curriculum or pedagogical approach is better or to take sides in deaf education debates. Instead, our goal is to uncover the links among pedagogical approaches used to teach deaf children in schools for the deaf, including their conceptions of languaculture, identity, and inclusion (both in the larger society and in deaf culture), and what they consider are the purposes of early education. Thus, our central concern is the role of kindergartens for the deaf as sites of acculturation into both deaf culture and larger national cultures.

We accomplish this effort by using a video-based ethnographic method ideally suited to the task of investigating languaculture, deaf culture, deaf communication, and deaf schooling (Bauman, 2008).

This method is a new application of the "video-cued multivocal eth-nography" method developed by Joseph Tobin and his colleagues in *Preschool in Three Cultures* (1989) and subsequent projects (Tobin, 1999). The core idea of this method is that an edited video showing a typical day in a classroom can function as a rich and provocative cue for a variety of discussions.

The specific steps of this method are to: (1) videotape one day in one kindergarten in a school for the deaf in each country; (2) edit the videotape down to 20 minutes; (3) lead focus-group discussions of the videotape with parents, teachers, and children from the classroom where we film, as well as with the other teachers and administrators in the school; (4) lead focus-group discussions of the videos shot in multiple other schools for the deaf in the same country; (5) lead cross-comparative focus-group discussions in all three countries of the videos from the three foreign countries; and (6) use the videos as cues for interviewing leaders in the field of deaf education in the three coun-tries. This multivoicedness approach enables these diverse stakeholders to play an important role in the discourse as they examine the videos that we produce. In this method, the videos function neither as data nor as description, but primarily as rich nonverbal cues designed to stimulate critical reflection and feedback.

Tobin, Wu, and Davidson's particular methodological contribu-tion was to combine the use of video as a tool for feedback (Spindler & Spindler, 1987) and as a "mnemonic device" (Asch & Asch, 1995, p. 48). In addition, they factored in Jay Ruby's (1982) admonition that ethnographic films be considered not objective data but reflexive mir-rors; James Clifford's (1983) call for ethnographies to be multivocal texts; and Mikhail Bakhtin's (1981) writings on heteroglossia, dialo-gism, and answerability. The result is a method in which videotape is used to provoke reflection not only from the teachers videotaped but also from their colleagues, their supervisors, and from their counter-parts in other cities and other countries.

The Hands & Voices organization and my research in the three different countries are examples of multivocal discourses by means of collaborative critical inquiry where power is diffused and given to those who usually are suppressed when discussing deaf education. The use of multivoicedness in these collaborative discourses enables "multiple voices participating" (Cummins, 2000, p. 237) in the shared pursuit on developing positive social constructions on languaculture, deaf education, and deafness. With the two summaries laid out, relevant future research considerations may provide not only some useful ways to highlight the normal spectrum when deciding to place the deaf child in a certain languaculture, but also ways that these two often divisive camps can coexist in collaborative inquiries on social justice issues relating to deafness and deaf education.

## THE CASE FOR MULTIPLE LANGUACULTURES

This book inquires into an "ideology of normalcy from the rule and hegemony of normates, to a vision of the body as changeable, unperfectable" (Davis, 2002, p. 39). One experience or pedagogy that may work for one child may not work for another, including determining which approach is more privileged, because everybody's situation is different and ought not to be confined in the realm of what is normal and deviant.

In relation to power and knowledge, science is accelerating faster than ethical debate and policymaking (Switzer, 2003). As long as defining deafness only by using parameters of normalcy continues to be a dominant part of the politics of deaf education, there may be more deviance designations in bureaucratic organizations to contain, regulate, and shape deafness with the "continuing neglect of diversity" (Horejes & Lauderdale, 2007, p. 21). The language of experts increases mystification and decreases the accessibility of public debate. Impairment does not cause disability; impairment causes social oppression by restricting activity (Linton, 2006).

Instead of continuing to fight a losing battle over which perception ought to be the most privileged mode of thought and/or what "impairment" means in our current history, this book has come to the conclusion that it is not the child who fails within a certain perception but the perception that fails the child. Instead of focusing on two narrow modes of thought, this book suggests exposing diverse communication choices—multiple languacultures for deaf people. I suggest that we need to start exploring deaf languacultures and the ways that unique languacultures are mediated and maintained as positive social constructs for the deaf child. One interdisciplinary and diverse approach is bilingualism as a possible form of a multilanguaculture (for comparison, see Marcia Moraes and Lourdes Diaz Soto's work on bilingual education in linguistic minority populations in Cummins, 2000). To add, bilingual education "is not only effective in maintaining a minority language, but also in *enhancing* the learning of a second language, such as English, far more so than a monolingual educational approach" (May, 2012, p. 133). Bilingualism has become an emerging force not just for linguistic minority populations (i.e., English Language Learners) but also within deaf education and society at large, and it shows promise in a shared pedagogy (both ASL and spoken English), where both groups "can understand the social constraints that inhibit progress" (Cummins, 2000, p. 237). The notion of bilingualism is not new. As indicated in Chapter 3, Sister Mary Ann Burke (1880) raised the possibility of a combined system in which sign language and spoken English could be used in different ways. These two languacultures for deaf people can coexist contingent on the child's advantages and disadvantages. This book suggests that the Milan 1880 incident may have stunted the potentiality of such an approach, but since bilingualism is starting to be welcome in academic debates, it is time to reconsider Burke's proposal of a combined system, that is, multiple languacultures for deaf people by means of bilingualism.

Cummins goes on to contend that "there are close to 150 empirical studies carried out during the past 30 or so years that have reported a positive association between additive bilingualism and students' linguistic, cognitive, or academic growth" (Cummins, 2000, p. 37). This positive association between multiple languacultures and their linguistic, cognitive, and/or academic growth may allow teachers to retreat from the academic canon or "cult of knowledge" and to rethink their role in these social institutions and its linguistic implications (Aronowitz & Giroux, 1991, p. 89). I suggest that bilingualism is one way for the divisive schools of thought to respect the diversity of linguistic "cultures" produced by different groups in the shared production of "collective memories, knowledge, social relations, and values within historically constituted relations of power" while, at the same time, preserving their unique cultures (Aronowitz & Giroux, 1991, p. 50). Bilingualism is still an ongoing work in progress even at Gallaudet University, which proclaims to be a bilingual university. Theoretical notions of bilingualism are very well documented, but actual praxis, empirical evidence, and the applied steps to make bilingualism work in a positive functional environment need more research despite the claim made in 1985 that "empirical evidence for the effectiveness of such program [bilingual] is often ambiguous" (Reagan, 1985, p. 275). These linguistic considerations for bilingualism still offer some opportunities to enhance diversity and multiple pathways to shared pedagogy, including the combination of sign language, spoken English, and cochlear implant technology (Coryell & Holcomb, 2007; Easterbrooks, 2002).

Bilingualism addresses the two summaries of this book as possible vehicles to progress. First, as deaf education wrestles with social constructions of languaculture and "normal" avenues to deaf education pedagogy, bilingualism provides a way to focus on the different skills that the student possesses and the ways that bilingualism may work best for that individual. For example, there may be deaf children who would benefit with ASL as their "native language," or what applied linguistics would call "L1," but who would be able to use spoken English as their second language (L2) while using their ASL (L1) as an anchor. A similar approach also works for those deaf students who would benefit from using spoken English as their L1 as they learn ASL (L2). Using bilingualism as a mechanism to "fit" with the child, the child no longer is "forced" to be confined within one languaculture; rather, the varying languacultures would mold a unique design to "fit" the child. This design would effectively eliminate any parameters of normalcy established by educational institutions, but instead, the child would choose which languaculture is most "natural" to him or her, thus, the most normal. The power of choosing languacultures is then given to the child as a gift, not as a means to "fix" his or her ostensible "impairment."

Second, sign-based and oral/auditory-based languacultures and schools for the deaf are here to stay, but can they coexist as a collective? Bilingualism may bridge the two diverse languacultures together in a collaborative project. Some sign-based schools argue that they are already incorporating bilingualism into their curriculum, but what most ASL deaf schools are incorporating is the written English along with ASL as their pedagogy, not the spoken English that is the premier goal of most oral schools. Thus, most ASL schools for the deaf incorporate a limited bilingual approach that restricts many deaf students from having the opportunity to learn how to speak (although many deaf schools do offer speech therapy, it is not incorporated as a primary pedagogical tool in the instruction but mainly offered on a "weekly" basis, if at all). In addition, schools for the deaf may want to conduct some research on immersion programs offered to hearing students that incorporate two whole languages (both spoken and written) and find strategic ways to incorporate the immersion curricula into the pedagogy for the deaf students. These immersion programs would not be identical, but would offer useful clues on instruction, attitudes, maintaining languacultures, and dealing with the larger forces of public schools who are still resistant to adopt bilingual programs as a positive. To be sure, not all deaf students will master a certain language whether it is spoken English or ASL, but at least they will be given a choice in finding the right languaculture that fits with their skills and abilities.

Bilingualism would also provide ways that "students' identity options and their views of their own potential are expanded as they engage directly to their lives and the power relations that exist both in their own society and globally" (Cummins, 2000, p. 263). Deaf students would be able to learn about their own society (the deaf community) and the larger society where hearing is the majority as well as the social constructions of difference and languacultures by means of power relations that exist within these boundaries.

Carol D. Lee, a former high school English teacher, primary grade teacher, school director, and past president of the American Educational Research Association (AERA), discusses the importance of the culture of everyday practices and the need to connect them to the classroom culture, specific languages as instructional discourse, the understanding of teacher knowledge, and student learning as well as to create what she calls a Cultural Modeling Framework (Lee, 2007). While her model focuses on African American students, many of her ideas coincide with deaf students as linguistic minorities when examining the school as a site of cultural practice and how such knowledge is constructed. More important, these analyses will "provide a deeper level of knowledge and practice and focusing policies and teaching tools such as curriculum, textbooks, and intervention resources" when providing the best effective pedagogy for deaf students (Little & Houston, 2003, p. 55).

Bilingualism offers ways that knowledge "begins with the everyday texts and then moves on to those canonical texts in which the social world is one about which we anticipate students will have greater prior knowledge and then moves on to canonical texts that are further removed from students' prior knowledge and life experiences (Lee, 2007, p. 50). There is "no place for any kind of supremacy in any country" (Moraes, 1996, p. 137), thus, introducing bilingualism as critical languaculture for the deaf would embrace multicultures, multilanguacultures, and different knowledge constructions and, most of all, would place the student in a position to claim his or her selfhood as a deaf person. Finally, bilingualism in the deaf school would enable the student to be in a position to learn various types of knowledge outlined by James Banks (1996, pp. 8–11), including personal/cultural, popular, mainstream academic, transformative academic, and school knowledge. By doing so, students would eventually be able to better "understand the perspectives of their own versions and interpretations of issues and events" rather than have some sort of ideological framework instilling their own narrow and static type of knowledge that has continued to fail deaf students throughout history.

## CONCLUSION

The notion of deafness is very complicated and deeply contested, including what the constraints for a "normal" deaf child ought to be. Young children, including deaf children, "unlike the adults [parents, teachers, audiologists, and psychologists] that surround them . . . are unconcerned with ideology, emotional ties to language and culture, and academic arguments for or against a particular pedagogical approach" (Erting, 2003a, p. 376). Instead, children are developing members under the ideological state apparatuses (or institutions like education) embedded with specific histories and cultures that will assist in constructing and organizing their life and its meanings (Althusser, 1970). Children enter deaf education as sites of acculturation/ enculturation where they learn a specific language and, in turn, develop cultural values and knowledge that would become meaningful to them—in both good and bad ways.

I am grateful that I have the audacity and disposition to let go of my bitterness at certain languacultures (whether I sided against sign language early on or whether I sided against oral-based pedagogy later on). It has been a long and frustrating journey, and along the way, I thought God was playing jokes on me, I thought I was going to be Quasimodo for the rest of my life, I thought I was deaf but then was relegated back to the margins and away from the very people on whom I relied for enculturation into the deaf community, and finally, I found myself at Gallaudet University where the very discussions in this book are taking place. I am still constantly learning about my identity as a deaf person. I am very appreciative acknowledging the important facets of multiple languacultures that I have both experienced and witnessed throughout my journey. The various times that I have navigated my boundaries have led me to a position today where I strongly feel aligned with E. M. Gallaudet's vision:

> It is a happy thing to us who are working in the interest of the deaf . . . that in this country we do not witness that division of our teachers into parties where a greater or less degree of bitterness of feeling exists, and where rival systems are combating each other with sometimes more earnestness than discretion, as has been the case in past years in many places on the other side of the globe; and it is a matter for which we cannot be too thankful that in this country we are working together, as is shown by the coming together on this occasion of the heads of institutions who represent the various systems and methods that are now pursued in the country.

> This paper is upon the combined method, which aims to unite all that is good in every system that may be employed for the benefit of the deaf. . . . Whether such combination in a single institution is possible or not, is a legitimate question for discussion. Some think it possible; others have a different opinion. If the presentation of this paper can draw out from those present to-day an expression of those different opinions, we shall all be benefited. (E. M. Gallaudet, 1880, p. 13)

Gallaudet's last sentence hits home for me: if this book can draw out the different opinions we have toward deaf education and find ways to organize these opinions into discourse, we all will benefit. As such, the book has tried to uncover some hidden knowledge by examining social constructions of what it means to be deaf under the guise of normalcy and deviance. The research has identified the purported significant differences in social constructions of normalcy and deviance to point to alternative perspectives when discussing deafness. If you are able to connect to some of the important messages in this book, then I have done my job; at the same time, I would be devastated "if someone hadn't shown my view to be incomplete or wrong five years down the line, for that would mean the field wasn't interesting enough to pursue" (Chomsky in Moraes, 1996, p. 19). Thus, I challenge scholars to find ways to elevate the ideas, themes, and theories of languaculture for the deaf and in deaf education. I challenge scholars to critically (yet constructively) examine the ways that the constructions on languacultures in this book can be further developed into some nascent critical theory of deafness and/or deaf languacultures. I want to build on Kendra Smith and MJ Bienvenu's (2007) inquiry, "What can we learn from feminist theory?" and not just limit discussion to feminist theory, but include other theories and ideas to form a Critical Deaf Theory (Gertz, 2004) or at least to pursue a critical systematic study on social constructed languacultures for the deaf in a theoretical framework. Such a framework would move from emic aspects toward healthy etic aspects of deafness in ways that open dialogue and collaborative inquiry on important issues like deaf education. Such a theory

> holds the promise of breaking the long tradition of the Deaf/
> hearing dichotomous position, and, in so doing, allows the
> cultural signifier "Deaf" to be self-defined and self-valued . . .
> [and] over time, the production of knowledge that more richly
> and accurately names and describes Deaf-hood will, we believe,
> improve the overall conditions of existence for Deaf people the
> world over. It is toward these ends that this article is dedicated.
> (Smith & Bienvenu, 2007, p. 63)

This book, too, is dedicated to these ends.

Has the current state of deaf education repeated history as George M. F. Hegel forewarned? In 1964, Congress commissioned what is now known as the Babbidge Report (originally titled "Education of the Deaf") for the secretary of the Health, Education, and Welfare Department by the Advisory Committee on the Education of the Deaf. In the Babbidge Report, Dr. Babbidge (former president of the University of Connecticut) and his advisees stated that

> [T]here is no reason to believe that we have reached the limit of human potential in educating the deaf. The longer we delay in supporting substantial, well-planned programs of research into more effective ways of teaching language . . . the more we waste the potential talents and skills of those maturing young people whose only difference is that they cannot hear. (Babbidge, 1965, p. xvii)

The time is now to realize the importance of its alternative social constrictions because "if we were to recognize the legitimacy of emic constructions of Deaf identity, the education of deaf children clearly would look much different than it does today" (Reagan, 2002, p. 58). The two summaries and the suggestions for future research, including bilingualism as multilanguacultures, described in this book are directed at contributing to a constructive reflective dialogue that will produce long-term outcomes not only for deaf students of future generations but also for a greater understanding of humankind and our connections to differences throughout the world (Artiles, 2003; Brown, 1996). It is clear that our current social construction of deafness and deaf education need reframing and that we need an alternative paradigm and/or theories of languacultures for deaf people. James Gee warns that "in the end we run out of words and meaning is rooted finally in judgment and action" (Gee, 1996, p. 293). Sister Mary Ann Burke foreshadowed Gee's warning regarding deaf education in 1880, when she said, "there is nothing left unsaid or unwritten; and that the whole subject is, as it were, exhausted," (Burke, 1880, p. 172).

Thus, the question really becomes this: Are we ready to undertake alternative ways of thinking and doing?

The possibilities are now.

# Afterword

*Pat Lauderdale*

What do you see when you imagine an individual who has been labeled as disabled? Do you imagine the hegemonic façade of someone begging for help with their cap in their hand or is the image of someone such as the theoretical physicist Stephen William Hawking?

In *Social Constructions of Deafness,* Thomas Horejes shatters the hegemonic façade of disablism. Some 25 years ago, I mentioned a related point about hegemony in the study of terrorism (Lauderdale, 1998). In the study of difference and the other, most scholars use the concept of hegemony as a synonym for domination much as they throw in references to Foucault on power. This vulgar use is at once much too narrow and too vacuous. Thomas Horejes's use of hegemony focuses on the state's "war of position" and those who dominate modes of production, that is, those who impose and promote crucial worldviews through cultural means. Such interpretations emerge from the control of central information sources, and ideas created by "objective" rule makers are presented as unbiased. The media provide the most obvious example of this process, and as most of civil society assumes the dominant interpretive framework, individuals use the meanings and ostensible truths derived from their interpretations as standards by which to judge others. Alternative ideas suggested by scholars such as Horejes are often dismissed as "biased," and in some instances, individuals or groups in civil society are defined as deviants, for example, sometimes as leaders and other times as troublemakers. The concept of hegemony challenges the idea of common sense by asking whether it is good sense.

The most useful concept of hegemony was created by Antonio Gramsci. In prison for over 10 years during the fascist regime of

Pat Lauderdale is a professor of Justice and Social Inquiry at Arizona State University in Tempe, AZ.

Mussolini, Gramsci reconceived the concept of hegemony to explain the encompassing tactics of the fascists. Acknowledging the obvious role of political economy but wanting to transcend the idea of false consciousness, he stressed the importance of understanding the manipulation of culture as a form of domination (compare Oliverio, 1998). Horejes uses hegemony in its Gramscian sense as a cultural concept rather than joining in the typical misuse of Gramsci's concept as a solely political or economic idea. For Gramsci and now Horejes, hegemony is an order in which a certain way of life and thought is dominant, where one worldview permeates customs and political and religious ideas, in particular, their intellectual and moral connotations. In their analysis of hegemony, they draw the distinction between civil and political society, with civil society being characterized by private relations within private organizations and political society is characterized by the state's use of coercive force. The war of position, in terms of the role of the state in society, usually is as a slow, protracted struggle that involves diverse means that include "nonviolent" aspects of civil society. Professor Horejes also suggests that hegemony is a "a theoretical idea to examine the various social control processes embedded in the cultural production of the everyday world in critical historical moments." Gandhi's anti-colonialist resistances in India or the more recent Occupy Wall Street exemplify wars of position.

The study of the power of law and deviance is most clearly demonstrated when new categories of deviance are being created or old categories are being transformed (Lauderdale, 2011). Under the Fugitive Slave Laws of the 1850s, for example, aiding and abetting an escaped slave was a crime, yet with the passage of the Thirteenth Amendment less than a decade later, slavery itself was the crime. Moreover, in 1800, the organization of a labor union was a crime, specifically, conspiracy in restraint of trade. By 1940, unions were legal, and employers were required by law to engage in collective bargaining. As we follow Professor Horejes's framework, we can examine the political and legal processes of how an accepted and socialized form of activity can become delegitimized, or vice versa.

In the United States, millions of dollars have been spent in recent years on social welfare, vocational rehabilitation, and employment programs that often have led to the marginalization of diverse people. In an earlier research publication, "Disablism Reflected in Law and Policy: The Social Construction and Perpetuation of Prejudice" (Horejes & Lauderdale, 2007), Tommy and I suggested that while there are widespread historical and cultural analyses of the problems associated with racism, sexism, classism, and other types of prejudice, there is very little on disablism. As with other prejudices, the examination of the origins and perpetuation of disablism is controversial. It is cloaked in narrow legal and policy analyses of the historical and cultural documentation on the notion of disability. The analysis of disablism typically has been misrepresented as only a health, economic, technical, or safety issue rather than as prejudice. The Americans with Disabilities Act of 1990 (ADA) became law with the assumption that it would provide equal accommodations for disabled people. We examined the institutions of education and the workplace to analyze "equal accommodations" under such policies and how they pose some serious and problematic political processes and consequences in shaping disability rights. Our analysis suggested that most disability policies remain rooted in a narrow medical model, despite some evidence of attempts to construct the politics of diversity and self-definition. Currently, we witness the growing crisis caused by an enormous backlog in the Department of Veterans Affairs for disabled American veterans. And, new research on hate crime examines violence in its myriad forms as they impact disabled people's lives (Roulstone & Mason-Bishop, 2012).

In major institutions such as education and medicine, a disabled person typically is examined as a case that can become a commodity, which can be classified, repaired, and recorded. Governmental agencies and bureaucratic organizations exercise their power and knowledge by means of ostensible scientific processes by using medical terminology, symptoms, "equal opportunity" solutions, and antidiscrimination rhetoric. Empirical examination by these agencies as "experts" further affirms their scientific control. The classification and normalization of disabled people becomes normalized within intellectual, social, and economic frameworks. The biological and cultural identity of the diverse disabled individuals is individualized and pulled apart. By using disciplinary techniques of biology as the powerful, scientific language of normalizing judgment and by examining the body, disability appears as devoid of history and culture. In a Weberian sense, this process makes it efficient, predictable, and rational for public policy to be presented in its idealized form, which would provide "equal opportunity" in education and the workplace, yet, without appropriate sociocultural consideration. And, most policy is explicated as a legal concept as if people are universal, homogenous, and normalized without respect to diversity.

Recently, the disability movement has fought to regain autonomy of sociocultural labels by attempting to go beyond the medical model and reveal why the means to an end are deeply important. Even something that on first glance appears simple and straightforward, for example, charity telethons to raise funds for "disabled" people, often segregate them and label them as deviant. Diversity is a more accurate description of disabled people than one that simply labels them as a heterogeneous group (Brown, 2011). Diversity includes, at least, the significant differences in the ranges and depths of individuals who are defined as having some type of disability as well as their place in society, which includes their socioeconomic status, gender, ethnicity, race, and age. The current thrust of pseudoscience to measure and normalize disablism continues to destabilize the much-needed self-determination of the international disability community. *Social Constructions of Deafness* is an important new step in research because it helps explain why disability policy requires a sociocultural model with the inclusion of diversity. Professor Horejes notes that communication for deaf people has been a tool to regulate language as knowledge and as a form of stigma with prejudice, lacking a human characteristic and an indicator of shaping languaculture for deaf children.

Information gleaned from our sensory experience is connected in a manner that simplifies understanding and recall. Schemes of interpretation provide us with frameworks for structuring and interpreting our experience. We often construct our world by assimilating it to schemas while accommodating them to their constraints. Erving Goffman (1974) similarly notes that situations are defined "in accordance with principles of organization that govern events"; he calls these organizing structure "frames." Making sense of the external world requires scanning the environment, selecting features that appear important, and taking information about those features and either storing it for future retrieval or using it as a basis for action. A cognitive schema, then, serves as an interpretive mechanism that structures and assigns meaning to incoming information. Popular media distributes much of the information.

Using apt and isolated events to make their point, popular media usually ignore the structure of harm, and the longer, often hidden, protracted processes. This summer, many read a horrific story of the murder of 12 people by a very disturbed individual who had dropped out of a doctoral program in Colorado. The story of this "Dark Knight" made headlines throughout the world for a number of days. Yet, at almost the same time, a story of 14 people being killed on the highway in a "truck accident" in Texas was relegated to the sidelines after a brief mention, and no mention was made of how many other people were killed in automotive "accidents" during the same time period. In the first instance, the intention and behavior of a very disturbed individual was to blame; however, the automotive deaths are left in the tumble of consequences and the false necessity of the paramount value of automotive travel. Yet, about 40,000 deaths occur yearly due to automotive accidents. Considering deafness in a similar way, Professor Horejes maintains that dominant perceptions of deafness create a one-sided framework that does not celebrate differences, diversity of language, culture, and positive constructions of deafness. One of the goals of his book is to provide alternative perspectives—a perspective through which deafness can be seen in a paradigm other than deviant or deficient.

Since individuals organize information in a schematic manner, we need to understand how individuals settle on one particular schema instead of another. We must understand why certain features of the environment are attended to and acted on while others are misinterpreted, ignored, or suppressed. This type of analysis requires us to examine the relationship between "schemes of interpretation" and social structures. Thomas Horejes illustrates how power is intimately connected with knowledge and those who generate and control knowledge are often perceived to speak the truth. "Truth" becomes linked in a circular relationship with systems of power that produce and sustain it as well as linked to effects of power that induce and extend it—a "regime" of truth. Stories of ostensible truth become deeply problematic.

In studying the "disabled" body, the biological and cultural identity of the diverse individual is pulled apart. The body as a social and historical construct becomes oblivious and docile. By using disciplinary techniques of medicine as the powerful, scientific language of normalizing judgment and examining the body, disability becomes devoid of history and culture. The processes are partially a result of trying to formally use the legal system, namely, in the workplace and education, while attempting to hegemonically use "accurate" empirical and scientific conclusions.

As an example of an important crack in the hegemonic façade of being disabled, consider parts of the story of Thomas Horejes. Of course, remember that if he had allowed society to effectively construct him as someone who is disabled and unable to do anything about it, he might have been "forced" to quit his education during late elementary school. Moreover, even approximately 70% of those rare individuals who are able to enroll in 2- and 4-year colleges quit without receiving a degree. I have known Professor Horejes for approximately 12 years, and I am familiar with his work as an undergraduate student, his work as an advocate for disabled people in Los Angeles, his achievements as a research assistant, his academic performance in graduate school, and his record as a scholar and teacher. He has usually needed little direction since his own standards already were clearly established. Tommy reveals that, throughout his speech therapy, he had a strong sense that his elementary school was more concerned with his hearing loss as a disadvantage rather than with his possible talents (including deafness) as advantages. The school officials were more focused on classifying him by means of audiological measurement and disciplining him to become "normal" based on the criteria of their ideology. At the end of fifth grade, he was the goalie of a soccer team that went undefeated that season as well as ran for and successfully became the student council president. In high school, he was a member of the varsity soccer, wrestling, and tennis teams. At Arizona State University, among a long list of his accomplishments, include being president of the Student Advisory Board, Disability Resource Center of Arizona State University, a Supreme Court Justice of the Associated Students of Arizona State University, and a member of the Governing Board of the National Youth Leadership Network. Clearly, Thomas is an exceptional person, yet I wonder how many other people defined as disabled simply were not able to throw off the deviant label of being disabled? And, where goes justice?

Consider that systematic explications of the sources of injustice include (a) analyses of how participants are excluded from the creation of agendas concerning justice and decision making regarding policy agendas; (b) the continued exposure of exploitation in labor relations; (c) an examination of the factors leading to the erosion of communities, collective identity, and the rights to equality, freedom, and justice; and (d) the long-term cost to nature (including humans) when justice is defined as separate and subservient to humans. Diversity is an important part of justice. We must recognize and respond to the dialectical nature of the conflict between totalization and particularism, between corporate monoculture and diversity, and between abstract universalism and collective identity. Variations in time and place suggest that traditional assumptions about the implementation of fairness and equality are inadequate, especially for people who are diverse. Ostensible development and progress in economics, science, and technology has been motivated partly by the desire to improve life and the desire to transcend the natural world and replace it with a human-made environment that is free from the uncertainties and indignities of pre- or post-modernity. Yet, this Frankensteinian approach to melding mind and machine appears to be a very old desire to control or conquer nature. It has contributed heavily to the destruction of our lives and continues to magnify the blind faith in technology and in the idea of progress itself. Artificial intelligence, various forms of nanotechnology, genetic engineering, in vitro fertilization, and related forms of biotechnology raise serious questions about the relation of identity and the body as well as about the wisdom of pretending to be God or, at least, the judge and jury without a judicious system of review.

For Professor Horejes, the social construction and maintenance of language influences the types of culture of a specific group, that is, languaculture. He uses languaculture as an important gravitating macroconcept throughout this book that connects many complex themes such as language(s), culture(s), identities, social constructions, normalcy, and deviance and that incorporates languaculture in the realm of institutions such as schools. Using countries as a comparative base with respect to the impact of languaculture, Professor Horejes presents a partial archaeology of American deaf education, specifically, the role of language (both sign language and spoken English).

Readers will learn in his book how he has examined significant issues in the field of deaf education, especially through his analysis of pedagogies in two different types of educational institutions and their impact on larger issues of justice. Professor Horejes correctly explicates the role of deaf education's institutional past, which is riddled by various deaf institutions each claiming to use the best and most effective pedagogical approach toward deaf education, including the role of ASL in the classroom settings. His research also has important value beyond the subject area and will become a significant contribution to interdisciplinary research on justice. That is, his research examines critical issues in politics and prejudice in U.S. disability education and policy. Please remember that most policy and research continue to frame disability narrowly as a health, economic, technical, and/or safety issue without a systematic analysis of the prejudice and/or stigma that is embedded and often magnified by those areas. His research raises the larger point that the politics of disability continue to solidify the concept of disablism, which magnifies and extends prejudice. He correctly notes that without critical, structural changes, the contemporary, dominant measuring and normalizing of "having a disability" will continue to destabilize the self-determination and collective determination of the disability community. All of us will suffer without such changes.

Let me close with a story since most of us remember stories longer than most of the other forms of learning. After noting my general agreement with Professor Horejes on his critiques of "deafness" and technology, a colleague suggested that we might be blind because modern forms of management and new technology would solve the problem of "deafness." In response, I told the colleague an ironic story that has been circulating concerning the quality of life. I have adapted the story for this afterword:

> A business consultant was at the pier of a small coastal village when a small boat with just one fisherperson docked. Inside the small boat were several large fish. The consultant noticed that the indigenous fisherperson was blind and complimented the disabled person on the quality of his fish and asked how long it took to catch them.

The disabled fisherperson replied, "Only a little while."

The consultant then asked, "Why don't you stay out longer and catch more fish?"

The fisherperson said, "I catch enough to feed my family."

The consultant then asked, "But what do you do with the rest of your time?"

The fisherperson replied, "I sleep late, fish a little, play with my children, take a nap with my wife, Emma, stroll into the village each evening where I sip wine and play music with my friends. I have a full and busy life."

The consultant scoffed, "I am a Stanford graduate and I can help you. You should spend more time fishing and with the proceeds, buy a bigger boat, and get a guide. With the proceeds from the bigger boat you could buy several boats so eventually you would have a fleet of fishing boats. Instead of selling your catch to a middleman, you would sell directly to the processor, eventually opening your own cannery. You would control the product, processing, and distribution. You could leave this small fishing village and move to a big city near you, then L.A., and eventually Beijing, where you will run your plutonomy enterprise."

The fisherperson asked, "But, how much time will this all take?"

To which the neoliberal replied, "10–20 years."

"But what then?"

The consultant laughed, "That's the best part. When the time is right, you would announce an IPO and sell your company stock to the public and become very rich, you would make millions."

"Millions? Then what?"

The consultant replied, "Then you can retire, and move to a small fishing village where you can sleep late, fish a little, play with your kids, take naps with your wife, stroll to the village where you can sip wine and play your music."

Such stories and language are appealing to many people; however, they often stop short of the whole story. The new story now includes the role of neoliberalism, where, for example, the blind indigenous fisherperson finds that his coastal fishing village has been sold to a multinational development company. The company will build a number of resorts, alter the landscape, end sustenance fishing, and destroy the nature of community, which was the intact life of the fisherperson. This scenario is becoming reality, but will it lead to a better quality of life?

# APPENDIX A

# METHODOLOGICAL ORIENTATIONS

This appendix discusses various methodological orientations for the gathering of original data in two schools for the deaf. The comparative method and grounded theory were selected as strategic tools for this analysis "because people who write about methodology often forget it is a matter of strategy" (Homans, 1949, p. 330; see also Denzin & Giardina, 2009). The purpose of the grounded theory, in the book, is not to test, confirm, or disconfirm existing theories, but rather to generate and uncover various levels of analyses and degrees of abstraction as a systematic investigation (Lauderdale, McLaughlin, & Oliverio, 1990) to provide an understanding of how these social control processes contribute to constructing deaf students as normal or deviant. These levels of analyses and degrees of abstraction via grounded theory provide various "lenses" of identifying data to be transformed into analytical information that may not have been possible previously without the interconnectedness of these levels and degrees. The intent of the grounded theory is to identify as much data as artifacts embedded in socially articulated discourses on the map so that I, as a researcher, am able to carefully select certain knowledge as emerging issues for analysis (Goodwin, 2002, p. 305; Denzin & Giardina, 2009, p. 29). This method provides the flexibility for "collecting and analyzing data that can help . . . conduct efficient fieldwork and create astute analysis" (Charmaz & Mitchell, 2001, p. 160). Thus, grounded theory and the comparative method were incorporated as strategic forms of methodological orientations to build and guide theoretical frameworks. The comparative method is used as a way to uncover similarities and differences between two deaf kindergartens; specifically, the classroom, students, and teachers as conceptual frameworks. These conceptual frameworks would guide theoretical ideas, including the diverse pedagogies and ideologies surrounding deafness and education. Grounded theory is used as a strategy to gather original data from these two schools to build into the three themes—pedagogy of language, culture in the classroom, and teacher knowledge.

The data collected include classroom observations, teacher interviews, and examination of student social interactions. The data were examined using videotaping, memo-making, note taking, observations, and interviews. The preliminary data then were transformed into thematic coding, often called axial coding, which relates codes to each other. Some of the information examined by means of thematic and axial coding includes the table/desk arrangements, the communication methods used, the symbolic interactions through communication, the use of technology, learning facilitation, and opinions on educational policies. Thematic and axial coding builds on conceptually integrated categories such as the physical ecology of the classroom, the complexities of culture, the types of performativity, the materiality applied, the communication used, the types of resistance, the use of technology, the teacher/student biographies, the knowledge facilitation, and the perception of effective instruction included in the classroom. Through dynamic comparisons of these concepts, some theoretical ideas connected these schools as social control institutions through which to examine the different constructions of deafness—that is, a "tale" of two classrooms. The result is detailed in Chapter 4.

These results build on theoretical themes and are examined fully in Chapter 5 as parts of the dynamic comparative analyses between the two classrooms, students, and teachers within the two deaf schools. This comparative framework then builds on elements of a grounded theory as a type of analysis for the study of deafness and deaf education. Figure A.1 provides a heuristic way to visualize the structure of the chapter.

## OVERVIEW OF METHODOLOGICAL ORIENTATIONS

It is crucial to select the types of methodological orientations and theoretical ideas that will provide the most meaningful data possible and, more important, will allow a search for theoretical

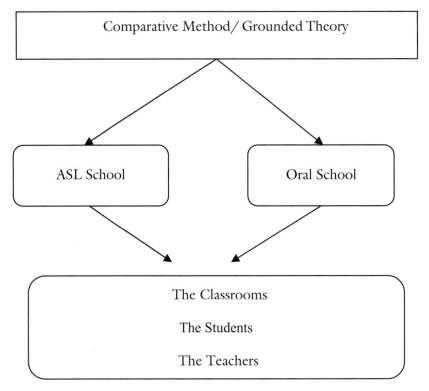

FIGURE A.1. Framework of the methodological orientation for Chapter 4.

ideas when discussing normalcy and deviance as constructions. This study involves exploratory research, so the research considers the comparative method for comparing two phenomena and grounded theory to build and guide theoretical frameworks for this study because

> a grounded theory emphasis on the comparative method . . . leads to (1) compare data from the beginning of the research, (2) compare data with emerging categories, and (3) demonstrate relations between concepts and categories. (Charmaz & Mitchell, 2001, p. 161).

A brief overview of each of the two orientations is necessary to understand their potential contribution toward the research here.

## Comparative Method

This research builds on the comparative method used by Shirley Heath's (1983) study on different educational institutions in two different communities with the purpose of raising larger societal issues, including the "interplay of people and historical and social conditions" (p. 7) as well as "the social and cultural context which created the input factors for individuals and groups" (p. 8). Thus, this orientation strives to incorporate the analytical findings as a possible springboard to more constructive dialogues within deaf education, its community, deafness, and contributions of these elements to larger issues of justice, deviance, and diversity.

The comparative method is one of the most effective methodological maps, which serves as a starting point for these types of analyses. These types and levels of analyses include the historical, social, economic, and political coordination on the sociological map (Lauderdale & Inverarity, 2003). For any comparative method, it is not possible to cover all points of interests at once; thus, there will be certain data sets, themes, and important points of interests within this research that will be left on the map to be explored and compared later by future researchers. Nonetheless, the use of comparative methods is a hallmark of the sociological investigation that "provides a body of descriptive and explanatory data, which allows us to see various practices and procedures in a wide context that helps to throw light" on the various educational institutions (Phillips, 1999, p. 15). This research is heavily rooted in the comparative methodology:

> [because] the production of facts is something beyond our power to command, and we can only bring them together as they have been spontaneously produced, the method used is one of indirect experimentation, or the comparative method. (Phillips, 1999, p. 16)

Relying on the comparative method as a mapping guide, this research uses Bowker and Star's (1999) classification analysis to uncover new, often hidden knowledge within two comparative complex educational institutions as ecologies. This orientation serves as a framework to uncover critical contrasting data such as the hidden social differences and the types of social equality constructed within the larger deaf education system in the name of ostensible progress. The purpose of the classification analysis is to examine the "interdependence of technical networks and standards, on the one hand, and the real work of politics and knowledge production on the other" (Bowker & Star, 1999, p. 34). It is also important to be able to examine the similarities and the differences of the theoretical frameworks to uncover the conflicting ontology, epistemology, and consequences of such social classifications, their processes, and formations (Steinmetz, 2005). More important, these classifications represent "contrasting ways of life and cultural beliefs," which in turn become what Pierre Bourdieu calls "classification struggles" (Du Gay, 1997, p. 93). It is these struggles that can become the site of contested meanings of normalcy and deviance, revealing cracks in hegemony, conflicting value systems; they can bring to light important knowledge not examined before or previously ignored.

There needs to be a firm recognition and distinction of the two different classroom ecologies before one can use the comparative method. All visual observations and data are clustered to allow comparisons "within and between" these classification systems, including the classroom, students, and teachers, by means of a dynamic comparative analysis (Figure A.2).

Bowker and Star's (1999) classification analysis offers a constructive approach for locating conceptual integrated categories to

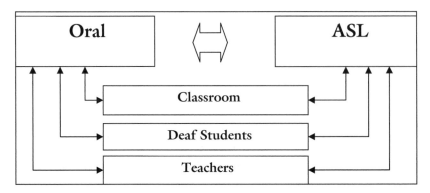

FIGURE A.2.   Two classifications for constant comparative analysis.

contribute to the functioning of classification systems. As a result of using this approach, two possibly different complex ecologies arise for analysis, each including their own diverse unique knowledge facilitation in the classroom (both explicit and hidden), the teacher's academic backgrounds, and the background of students (e.g., demographics and socioeconomic statuses). Other analyses will include the embeddedness of technology in the classroom; the embodiment of the materiality of "speech" (both vocal and nonvocally); and the various arrangements of membership validation, including the requirements to "enter" an educational institution.

These classification systems are further examined as a "gestalt switch" to provide a holistic examination of their role within the classification system (Bowker & Star, 1999, p. 34). Examining these classification systems serves as a method to analyze the interdependent system in practice and to possibly expose larger structural forces that maintain the social organization of the two schools. Along with the comparative method as a guiding methodological map, the use of grounded theory was major tool of the fieldwork gathered in this research.

## Grounded Theory

Barney Glaser and Anselum Strauss (1967) outline several general procedures that are fundamental to grounded theory, including (a) the selection of theoretical sampling; (b) constant comparisons of the sampling and integration of the data, systematic asking of generative and concept-relating questions, and systematic open and axial coding procedures; (c) the use of axial coding and thematic coding to construct comparative phenomena or concepts to build theoretical frameworks; and (c) the creation of these theoretical frameworks for comparisons to build a stronger grounded theory (Charmaz, 2006). The seven procedural stages I used for grounded theory were (a) the selection of the classroom, students, and teachers within the ASL school and oral school to frame the theoretical sampling; (b) data collection by means of coding, memo-making, note taking, videotaping, observations, and interviews; (c) an analysis and comparison of the data collection to discover patterns and codes; (d) the emergence and classification of thematic and axial coding by means of comparing codes from the data collection; (e) the development of conceptual integrated categories for constant comparisons; (f) the construction of a theoretical framework from comparative conceptual integrated categories; and (g) the development of elements of a grounded theory of deaf education for Chapter 4 (Figure A.3).

The procedures of grounded theory allow for attaining conceptual "density" and variation to be formed as comparative conceptual integration of categories (Denzin & Lincoln, 2005). The conceptual integrated categories compared by means of theoretical sampling contribute to the examination of the issues being studied, that is, the diverse social phenomena of normalcy and deviance occurring in deaf education. These samplings, developed by Glaser and Strauss (1967), were to help ensure "that the sample(s) are theoretically representative with respect to the problem and the population being studied," including

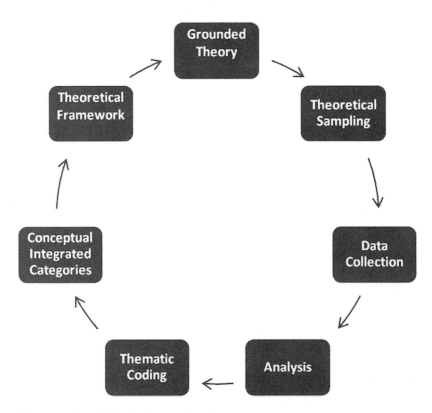

FIGURE A.3. Model of grounded theory.

the construction of the social and historical structures between the two classification systems (Erting, 1981, p. 232). Theoretical sampling also means "going back to the field to gather specific data to fill in gaps within categories, to elaborate the analysis of these categories [ASL and oral schools], and to discuss variation within and between them" (Charmaz & Mitchell, 2001, p. 168). For this research, the classroom, teachers, and students within the ASL classroom and the oral classroom make up the theoretical sampling, which serves as a framework for comparative analysis (Figure A.4).

On entering the schools, data were collected through handwritten notes, observations, interviews, and videotaping of the students' social interactions. The field notes were then digitally typed in NUD*IST, qualitative software that is programmed to detect recurring words from the field notes. These recurring words were highlighted (or "tagged"), analyzed, and coded (open and axial coding to connect "key" data). The digital copy of the field notes was printed with the highlighted words present, which allowed identifying the highlighted words several times for meaning in each sentence; connecting the same word in other sentences during other dates of observations; and searching for latent ideas, including where and when the term originated. This procedure also included who or what was the precursor of these original highlighted words. Then, several highlighted words were anchored to develop connections for comparisons. Ideas were written by hand in the margins and used as memos at all steps of the process. After the

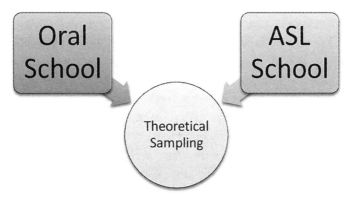

Figure A.4.   The design of theoretical sampling.

initial round of coding, relationships about the data were discovered by means of axial coding, and analytic memos were written to find emerging definitions and themes, which allowed highlighted words to become thematic codes that would become representative of the many patterns found through the continuous observations made in both schools as important concepts of analysis. Then these thematic codes were arranged as conceptual frameworks for structural analysis, or what Strauss and Corbin (1997) call "sorting out data," to be made into a theoretical framework (Figure A.4). The classroom, students, and teachers as sites of comparative analyses were elaborated and fleshed out by these thematic codes that would serve to construct the "types" of knowledge maintained and organized. These comparative analyses were then built into narrative descriptions or "more general perspectives, themes, and dimensions" in Chapter 5 (O'Day & Killeen, 2002, p. 9). The elements of the grounded theory became a process of "simultaneous data-collection and analysis, [in] pursuit of emergent themes [by means of thematic and axial codes] and theoretical sampling that becomes . . . integration of categories into a theoretical framework that specifies causes, conditions, and consequences of the process(es)" (Charmaz & Mitchell, 2001, p. 160).

Although grounded theory is recognized as a flexible methodological approach, the sampling by means of grounded theory will temporarily exclude some of the other important data/themes/issues in the research. Some possible samplings that were excluded included the mainstreaming schools (e.g., a combination of both deaf and hearing students) and schools that offer different types of communication pedagogy for the deaf (e.g., cued speech). This process delves into certain specific knowledge for a grounded theory: framing the sampling for the ASL and oral classroom for comparative purposes. Then, the findings and elements of the current grounded theory may be able to incorporate the previously disassociated data/themes/issues together as future theoretical sampling into integrated categories and then theory building. This circular process may build toward another grounded theory to connect different knowledge into another layer of analysis.

This procedure may help the data/themes/issues to uncover knowledge, which will add another layer of analysis that continues to be contested dynamically and interwoven rather than confined into static and fixed sites of information (Gerson & Horowitz, 2002, p. 199; see also Paul Atkinson's (1992) writing up and down in the "texts-of-the-field"). The elements of a grounded theory are a means, not an end, of the research design; thus, this orientation's goal is to move this rich data into various levels of analysis. The elements of a grounded theory are the means to provide more useful data within the theoretical sampling for other researchers to further create other methods to examine the "types of knowledge" in deaf education and deafness in general. Some of this discovered knowledge will possibly provide disconfirming evidence that will apply to other orientations.

For some scholars, grounded theory is traditionally done before a literature review to enable the researcher to go in the field naively with no ostensible researcher bias (Glaser, 1998). However, the archaeology of deaf education in Chapter 3 shows that there is little or no cross-comparative literature between the two types of school; thus, it is necessary to show that there is a need for a comparative method between the two schools to uncover knowledge and evidence that had been viewed as invincible (Strauss & Corbin, 1997).

This chapter now moves to the research setting as the scope for analysis, which serves as the foundation for the comparative study while allowing grounded theory to serve as its systematic tool to examine these two social control organization often embedded in educational institutions.

## RESEARCH SETTING

The research setting consists of studying two classification systems with two different educational pedagogies; Magnet School, where students use ASL, and Central School, where students use the oral method. These two schools with self-contained classrooms of deaf students are often categorized in two different types of educational settings that contrast in educational pedagogy, including the placement and nonplacement of ASL in the child's educational and social development (Power & Leigh, 2000; Wilbur, 2000).

The mainstreaming classification system (e.g., schools where deaf students are assimilated with hearing students in the classroom) will be left on the map for future research. The selection of the two different types of classifications does not claim the mainstreaming classification system and its understanding to the overall deaf education system as irrelevant, but it requires different methodological approaches and tools of examination. The different approaches include the multidimensional memberships in the mainstreaming classroom (i.e., both deaf and hearing students), the complex criteria of social identity when exposed as the minority deaf student (as opposed to being the full majority in a self-contained classroom), the role of interpreters in the classroom setting, and the general background and pedagogical instruction of the teacher (as opposed to specialized training of teachers for the deaf). More important, the mainstreaming system does not have the specialized pedagogical use of a unique language other than English, which is a primary focus of this study when determining how the social constructions of language have been cast as normal or deviant (i.e., oral versus ASL). The examinations of the mainstreaming classification systems are not a part of this study.

I was able to contact the principals of both schools through email. I explained that I was a deaf doctoral student at Arizona State interested in possibly observing their classroom "several times" and that I would like to meet with them in person to discuss these ideas. When I met with the principals, I came prepared with consent forms that mirrored the template forms provided by my university's Office of Research Integrity and Assurance. I informed them that I would be a co-investigator conducting the research under the supervision of Dr. Pat Lauderdale, my dissertation chair, as primary investigator and to contact him for any technical and administrative questions. I was able to "switch" my language modality to fit in with the school's pedagogy to affirm that I shared "similar traits" with the school. Specifically, at the ASL school, communication between the principal and me was conducted in sign language while, conversely, oral communication methods were used at meetings in the oral school. Once I got the schools' signed consent, I proceeded to complete two Institutional Review Board (IRB) forms for my university's approval. The first IRB form focused on classroom observations and the second form included the opportunity to videotape. From that point on, what became "several observations" turned into frequent observations, as I was able to gain the trust of the two principals. It is important to note that the principal at the ASL school offered me the opportunity to observe as many different classes with different teachers as possible while the oral school limited me to observing one teacher in one classroom.

I took the opportunity to observe other ASL classrooms with other ASL teachers, but I was restricted from including their data in this study to meet the constraint of the comparative method. I asked the principal in the oral school several times if I could observe other classrooms, and I was informed that it would not be necessary since she claimed that the other oral classrooms would be the "same" because they are "strictly" (her word) bound to follow a specific curriculum that is known as the Moog curriculum. Although the study was limited to two schools to allow an equal comparison, these two schools—as a part of my theoretical sampling— still can become important sites of analyzing and examining its important contribution in the implications of normalcy and deviance.

## THEORETICAL SAMPLING

The two classrooms, the students, and the teachers were selected as my theoretical sampling. Then, through data collection, the data were transformed into thematic and axial coding, which were often interwoven but contributed differently in each conceptual framework and sampling. For example, discussing the academic background of the teacher in one framework also has an impact on the students' learning process in another framework. Further, the academic background of the teacher also indicates the "type" of classroom (another framework) to be framed (i.e., the arrangement of the students' desks and the use of technology to fit in their teaching pedagogical background). The next section organizes the classroom, students, and teachers to deconstruct conceptually integrated categories by means of thematic and axial codes into important theoretical frameworks. This part is organized structurally to examine how each conceptually integrated category contributes closely with each sampling in one layer of analysis for comparative purposes.

### Classrooms

The classroom is a representation of space with social meanings that contribute to the social functions of the school as a social organization (Harrison & Dourish, 1996). Examining the classroom as a place includes analyzing the classroom in terms of its social meanings and using its space as an abstract perception of the lived experiences within the classroom. Michel Foucault contended that the physical places of school buildings and grounds were designed as "pedagogical" machines, constructing functional sites through space and social meanings (Foucault, 1977/1995). In addition to the school buildings and grounds, classrooms are also a reflection of these functional sites as place because these classrooms contribute to the overall space and the social meanings of the school itself. In observing the classrooms, I used axial and thematic codes to build on the conceptually integrated categories, including the physical ecology of the classroom, complexities of the culture in the classroom, materiality applied, and the types of performativity used in the classroom. These spaces and social meanings contributed to the conceptually integrated categories to build classroom as a site of analysis of social constructions (Figure A.5).

Figure A.5 show the four emergent conceptually integrated categories that I used to elaborate the classroom as a site of analysis. The conceptually integrated categories revealed by thematic and axial codes became the important indicators of the types of classroom construction

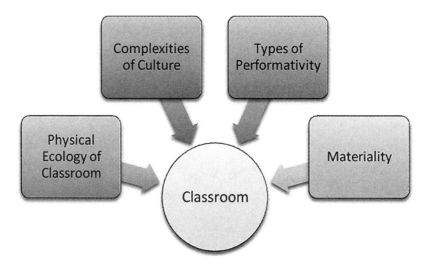

FIGURE A.5.   Four conceptually integrated categories through which to analyze the classroom.

in the respective kindergartens (Figure A.6). The codes contrasted the classrooms with each other, thus enabling me to provide a stronger constructive comparative analysis. This analysis also led to two strong and distinctive comparable samplings (the kindergarten classrooms) that would contribute to important elements of the grounded theory. The classroom as a sampling enabled me to study and analyze the process of certain types of constructions that simultaneously influenced the "normal" classroom to maintain its ideological notion of what a classroom ought to be. To build the four conceptually integrated categories to analyze the classrooms, I analyzed several axial codes that were recurring throughout my field notes by using NUD*IST software. These axial codes became emergent thematic codes to contribute to the overall examination of the classroom for meanings (Figure A.6). Again, these codes were often found interwoven with other conceptually integrated categories, but for comparative purposes, they were structured under four specific categories.

**Physical ecology of the classroom.** The physical ecology of the classroom such as the physical structure of the classroom, including the arrangement of the teacher/students' table, desks, and chairs within the classroom were analyzed as a product of human social and cultural activity (See Artiles, 2003, for FirstSpace analysis;

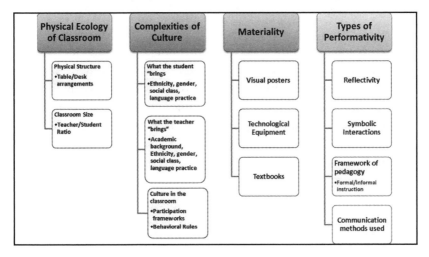

FIGURE A.6. Various codes that contribute to conceptually integrated categories within the classroom.

Gallego, Cole, & Laboratory of Comparative Human Cognition, 2001, for "classroom culture"). These structural designs reflected the reproduction of patterns of social stratification and constructions by social control institutions, including human social and cultural activities (Bourdieu & Passeron, 1977; Gallego et al., 2001). While observing, some questions emerged, for example, how is the classroom ecology set up to maximize the teacher's way of instruction? Are students arranged in a "face-to-face" approach with other students or are they arranged in a manner in which the teacher presents herself/himself as the main "focus" of the classroom? I also observed the various classroom sizes, including the teacher/student ratio. These observations contributed toward the physical ecology of the classroom as one conceptually integrated category.

**Complexities of culture.** As I organized the observational data of the classroom into axial codes, the classrooms became sites of complex ecologies embedded with symbolic activities and artifacts that construct the complexities of culture in the classroom, including what the student "brings" to the class, what the teacher "brings" to the class, and the "classroom" culture. Complexities of culture, in this respect, are the embodiment of various features, including

> patterns, explicit and implicit, of and for behavior acquired and transmitted by symbols, consisting of the distinctive achievement of human groups, including their embodiment in artifacts; the essential core of culture consist of traditional (i.e., historically derived and selected) ideas and especially their attached values cultural systems [that] may on one hand be considered as products of action, on the other as conditioning elements of further action. (Kroeber & Kluckhohn in Gallego et al., 2001, p. 953)

The complexities of culture in the classroom were observed through the student participation in both formal and informal academic practices. The activities in the overall classroom context are "often organized in ways that help young people develop identities as members of that practice" (Lee, 2007, p. 26). Some parameters of what the student and teacher "bring" to the classroom include ethnicity, gender, social class, language practices, and participation repertories. I was able to observe and document some educational and cultural aspects of the classroom such as participation frameworks, behavioral rules, turn-taking procedures, and criteria for success or failure. Overall, the complexities of culture in the classroom that I observed manifested into thematic codes. These codes included the ecology of interactions, traffic management in interaction, and the type of knowledge constructed and developed into the cultures in the classroom, an important conceptually integrated category (Gallego et al., 2001).

**Materiality.** My thematic and axial codes helped identify another conceptually integrated category—materiality in the classroom. I was able to document the different types of "materials" present, including visual posters, the manual ASL alphabet poster, the auditory technical equipment, and the types of textbooks. Did the teacher use satire in an attempt to make the connection between "everyday" knowledge and "academic" knowledge? These questions elicited certain types of information conveyed through poetry, storytelling, and visual materials such as televisions. Were these types of information in textbooks designed visually or textually? Do these textbooks include certain types of cultures such as sign language or any indication of deafness? I examined the diverse curricula by noting the variety of educational tools such as books, structured toys, and flash cards. Information about the various types of policy influences such as the financial resources available by the school to make the class "updated" with the latest technology (i.e., SmartBoard®), and how the school mandates each classroom and curriculum to be structured to meet its accountability standards was also sought.`

**Types of performativity.** The various types of performance used by the teacher/students emerged as the fourth conceptually integrated category showing important contributors to influence the classroom as a site of analysis. The types of performativity observed included reflexivity and symbolic interaction as thematic codes. Observing the actual instructional processes in the classroom, various educational topics and method as basic educational framework of pedagogy for the deaf students were documented and videotaped. In the classroom, I observed the overall communicative methods used and the portrayal of comprehension between the teacher and the students as well as the students among other students. I sought to observe instances of diverse instructional pedagogy incorporating formal (academic) and informal (social and cultural) types of knowledge into the classroom activities. In addition, I observed unstructured (i.e., recess, independent play time with toys) and structured (storytelling, playing on the computer) types of play for comparison. These thematic codes contributed to developing the types of performativity in the classroom as a comparative category for analysis.

## Students

My examinations of deaf students became important sites of analysis within the deaf schools. The schools as educational institutions relied greatly on deaf students to function; without the presence of social issues on deafness and deaf students, there would be no need for deaf education institutions nor for teachers of the deaf. Thus, deaf students play a very critical role in social control processes that contribute to shaping certain ideologies in the deaf educational system. The research focuses only on the deaf students' contribution in the deaf classroom and encourages future researchers to connect the analyses of this study to the many other social control processes that surround deaf students.

Throughout my observations of the students and development of axial and thematic codes, I uncovered four emergent conceptually integrated categories for comparative analysis: communication, resistance, technology, and student biographies (Figure A.7). Once again, the data gathered were transformed into information by means of axial and thematic codes through NUD*IST software, which was then analyzed as conceptually integrated categories to become structural categories for comparisons.

These categories were further broken down by axial and thematic codes during my data collection and analysis (Figure A.8). These concepts presented the most comparative analysis possible between the students within the two classrooms; that is, the codes contrasted

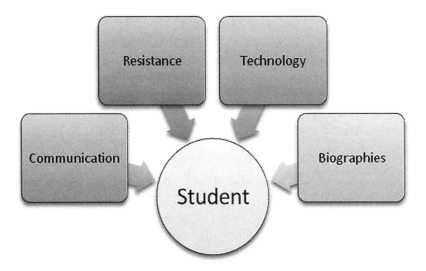

Figure A.7.  Four conceptually integrated categories to analyze the students.

greatly. The examination and comparison of these concepts provide a way to better compare the students as a site of analysis.

**Communication use.** The use of communication was the most visual and most important aspect of my data collection. As I organized the data, I detected many emergent issues that would build the communication use as an important axial and thematic code. In the classroom, I observed the deaf students' communication both toward the teacher and toward other students as well as the symbolic interaction between these exchanges of both informal and formal information. Formal information became described as organized and structured data constructed by the teacher. I observed the ways that the students conducted themselves in terms of the manner in which they recognized the rules they must adhere to in these formal settings. Equally as important, I observed the ways students contest informal information with formal information because these types of information could "represent the students' attempts to work out a connection between the two discourses [formal and informal]" to make sense of the overall information being portrayed (Gallego et al., 2001, p. 971). This contested knowledge also may reveal the types

## Students

Figure A.8.  Various codes that contributed to the conceptually integrated student categories.

of resistance portrayed by the students when given certain types of information.

**Resistance.** The notion of resistance and agency became another important conceptually integrated category that was found through axial and thematic coding. I examined in the deaf students' exchange of "knowledge" and how the facilitation of that knowledge was accepted and/or resisted (McFadden, 1995). I especially observed the levels of individual and group agency in the classroom and detected any resistance applied toward/by the deaf student both in formal and informal educational activities. Throughout my observations, when resistance is applied, for example, the repetition (or suppression) of specific language, it gave more leverage to the teacher and the classroom instruction, thereby strengthening the apparatus of the classroom (Fernandes, 1988).

**Technology.** The presence of technology, namely, the student's use of hearing aids/cochlear implants/FM systems was another conceptually integrated category. Throughout my observations, I documented technology and whether it served an important role as a possible embedded material in the overall function of the specific deaf educational pedagogy. I observed how technology was used through educational instruction and how the students incorporated this technology (e.g., hearing aids and/or cochlear implant) in their educational learning process.

**Biographies.** I also documented the biographies of the students, including their ethnicity, gender endowment, first names, the "types" of clothes they wore, which possibly reflected socioeconomic status, and their over-all demeanor in the educational setting. I observed their personalities—whether they were outspoken, the types of behavior they exhibited, their level of respect for authority and other students—and how they incorporated their own personalities into the academic classroom. The presence of technology used by the students and their biographies make up the "types" of membership they bring into the educational surrounding. In this aspect, I examined the ways in which their membership may be accepted by others since they involve both a "sense of identity as well as a level of acceptance by others" (Lee, 2007, p. 12). Organizing my data by means of thematic and axial codes led me to construct biographies as an important conceptually integrated category that would build on the students as an emerging theme for analysis.

## Teachers

Throughout my observations, teachers became a very important comparative concept, particularly, to examine their role in deaf education. Through my observations, I noticed that teachers became strong facilitators in the student's academic achievement, for example,

> actively observing and looking for patterns in details observed will lead students to search their existing knowledge base, to attend to connections between their existing knowledge base and the target problem, and be metacognitive by describing their own reasoning process. (Lee, 2007, p. 134)

In my analysis, the teacher plays a critical role in the classroom by shaping the student's cognitive, linguistic, and learning process. Through my observations and coding, three major conceptually integrated categories emerged that contributed strongly in the analysis of the teachers: the type of teacher facilitation, perception of effective instruction, and their biographies (Figure A.9).

These three concepts are further broken down by various axial and thematic codes (Figure A.10).

**Knowledge facilitation.** How the teacher facilitates certain types of knowledge as well as shapes the student's educational and social process through the specific selected language pedagogy was carefully observed by means of field notes and videotaping. I looked at the ways that the teacher mediated textual symbols (i.e., flash cards) into educational information. In addition to observation, I interviewed teachers, asking concrete and abstract open-ended questions regarding their knowledge and views on deaf education in general.

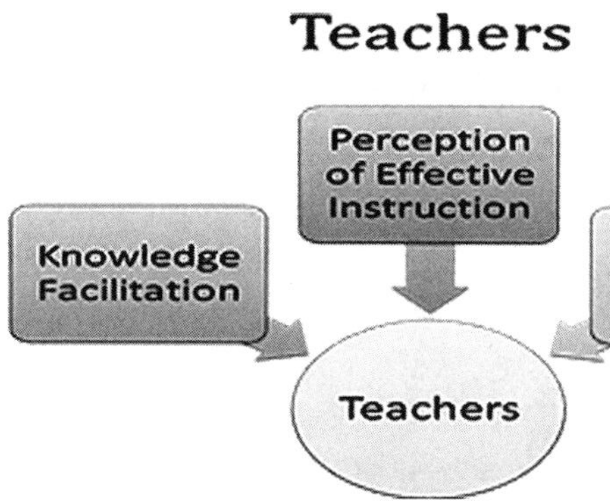

## Teachers

FIGURE A.9.   Three conceptually integrated categories through which to analyze the teachers.

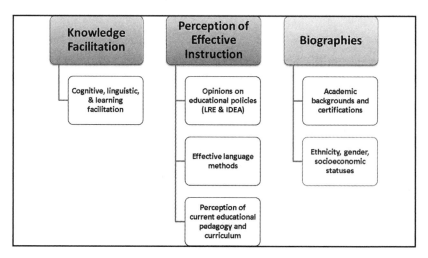

FIGURE A.10.   Various codes that contribute to the conceptually integrated categories.

**Perception of effective instruction.** Throughout my interviews and observations, the perception of effective instruction emerged as critical analysis. In interviews, the teachers were asked about their perception of effective instruction, including their assessment of the least restrictive environment (LRE) under the IDEA and NCLB legislation. They were asked to list the values that they believe are instrumental to the deaf child's education, their attitudes about "effective" ASL and oral methods, and their overall assessment of their school's language pedagogy in the academic setting. I also observed how they incorporated their teaching preference into the classroom instruction, for example, the ways they used specific language and how they mediated certain types of relationships with the students.

**Biographies.** The last concept that emerged from my axial and thematic codes were the teacher's biographies. I sought to examine whether the teachers possessed teacher credentials and further professional development certifications to provide a better understanding of how these teachers are structured by outside influences to become "better" teachers. The teachers' academic backgrounds were explored to gain a greater understanding of their training and how they may incorporate it into the classroom (i.e., bringing their "culture" in the classroom). This variable became crucial because the academic background and training of the teacher build on teacher knowledge. Through my observations, I was able to see how they used their prior teacher knowledge to facilitate and impose certain knowledge toward deaf students. I also documented their age-range, ethnicity, and overall management style in the classroom, which would build on teacher biographies as a concept.

## Structural Dimensions

The classrooms, students, and teachers as a theoretical sampling for comparative analysis are not intended to be studied on their own; the sampling offers a structural way to frame important conceptually integrated categories that are interwoven and often serve to influence one another. These conceptually integrated categories, as a collective, build on structural dimensions of deaf educational practices to develop elements of a grounded theory of deafness, including its constructions. These samplings as comparative sites of analysis (classroom, students, teachers) using conceptual integrated categories allow me to build these organized analyses into narratives and to contribute to the overall structural dimensions for elements of a grounded theory of deafness (Strauss & Corbin, 1997). These conceptual categories are transformed into theoretical information by means of narratives as structural dimensions that can be analyzed and framed as theoretical themes to uncover hidden knowledge that may have not been made visible before. These themes include the diverse pedagogies of language, culture in the classroom, and teacher knowledge. These themes contribute to the construction of languaculture for deaf people. Chapter 4 presented some narrative descriptions of these classrooms to build onto structural and theoretical frameworks in Chapter 5 to identify the various constructions of deafness as a whole. More important, my findings and analyses offer a way to examine the larger implications of deafness by means of the diverse educational practices constructed for deaf students (Little & Houston, 2003, p. 55). These methodological orientations and theoretical themes offer opportunities to examine the dynamics being contested in the two schools and to understand how they may contribute to the overall ideologies manifested within the realm of deafness and deaf education.

# REFERENCES

Agar, M. (1994). *Language shock: Understanding the culture of conversation*. New York, NY: William Morrow and Company.

Akamatsu, C., & Andrews, J. (1993). It takes two to be literate: Literacy interactions between parent and child. *Sign Language Studies, 81,* 333–360.

Alexander Graham Bell Association for the Deaf and Hard of Hearing. (2009). *Speaking volumes*. Retrieved from http://www.oraldeafed .org/materials/info-spkvol.html

Allen, B., Meyers, N., Sullivan, J., & Sullivan, M. (2007). Using American Sign Language in assessing the end-of-life-care educational needs of deaf persons: Lessons on language, culture, and research practices. In T. Kroll, D. Keer, P. P. Placek, J. Cyril, & G. Hendershot (Eds.), *Towards best practices for surveying people with disabilities* (Volume 1, pp. 47–69). New York, NY: Nova Science Publishers.

Althusser, L. (1970). Ideology and ideological state apparatuses. Lenin and Philosophy and Other Essays, *Monthly Review Press.* Retrieved from http://www.marxists.org/references/archive/ althusser/1970/ideology.htm.

American Psychiatric Association (APA). (1968). *Diagnostic and Statistical Manual of Mental Disorders II.* Washington, DC: Author.

American Psychiatric Association (APA). (1980). *Diagnostic and Statistical Manual of Mental Disorders III.* Washington, DC: Author.

American Psychiatric Association (APA). (2000). *Diagnostic and Statistical Manual of Mental Disorders IV.* Washington, DC: Author.

Amman, J. C. (1694). *The talking deaf man: Or, a method proposed whereby he who is born deaf may learn to speak*. London, UK: Tho. Hawkins.

Amman, J. C. (1700). *Dissertatio de loquela*. Amsterdam, Netherlands: J. Wolters.

Andrews, J. F., & Leigh, I. W. (2004). *Deaf people: Evolving perspectives from psychology, education and sociology*. Boston, MA: Allyn & Bacon.

Andrews, J. F., & Franklin, T. C. (1997). Why hire deaf teachers? *Texas Journal of Speech and Hearing, 12*(1), 12013. (ERIC document:ED 425 600)

Aronowitz, S., & Giroux, H. (1991). *Postmodern education: Politics, culture, and social criticism*. Minneapolis, MN: University of Minnesota Press.

Aronowitz, S., & Giroux, H. (1993). *Education: Still under siege*. Westport, CT: Bergin & Garvey.

Artiles, A. J. (2003). Special education changing identity: Paradoxes and dilemmas in views of culture and space. *Harvard Educational Review, 73*(2), 164–247.

Asch, T., & Asch, P. (1995). Film in ethnographic research. In P. Hocking (Ed.), *Principles of visual anthropology* (pp. 335–362). New York, NY: Mouton de Gruyter.

Atkins v. Virginia, 536 U.S. 304, 122 S.Ct. 2242 (2002).

Atkinson, P. (1992). Understanding ethnographic texts. *Qualitative Research Methods Series, 25*. Newbury Park, CA: Sage.

Babbidge, H. (1965). *Education of the deaf in the United States: Report of the Advisory Committee on Education of the Deaf*. Washington, DC: U.S. Government Printing Office.

Bagga-Gupta, S. (2000). Visual language environments: Exploring everyday life and illiteracies in Swedish deaf bilingual schools. *Visual Anthropology, 15*(2), 95–120.

Bailes, C. N. (1999). *Primary-grade teachers' strategic use of American Sign Language in teaching English literacy in a bilingual school setting*. (Doctoral dissertation). Available from ProQuest Dissertations and Theses database. (UMI No. 9926724)

Bailes, C. N. (2001). Deaf-centric teaching: A case study in ASL-English bilingualism. In L. Bragg (Ed.), *Deaf world: A historical reader and primary source book* (pp. 211–233). New York, NY: New York University Press.

Bakhtin, M. (1981). *The dialogic imagination: Four essays by M. M. Bakhtin* (C. J. Emerson & M. Holquist, Trans.). Austin, TX: University of Texas Press.

Banks, J. A. (1993). The canon debate, knowledge construction, and multicultural education. *Educational Researcher, 22*, 4–14.

Banks, J. A. (1996). *Multicultural education, transformative knowledge, and action.* New York, NY: Teachers College, Columbia University Press.

Banks, J. A. (2000). The social construction of difference and the quest for educational equality. In R. S. Brandt (Ed.), *Education in a new era* (pp. 21–45). Alexandria, VA: Association for Supervision and Curriculum Development.

Barnartt, S., & Scotch, R. (2002). *Disability protests: Contentious politics, 1970–1999.* Washington, DC: Gallaudet University Press.

Barth, F. (1969). *Ethnic groups and boundaries.* Boston: Little Brown.

Bat-Chava, Y., & Deignan, E. (2001). Peer relationships of children with cochlear implants. *Journal of Deaf Studies and Deaf Education, 6*, 186–199.

Bauman, H-D. (Ed.). (2008). *Open your eyes; deaf studies talking.* Minneapolis: University of Minnesota Press.

Bauman, H-D., & Murray, J. (2010). Deaf studies in the twenty-first century: Deaf-gain and the future of deaf studies. In M. Marschark & P. E. Spencer (Eds.), *Oxford handbook of deaf studies, language, and education* (Vol. 2, pp. 210–225). New York, NY: Oxford University Press.

Baynton, D. (1999). Savages and deaf-mutes: Evolutionary theory and the campaign against sign language in the nineteenth century. In J. V. Cleve (Ed.), *Deaf history unveiled: Interpretations from the new scholarship* (pp. 92–112). Washington, DC: Gallaudet University Press.

Baynton, D. (2001). Disability and the justification of inequality in American history. In P. Longmore & L. Umansky (Eds.), *The new disability history: American perspectives* (pp. 33–57). New York, NY: New York University Press.

Becker, H. S. (1961). Schools and systems of stratification. In A. H. Halsey, J. Floud, & C. A. A. Anderson (Eds.), *Education, economy, and society* (pp. 93–104). New York, NY: Free Press.

Beckett, A. (2006). Understanding social movements: Theorising the disability movement in conditions of late modernity. *The Sociological Review, 54*(4), 734–752.

Bell, A. G. (1872a). Results of experiments with visible speech. In *Joint Documents of the State of Michigan* (Vol. 3). Lansing: W. S. George & Co. Retrieved from http://books.google.com/books/?id=FBwoAQAAMAAJ

Bell, A. G. (1872b). Visible speech as a means of communicating articulation to deaf-mutes. *American Annals of the Deaf and Dumb, 17*(1), 1–21.

Bentler, R. (2009). Hearing aid innovations: 100+ years later. *The Volta Review, 109*(1), 33–43.

Berger, J. (2005). Uncommon schools: Institutionalizing deafness in early-nineteenth-century America. In S. Tremain (Ed.), *Foucault and the government on disability* (pp. 153–171). Ann Arbor, MI: University of Michigan Press.

Bettie, J. (2003). *Women without class: Girls, race, and identity.* Berkeley, CA: University of California Press.

Biennial Report of the Directors and Officers of the Minnesota Institution. (1884). In *Proceedings of the Fifth National Conference of Superintendents and Principals of Institutions for Deaf Mutes.* Minneapolis, MN: Johnson, Smith & Harrison.

Bourdieu, P. (1992). *The logic of practice* (R. Nice, Trans.). Cambridge, UK: Polity Press.

Bourdieu, P., & Passeron, J. C. (1977). *Reproduction in education, society, and culture.* London, UK: Sage.

Bowe, F. (2003). Transition for deaf and hard-of-hearing students: A blueprint for change. *Journal of Deaf Studies and Deaf Education, 8*(4), 485–493.

Bowker, G., & Star, J. (1999). *Sorting things out: Classification and its consequences.* Boston, MA: MIT Press.

Branson, J., & Miller, D. (2002). *Damned for their difference: The cultural construction of deaf people as disabled.* Washington, DC: Gallaudet University Press.

Breivik, J-K. (2005). *Deaf identities in the making: Local lives, transitional connections.* Washington, DC: Gallaudet University Press.

Brittanica Biographies. (2012). Alexander Graham Bell. Retrieved from http://www.britannia.com/bios/bell.html.

Brown, S. E. (1996). *Disability culture: A fact sheet.* Las Cruces, NM: Institute on Disability Culture.

Brown, S. E. (2003). *Movie stars and sensuous scars: Essays on the journey from disability shame to disability pride.* Bloomington, IN: iUniverse.com.

Brown, S. E. (2011). *Surprised to be standing: A spiritual journey.* New York, NY: CreateSpace Independent Publishing Platform.

Brown v. Board of Education of Topeka, 347 U.S. 483 (1954).

Brueggemann, B. J. (2004). *Literacy and deaf people: Cultural and contextual perspectives.* Washington, DC: Gallaudet University Press.

Brueggemann, B. J. (2010). On (almost) passing. In L. J. Davis (Ed.), *The disability studies reader* (pp. 210–219). New York, NY: Routledge.

Brusky, A. (1995). Making decisions for deaf children regarding cochlear implant: The legal ramifications of recognizing deafness as a culture rather than a disability. *Wisconsin Law Review,* 237–270.

Buchanan, R. M. (1999). *Illustrations of equality: Deaf Americans in school and factory 1850–1950.* Washington, DC: Gallaudet University Press.

Buchmann, C., & Hannum, E. (2001). Education and stratification in developing countries: A review of theories and research. *Annual Review of Sociology, 27,* 77–102.

Buck v. Bell, 274 U.S. 200, 207 (1927).

Bunge, M. (1999). *Social science under debate: A philosophical perspective.* Toronto, Canada: University of Toronto Press.

Burch, S., & Sutherland, I. (2006). Who's not yet here? American disability history. *Radical History Review 94,* 127–147.

Burchardt, T. (2004). Capabilities and disability: the capabilities framework and the social model of disability. *Disability & Society, (19)7,* 735–751.

Burke, M. A. (1888). Views on the combined method. *American Annals of the Deaf, 25*(3), 169–230.

Butler, J. (1993). Critically queer. *GLQ: A Journal of Lesbian and Gay Studies 1*(1), 17–32.

Butler, J. (2000). Critically queer. In A. Tripp (Ed.), *Gender: Readers in cultural criticism* (pp. 154–181). New York, NY: Palgrave.

Carlisle, J., & Stone, A. (2005). Exploring the role of morphemes in word reading. *Reading Research Quarterly, 40,* 428–449.

Charmaz, K. (2006). *Constructing grounded theory: A practical guide through qualitative analysis.* London, UK: Sage.

Charmaz, K., & Mitchell, R. (2001). Grounded theory in ethnography. In P. Atkinson (Eds.), *Handbook of ethnography* (pp. 160–174). London, UK: Sage.

Charrow, V. R., & Wilbur, R. B. (1975). The deaf child as a linguistic minority. *Theory into Practice, 14*(5), 353–359.

Chudgar, A., & Luschei, T. (2009). National income, income inequality, and the importance of schools: A hierarchical cross-national comparison. *American Educational Research Journal, 46*(3), 626–658.

Clifford, J. (1983). On ethnographic authority. *Representations, 2*(Spring), 118–146.

Code, L. (1991). *What can she know? Feminist theory and the construction of knowledge.* Ithaca, NY: Cornell University Press.

Collins, P. H. (1999). Moving beyond gender. In M. Ferree, J. Lorber, & B. Hess (Eds.), *Revisioning gender* (pp. 61–284). Thousand Oaks, CA: Sage.

Commerson, R. C. (2008). *Media, power, and ideology: Re-presenting DEAF.* (Master's thesis). Gallaudet University, Washington DC. Retrieved from http://vimeo.com/12817361

Conrad, P., & Schneider, J. (1992). *Deviance and medicalization: From badness to sickness.* Philadelphia, PA: Temple University Press.

Cooper, K., & White, R. (2009). Distinguished performances: The educative role of disciplines in qualitative research in education. *International Review of Qualitative Research, 2*(2), 167–188.

Cornwell, L. (2005). American Sign Language gains popularity as foreign language. *Hamilton (Ohio) Journal-News.*

Coryell, J., & Holcomb, T. (2007). The use of sign language and sign systems in facilitating the language acquisition and communication of deaf students. *Language, Speech, and Hearing Services in Schools 28,* 384–394.

Cummins, J. (1986). Empowering minority students: A framework for intervention. *Harvard Educational Review, 56,* 18–56.

Cummins, J. (2000). *Language, power, and pedagogy: Bilingual children in the crossfire.* Toronto, Canada: Multilingual Matters.

Cummins, J. (2006). Pedagogies of choice: challenging coercive relations of power in classrooms and communities. *International Journal of Bilingual Education and Bilingualism, 12*(3), 261–271.

Davis, L. J. (1995). *Enforcing normalcy: Disability, deafness, and the body.* New York, NY: Verso.

Davis, L. J. (2002). *Bending over backwards: Disability, dismodernism & other difficult positions.* New York, NY: New York University Press.

DeafMom. (2011). Hands & Voices in Maine [Web log post]. Retrieved from http://deafmomworld.com/hands-voices-in-maine/

Deaf Youth USA. (2010). *"D" "d"—POINTLESS.* [Digital video]. Retrieved from http://www.youtube.com/watch?v = 4OTq6Q5 6tyg&feature = player_embedded

Delvin, R. F., & Pontheir, D. (2006). *Critical disability theory: Essays in philosophy, politics, policy, and law.* Vancouver, Canada: University of British Columbia Press.

Denzin, N., & Giardina, M. (2009). Qualitative inquiry and social justice: Toward a politics of hope. In N. Denzin & M. Giardina (Eds.), *Qualitative inquiry and social justice* (pp. 12–50). Walnut Creek, CA: Left Coast Press.

Denzin, N., & Lincoln, Y. (2003). *The landscape of qualitative research* (2nd ed.). Thousand Oaks, CA: Sage.

Denzin, N., & Lincoln, Y. (2005). *The Sage handbook of qualitative research.* Thousand Oaks, CA: Sage.

DePoy, E., & Gilson, S. (2004). Disability, identity, and cultural diversity. *Review of Disability Studies, 1*(1), 16–24.

Derrida, J. (1974). *Of grammatology.* Baltimore, MD: Johns Hopkins University Press.

DesJardin, J., Ambrose, S. E., & Eisenberg, L. S. (2008). Literacy skills in children with cochlear implants: The importance of early oral language and joint storybook reading. *Journal of Deaf Studies and Deaf Education, 14*(1), 22–43.

Donoghue, C. (2003). Challenging the authority of the medical definition of disability: An analysis of the resistance to the social constructionist paradigm. *Disability & Society, 18*(2), 199–208.

Donovan, S., & Cross, C. (Eds.). (2002). *Minority students in special and gifted education.* Washington, DC: National Academy Press.

DuBois, W. E. B. (1897). Strivings of the negro people. Retrieved from http://www.theatlantic.com/magazine/archive/1897/08/strivings-of-the-negro-people/5446/

Du Gay, P. (1997). *Production of culture/cultures of production.* London, UK: Sage.

Durkheim, E. (1997). *The division of labor in society.* New York, NY: Free Press. (Original work published 1893)

Easterbrooks, S. R. (2002). *Language learning in children who are deaf and hard of hearing: Multiple pathways.* Boston, MA: Allyn and Bacon.

Education for All Handicapped Children Act Amendments of 1990 (Pub. L. No. 101-476) 20 U.S.C. 1401 *et seq.* (1990).

Edwards, R. A. R. (2010). "Hearing aids are not deaf": A historical perspective on technology in the deaf world. In L. J. Davis (Ed.), *The disability studies reader* (pp. 223–236). New York, NY: Routledge.

Emens, E. (2008). Integrating accommodation. *University of Pennsylvania Law Review, 156*(4), 839–922.

Emerson, R. (2001). Producing ethnographies: Theory, evidence and representation. In R. Emerson (Ed.), *Contemporary field research* (2nd ed., pp. 281–316). Prospect Heights, IL: Waveland Press.

Emerson, R., Fretz, R., & Shaw, L. (1995). *Writing ethnographic fieldnotes.* Chicago, IL: University of Chicago Press.

English, K., & Church, G. (1999). Unilateral hearing loss in children: An update for the 1990s. *Language, Speech, and Hearing Services in Schools, 30,* 26–31.

Erevelles, N. (2002). Voices of silence: Foucault, disability, and the question of self-determination. *Studies in Philosophy and Education, 21*(1), 17–35.

Erevelles, N. (2005). Signs of reason: Riviere, facilitated communication, and the crisis of the subjects. In S. Tremain (Ed.), *Foucault and the government on disability* (pp. 45–64). Ann Arbor, MI: University of Michigan Press.

Eriks-Brophy, A., Durieux-Smith, A., Olds, J., Fitzpatrick, E., Duquette, C., & Whittingham, J. (2007). Facilitators and barriers to the integration of orally educated children and youth with hearing loss into their families and communities. *The Volta Review, 107*(1), 5–36.

Erting, C. J. (1981). An anthropological approach to the study of communicative competence of deaf children. *Sign Language Studies, 32*, 221–238.

Erting, C. J. (1982). Deafness, communication, and social identity: An anthropological analysis of interaction among parents, teachers, and deaf children in a preschool. (Doctoral dissertation, American University). *Dissertation Abstracts International, 43*(11), 3641. (UMI No. 8306972)

Erting, C. J. (1985). Cultural conflict in a school for deaf children. *Anthropology and Education Quarterly, 16*(3), 225–243.

Erting, C. J. (1987). Socialization in families with deaf children. *Gallaudet encyclopedia of deaf people and deafness.* New York, NY: McGraw-Hill.

Erting, C. J. (1988). Acquiring linguistic and social identity: Interaction of deaf children with a hearing teacher and a deaf adult. In M. Strong, (Ed.), *Language learning and deafness* (pp. 192–219). New York, NY: Cambridge University Press.

Erting, C. J. (1994). *Deafness, communication, social identity: Ethnography in a preschool for deaf children.* Burtonsville, MD: Linstok Press.

Erting, C. J. (2003a). Language and literacy development in deaf children: Implications of a sociocultural perspective. In B. Bodner-Johnson & M. Sass-Lehrer (Eds.), *The young deaf or hard of hearing child: A family-centered approach to early education* (pp. 373–398). Baltimore, MD: Paul H. Brooks.

Erting, C. J. (2003b). Signs of literacy: An ethnographic study of American Sign Language and English literacy acquisition. In B. Bodner-Johnson & M. Sass-Lehrer (Eds.), *The young deaf or hard of hearing child: A family centered approach to early education* (pp. 455–467). Baltimore, MD: Paul H. Brooks.

Erting, C. J., Johnson, R. C., Smith, D. L., & Snider, B. C. (Eds.). (1994). *The deaf way: Perspectives from the International Conference on Deaf Culture*. Washington, DC: Gallaudet University Press.

Erting, C. J., & Pfau, J. (1997). *Becoming bilingual: Facilitating English literacy development using ASL in preschool*. Washington, DC: The Laurent Clerc National Deaf Educational Center, Gallaudet University.

Erting, C. J., Prezioso, C., & Hynes, M. (1994). The interactional context of deaf mother-infant communication. In V. Volterra and C. J. Erting (Eds.), *From gesture to language in hearing and deaf children* (pp. 97–106). Washington, DC: Gallaudet University Press.

Fay, E. A. (1880). (Ed.). Proceedings of the Fourth National Conference of Superintendents and Principals of Institutions for Deaf Mutes. *American Annals of the Deaf and Dumb* 25(3), 169–223. Retrieved from http://dspace.wrlc.org/doc/bitstream/2041/67603/AADDvol25no3display.pdf

Fay, E. A. (1878). The mental life of deaf mutes as related to their education and care. In *Proceedings of the Ninth Convention of American Instructors of the Deaf and Dumb* (pp. 68–76). Columbus, OH: Ohio Institution for the Deaf and Dumb.

Feinberg, W., & Soltis, J. (2004). *School and society*. (3rd ed.). New York, NY: Teachers College Press.

Fernandes, J. K., & Myers, S. S. (2009). Inclusive deaf studies: Barriers and pathways. *Journal of Deaf Studies and Deaf Education, 15*(1), 17–29. doi:10.1093

Fernandes, J. V. (1988). From the theories of social and cultural reproduction to the theory of resistance. *British Journal of Sociology of Education, (9)*2, 169–180.

Fischer, S. D. (2007). Ringo and mikan: deaf vs. Deaf in Japan. *Journal of Deaf Studies and Deaf Education, 13*(1), 152.

Fishman, J. A. (Ed.). (1968). *Readings in the sociology of language*. The Hague, Netherlands: Mouton.

Fleisher, D., & Zames, F. (2001). *The disability rights movement: From charity to confrontation*. Philadelphia, PA: Temple University Press.

Fordham, S. (1988). Racelessness as a factor in black students' school success: Pragmatic strategy or pyrrhic victory? *Harvard Educational Review, 58*(1), 54–85.

Foster, S., & Kinuthia, W. (2003). Deaf persons of Asian-American, Hispanic American, and African American backgrounds: A study of intraindividual diversity and identity. *Journal of Deaf Studies and Deaf Education, 9*(3), 271–290.

Foucault, M. (1995). *Discipline and punish: The birth of the prison.* (A. Sheridan, Trans.). New York, NY: Vintage Books Press. (Original work published 1977)

Foucault, M. (1998). *Madness and civilization: A history of insanity in the age of reason.* (R. Howard Trans.). New York, NY: Vintage Press. (Original work published 1965)

Foucault, M. (1975). *I, Pierre Rivièr, having slaughtered my mother, my sister, and my brother . . .:* A case study of parricide in the nineteenth century. (F. Jellinek, Trans). Lincoln, NE: University of Nebraska Press.

Freire, P. (2004). *Pedagogy of hope: Reliving pedagogy of the oppressed.* (R. R. Barr, Trans.). New York, NY: Continuum. (Original work published 1992)

Gabel, S., & Peters, S. (2004). Presage of a paradigm shift? Beyond the social model of disability toward resistance theories of disabilities. *Disability & Society, 19*(6), 585–600.

Gallaudet, E. M. (1880). Fourth National Conference of Superintendents and Principals of Institutions for Deaf Mutes. *American Annals of the Deaf, 25*(3), 169–230.

Gallaudet Research Institute. (2008). *Regional and national summary report of data from the 2007–08 annual survey of deaf and hard of hearing children and youth.* Washington, DC: Author.

Gallaudet Research Institute. (2002). *Regional and national summary report of data from the 2001–2002 annual survey of deaf and hard of hearing children and youth.* Washington, DC: Author.

Gallaudet Research Institute. (2010). *Regional and national summary report of data from the 2009–2010 annual survey of deaf and hard of hearing children and youth.* Washington, DC: Author.

Gallego, M. A., Cole, M., & Laboratory of Comparative Human Cognition. (2001). Classroom cultures and cultures in the classroom. In V. Richardson (Ed.), *Handbook of research on teaching* (4th ed., pp. 951–997). Washington, DC: American Educational Research Association.

Gane, M. (Ed.). (1986). *Towards a critique of Foucault*. London, UK: Routledge.

Gannon, J. (1981). *Deaf heritage: A narrative history of deaf America*. Silver Spring, MD: National Institute for the Deaf Press.

Garrett, E. (1883). A plea that the deaf-"mutes" of America may be taught to speak. *American Annals for the Deaf, 28*(1), 15–20.

Gassett, J. (1961). *Meditations on Quixote*. New York, NY: Norton Press. (Original work published in 1914)

Gee, J. P. (1990). *Social linguistics and literacies: Ideology in discourse*. London, UK: The Falmer Press.

Gee, J. P. (1993). *An introduction to human language: Fundamental concepts in linguistics* (pp. 8–10). Englewood Cliffs, NJ: Prentice Hall.

Gee, J. P. (1996). *Social linguistics and literacies: Ideology in discourses*. (2nd. ed.). London, UK: Taylor & Francis.

Geers, A., Moog J., Biedenstein, J., Brenner, C., & Hayes, H. (2009). Spoken language scores of children using cochlear implants compared to hearing age-mates at school entry. *Journal of Deaf Studies and Deaf Education, 14*(3), 371–385.

Geers, A., & Nicholas, J. (2003). Hearing status, language modality, and young children's communicative and linguistic behavior. *Journal of Disability Studies and Deaf Education, 8*(4), 422–437.

Gerson, K., & Horowitz, R. (2002). Observation and interviewing: Options and choices in qualitative research. In T. May (Ed.), *Qualitative research in action* (pp. 199–224). London, UK: Sage.

Gertz, E. N. (2004). *Dysconscious audism and critical deaf studies: Deaf crit's analysis of unconscious internalization of hegemony within the Deaf community*. Dissertation Abstracts International, 64 (08), 2835. (UMI No. 3100674)

Gillespie, J. A. (1888). Aural instruction. In *Proceedings of the (Gallaudet) Sixth National Conference of Superintendents and Principals of Institutions for Deaf Mutes. Jackson, Miss.* Gallaudet University Archives, Washington, DC.

Giroux, H. (1992). *Border crossings: Cultural workers and the politics of education*. London, UK: Routledge.

Giroux, H., & Simon, R. (1989). Popular culture and critical pedagogy: Everyday life as a basis for curriculum knowledge. In H. Giroux (Ed.), *Critical pedagogy, the state, and cultural struggle: Teacher empowerment and school reform* (pp. 236–253). Albany, NY: State University of New York Press.

Glaser, B. G. (1998). *Doing grounded theory—Issues and discussions*. Mill Valley, CA: Sociology Press.

Glaser, B. G., & Strauss, A. (1967). *The discovery of grounded theory: Strategies for qualitative research*. Chicago, IL: Aldine Press.

Glickman, N. (1993). *Deaf identity development: Construction and validation of a theoretical model*. (Unpublished doctoral dissertation). University of Massachusetts, Amherst, MA.

Glickman, N. S. (1996). The development of culturally deaf identities. In N. S. Glickman & M. A. Harvey (Eds.), *Culturally affirmative psychotherapy with deaf persons* (pp. 115–153). Mahwah, NJ: Lawrence Erlbaum.

Glickman, N., & Gulati, S. (2003). *Mental health care of deaf people: A culturally affirmative approach*. Mahwah, NJ: Lawrence Erlbaum.

Goffman, E. (1959). *The presentation of self in everyday life*. Garden City, NY: Doubleday Anchor Press.

Goffman, E. (1968). *Stigma: Notes on the management of spoiled identity*. Englewood Cliffs, NJ: Prentice-Hall.

Goffman, E. (1974). *Frame analysis: An essay on the organization of experience*. New York, NY: Harper and Row.

Goodwin, C. (1994). Professional vision. *American Anthropologist, 96*(3), 606–633.

Goodwin, C. (2002). Professional vision. In D. Weinberg (Ed.), *Qualitative research methods* (pp. 281–312). Malden, MA: Blackwell Press.

Gould, J. J. (1996). *Mismeasure of man*. New York, NY: W.W. Norton.

Gramsci, A. (1971). *Selections from the prison notebooks*. London, UK: Lawrence and Wishart.

Guiberson, M. (2005). Children with cochlear implants from bilingual families: Considerations for intervention and a case study. *The Volta Review, 105*(1), 29–39.

Guinier, L. (2001). Rethinking power, rethinking theater: A conversation between Lani Guinier and Anna Deavere Smith. *Theater*, *31*(3), 31–45.

Gwaltney, J. L. (1970). *The thrice shy cultural accommodation to blindness and other disasters in a Mexican community*. New York, NY: Columbia University Press.

Habermas, J. (1972). Knowledge and human interests (J. Shapiro, Trans.). Boston, MA: Beacon Press.

Hall, J. (2002). Narrowing the breach: Can disability culture and full educational inclusion be reconciled? *Journal of Disability Policy Studies, 13*(3), 144–152.

Hands & Voices. (2005). The reform movement: Changes for deaf ed imminent. Retrieved from http://www.handsandvoices.org/articles/education/deaf_ed_reform/blueprint.html.

Haraway, D. (2003). Situated knowledges: The science question in feminism and the privilege of partial perspective. In N. Denzin & Y. Lincoln (Eds.), *Turning points in qualitative research: Tying knots in a handkerchief* (pp. 21–47). Crossroads in Qualitative Inquiry Series. Walnut Creek, CA: Alta Mira Press.

Harrison, S., & Dourish, P. (1996). Re-place-ing spaces: The roles of place and space in collaborative systems. In *Proceedings of the 1996 ACM Conference on computer supported cooperative work* (pp. 67–76). Cambridge, MA: Association for Computer Machinery.

Harry, B., & Klingner, J. (2006). School structure: Institutional bias and individual agency. In B. Harry & J. Klingner (Eds.), *Why are so many minority students in special education? Understanding race and disability in schools* (pp. 23–39). New York, NY: Teachers College Press.

Hart, B., & Risley, T. (1995). *Meaningful differences in the everyday experience of young American children*. Baltimore, MD: Paul H. Brookes.

Heath, S. B. (1983). *Ways with words: Language, life and work in communities and classrooms*. New York, NY: Cambridge University Press.

Hegel, G. M. (1981). *Lectures on the philosophy of history*. (H. B. Nisbet Trans.) Cambridge, UK: Cambridge University Press. (Original work published 1837)

Hehir, T. (2002). Eliminating ableism in education. *Harvard Educational Review, (72)*1, 1–33.

Hehir, T. (2005). *New directions in special education: Eliminating ableism in policy and practice.* Cambridge, MA: Harvard University Press.

Hermans, D., Knoors, H., Ormel, E., & Verhoeven, L. (2008). Modeling reading vocabulary learning in deaf children in bilingual education programs. *Journal of Deaf Studies and Deaf Education, 13,* 155–174.

Higgins, P. C., & Nash, J. (Eds.). (1987). *Understanding deafness socially.* (2nd ed.). Springfield, IL: Charles C. Thomas.

Hoffmeister, R. (1990). "ASL and its implications for language." In H. Bornstein (Ed.), *Manual communication: Implications for education* (pp. 81 – 107). Washington, DC: Gallaudet University Press.

Hoffmeister, R. (1996). Cross-cultural misinformation: What does special education say about deaf people. *Disability & Society, 11*(2), 171–189.

Homans, G. C. (1949). The strategy of industrial sociology. *The American Journal of Sociology, 54*(4), 330–337. Chicago, IL: The University of Chicago Press.

Hooks, B. (1994). *Feminist theory from margin to center.* Boston, MA: South End Press.

Hott, L., & Garey, D. (Producers). (2007). *Through Deaf Eyes* [DVD]. Washington, DC: WETA-TV. Available from PBS Home Video.

Horejes, T. (2009a). Constructions of deafness: Exploring normalcy and deviance within specific social representations. *Journal of Human Development, Disability, and Social Change, 18*(2), 7–22.

Horejes, T. (2009b). Constructions of deafness and deaf education: Exploring normalcy and deviance. Doctoral dissertation, Arizona State University–Tempe, AZ. Retrieved from *Dissertations & Theses* [Full Text], http://udini.proquest.com/view/constructions-of-deafness-and-deaf-pqid:1968618631/ (Publication No. AAT 3391838)

Horejes, T., & Lauderdale, P. (2007). Disablism reflected in law and policy: The social construction and perpetuation of prejudice. *Review of Disability Studies, 3*(3), 13–23.

Hughes, B., & Paterson, K. (1997). The social model of disability and the disappearing body; Towards a sociology of impairment. *Disability & Society, 12*(3), 325–340.

Humphries, T. (1977). *Communicating across cultures (deaf-/hearing) and language learning.* Unpublished doctoral dissertation, Union Institute and University, Cincinnati, OH.

Humphries, T., & MacDougall, F. (1999). "Chaining" and other links: Making connections between American Sign Language and English in two types of school settings. *Visual Anthropology Review, 15*(2), 84–94.

Hyde, M. (2009). Inclusion in an international context. In *Deaf people around the world: Educational and social perspectives* (pp. 352–367). Washington, DC: Gallaudet University Press.

Hymes, D. (1964). Towards ethnographies of communication. In J. Gumperz & D. Hymes (Eds.), *The ethnography of communication.* [Special issue] *American Anthropologist 66*(6), 1–34.

Hymes, D. (1966). *On communicative competence.* Paper presented at the Research Planning Conference on Language Development among Disadvantaged Children, Yeshiva University, New York.

Individuals with Disabilities Education Act, Pub. L. No. 101-476, 104 Stat. 1142 (1990), codified at 20 U.S.C. §1400 et seq.

Ivanic, R. (1998). Introduction. In R. Ivanic, *Writing and identity: The discoursal construction of identity in academic writing* (pp. 1–34). Philadelphia, PA: John Benjamins.

Jackson, P. (1968). *Life in classrooms.* Chicago, IL: University of Chicago Press.

Jamieson, J., & Pedersen, E. (1993). Deafness and mother-child interaction: Scaffolded instruction and the learning of problem-solving skills. *Early Development and Parenting, 2,* 229–242.

Janesick, J., & Moores, D. (1992). Ethnic and cultural considerations. In T. Kluwin, D. Moores, & M. A. Gaustad (Eds.), *Toward effective public school programs for deaf students: Context, processes, and outcomes* (pp. 49–65). New York, NY: Teachers College Press, Columbia University.

Johnson, A. (2000). *Privilege, power, and difference.* Boston, MA: McGraw Hill.

Johnson, J. L. (2011). International leaders summit: Using dialogue to center the conversation on the education of deaf children and youth in the 21st century. *American Annals of the Deaf, 156*(2), 75–86.

Johnson, R. E. (1991). Sign language, culture and community in a traditional Yucatec Maya village. *Sign Language Studies, 73,* 461–474.

Johnson, R. E., & Erting, C. (1989). Ethnicity and socialization in a classroom for deaf children. In C. Lucas (Ed.), *The sociolinguistics of the deaf community* (pp. 41–84). San Diego: Academic Press.

Johnson, R. E., Liddell, S. K., & Erting, C. J. (1989). *Unlocking the curriculum.* (GRI Working Paper No. 89-3). Washington, DC: Gallaudet Research Institute.

Jones, M. (2002). Deafness as culture: A psychosocial perspective. *Disability Studies Quarterly, 22*(2), 51–60.

Kagan Unlimited. (2009). The Stealth S.S.A. secret sound amplifier. Retrieved from http://www.stealthssa.com/

Karchmer, M. A., & Mitchell, R. E. (2003). Demographic and achievement characteristics of deaf and hard of hearing students. In M. Marschark & P. E. Spencer (Eds.), *Oxford handbook of deaf studies, language, and education* (pp. 21–37). New York: Oxford University Press.

Kelly, R. R., Lang, H. G., & Pagliaro, C. M. (2003). Mathematics word problem solving for deaf students: A survey of practices in grades 6–12. *Journal Deaf Studies & Deaf Education, 8,* 104–119.

Kelly, G., Luke, A., & Green, J. (2008). What counts as knowledge in educational settings. *Review of Research in Education, 32,* vii–x.

Kent, B. A. (2003). Identity issues for hard-of-hearing adolescents aged 11, 13, and 15 in mainstream setting. *Journal of Deaf Studies and Deaf Education, 8*(3), 315–324.

Kim, M., King, K., & Veno, J. (2009). *Narrative development of children with hearing loss as language socialization: An ethnographic study on discourse patterns in classrooms.* Paper presented at the American Educational Research Association Conference, San Diego, CA.

Kinsel, T. A. (1891). The early stages in deaf education. *American Annals of the Deaf and Dumb, 36*(3), 211–221.

Kluwin, T., Moores, D., & Gaustad, M. A. (Eds.). (1992). *Toward effective public school programs for deaf students: Context, processes, and outcomes.* New York: Teachers College, Columbia University Press.

Koester, L., Papousek, H., & Smith-Gray, S. (2000). Intuitive parenting, communication, and interaction with deaf infants. In P. Spencer, C. Erting, & M. Marschark (Eds.), *The deaf child in the family and at school* (pp. 55–72). Mahwah, NJ: Lawrence Erlbaum.

Komesaroff, L. (2002). Applying social critical literacy theory to deaf education. *Australian Journal of Language and Literacy, 25*(2), 37–46.

Komesaroff, L. (2008). Bilingual education. In L. Komesaroff (Ed.), *Disabling pedagogy: power, politics, and deaf education* (pp. 51–76). Washington, DC: Gallaudet University Press.

Kroeber, A. L., & Kluckhohn, C. (1952). *Culture: A critical review of concepts and definitions.* Harvard University Peabody Museum of American Archeology and Ethnology Papers 47.

Kuhn, T. (1996). *The structure of scientific revolutions* (3rd ed.). Chicago, IL: The University of Chicago Press.

Kuntze, M. (1993). Deaf bilingualism and biculturalism: Formulating definitions, approaches and language policy. In *ASL in schools: Policies and curriculum* (pp. 129–136). Washington, DC: College for Continuing Education, Gallaudet University.

Kuntze, M. (2000). Codeswitching in ASL and written-English language contact. In K. Emmorey & H. Lane (Eds.), *Signs of language revisited: An anthology to honor Ursula Bellugi and Edward Klima* (pp. 287–302). Mahwah, NJ: Lawrence Erlbaum.

La Bue, M. A. (1995). Language and learning in a deaf education classroom: Practice and paradox. In C. Lucas (Ed.), *Sociolinguistics in deaf communities* (pp. 164–220). Washington, DC: Gallaudet University Press.

Ladd, P. (2003). *Understanding deaf culture: In search of deafhood.* Toronto, Canada: Multilingual Matters.

Ladson-Billings, G., & Tate, W. (1995). Toward a critical race theory on education. *Teacher's College Record, 97*(1), 47–68.

Lane, H. (1989). *When the mind hears: A history of the deaf.* New York, NY: Vintage Press.

Lane, H. (1994). Constructing deafness in France and the United States. In The French-American Foundation (Ed.), *Parallel views: Education and access for Deaf people in France and the United States* (pp. 3–22). Washington, DC: Gallaudet University Press.

Lane, H. (1995). Constructions of deafness. *Disability & Society, 10*(2), 171–190.

Lane, H. (1999). *The mask of benevolence.* (2nd ed.). San Diego, CA: DawnSignPress.

Lane, H. (2005). Ethnicity, ethics, and the deaf-world. *Journal of Deaf Studies and Deaf Education, 10*(3), 291–310.

Lane, H. (2006). *The deaf experience: Classics in language and education.* Washington, DC: Gallaudet University Press.

Lane, H., & Grosjean, F. (Eds.). (1980). *Recent perspectives on American sign language.* Hillsdale, NJ: Lawrence Erlbaum.

Lane, H., Pillard, R., & Hedberg, U. (2011). *The people of the eye: Deaf ethnicity and ancestry.* New York, NY: Oxford University Press.

Lankshear, C., & McLaren, P. L. (1993). *Critical literacy: Politics, praxis, and the postmodern.* Albany, NY: State University of New York Press.

Lareau, A. (1989). Common problems in field work: A personal essay. In A. Lareau (Ed.), *Social class and parental intervention in elementary education* (pp. 197–233). New York, NY: Falmer Press.

LaSasso, C., & Lollis, J (2003). Survey of residential and day schools for deaf students in the United States that identify themselves as bilingual-bicultural programs. *Journal of Deaf Studies and Deaf Education, (8)*1, 79–91.

Lauderdale, P. (1998). Afterword: Terror, hegemony and jurisprudence. In A. Oliverio, *The state of terror* (pp. 147–154). Albany, NY: State University of New York Press.

Lauderdale, P. (Ed.). (2003). *A political analysis of deviance.* Toronto, Canada: de Sitter Publications.

Lauderdale, P. (2011). *A political analysis of deviance* (3rd ed.). Whitby, Canada: de Sitter Publications.

Lauderdale, P., & Amster, R. (2006). Power and deviance. (2nd ed.). In L. Kurtz (Ed.), *Violence, peace, and conflict* (Vol. 3, pp. 123–134). New York, NY: Academic Press.

Lauderdale, P., & Inverarity, J. (2003). From apolitical to political analyses of deviance. In P. Lauderdale (Ed.), *A political analysis of deviance* (pp. 15–46). Toronto, Canada: de Sitter Publications.

Lauderdale, P., McLaughlin, S., & Oliverio, A. (1990). Levels of analysis, theoretical orientations and degrees of abstraction. *The American Sociologist, 21*(1), 29–40.

Lederberg, A. R., & Spencer, P. (2009). Word-learning abilities in deaf and hard of hearing preschoolers: Effect of lexicon size and language modality. *Journal of Deaf Studies and Deaf Education, 14*(1), 44–62.

Lee, C. D. (2007). *Culture, literacy, and learning: Taking bloom in the mist of the whirlwind.* New York, NY: Teachers College Press.

Leigh, I., Maxwell-McCaw, D., Bat-Chava, Y., & Christiansen, J. (2009). Correlates of psychosocial adjustment in deaf adolescents with and without cochlear implants: A preliminary investigation. *Journal of Deaf Studies and Deaf Education, 14*(2), 244–259.

LeMaster, B. (2002). School language and shifts in Irish deaf identity. In L. Monaghan, C. Schmaling, K. Nakamura, & G. H. Turner (Eds.), *Many ways to be deaf,* (pp. 153–172). Washington, DC: Gallaudet University Press.

Linton, S. (2006). Reassigning meaning. In L. J. Davis (Ed.), *The disability studies reader* (pp. 161–172). London: Routledge.

List, G. (1999). Deaf history: A suppressed part of general history. In J. V. Van Cleve (Ed.), *Deaf history unveiled: Interpretations from the new scholarship* (pp. 113–126). Washington, DC: Gallaudet University Press.

Little, M., & Houston, D. (2003). Comprehensive school reform: A model based on student learning. *Journal of Disability Policy Studies, 14*(1), 54–62.

Lividas, G. (2010). Deaf education: A new philosophy. Retrieved on August 2012 at *http://www.rit.edu/research/biox_story.php?id = 35*

Lombardo, P. (2009). Involuntary sterilization. In S. Burch & P. K. Longmore (Eds.), *Encyclopedia of disability history* (pp. 503–504). New York, NY: Facts on File Press.

Longmore, P. (2003). *Why I burned my book: And other essays on disability.* Philadelphia, PA: Temple University Press.

Lou, M. W. (1988). The history of language use in the education of the deaf in the United States. In M. Strong (Ed.), *Language*

_References_  269

*learning and deafness* (pp. 75–98). Cambridge, UK: Cambridge University Press.

Lucas, C. (Ed.). (1995). *Sociolinguistics in deaf communities.* Washington, DC: Gallaudet University Press.

Luckner, J. L. (2006). Evidence-based practices and students who are deaf. *Communication Disorders Quarterly, 28*(1), 49–52.

Luckner, J. L., & Bowen, S. (2006). Assessment practices of professionals serving students who are deaf or hard of hearing: An initial investigation. *American Annals of the Deaf, 151*(4), 410–417.

Luckner, J. L., & Muir, S. (2002). Suggestions for helping students who are deaf succeed in general educational settings. *Communication Disorders Quarterly, 24*(1), 23–30.

Luckner, J. L., Muir, S. G., Howell, J. J., Sebald, A., & Young, J. (2005). An examination of the research and training needs in the field of deaf education. *American Annals of the Deaf, 150*(4), 358–368.

MacKinnon, C. A. (1994). *Only words.* Cambridge, MA: Harvard University Press.

Mannheim, K. (1936). *Ideology and utopia.* London, UK: Kegan Paul/Trench, Trubner.

Margolis, E., Soldatenjo, M., Acker, S., Gair, M. (2001). Peekaboo: Hiding and outing the curriculum. In E. Margolis (Ed.), *The hidden curriculum in higher education* (pp. 1–18). New York, NY: Routledge.

Markowitz, H., & Woodward, J. (1978). Language and the maintenance of ethnic boundaries in the deaf community. *Communication and Cognition, 11,* 29–38.

Marschark, M., Convertino, C., & Larock, D. (2006). Optimizing academic performance of deaf students: Access, opportunities, and outcomes. In D. Moores & D. Martin (Eds.), *Deaf learners: Developments in curriculum and instruction* (pp. 179–200). Washington, DC: Gallaudet University Press.

Marschark, M., Lang, H., & Albertini, J. A. (Eds.). (2002). *Educating deaf students: From research to practice.* New York, NY: Oxford University Press.

Marschark, M., & Spencer, P. E. (Eds.). (2010). *Oxford handbook of deaf studies, language, and education* (Vol. 2). New York, NY: Oxford University Press.

Marx, K. (1996). *Das kapital*. Washington, DC: Gateway Editions. (Original work published 1867)

Mason, D., & Ewoldt, C. (1996). Whole language and deaf bilingual/bicultural education—Naturally! *American Annals of the Deaf, 4*, 293–297.

Maudin, J. G. (2007). Life goes on: Disability, curriculum, and popular culture. In S. Springgay & D. Freedman (Eds.), *Curriculum and the cultural body* (pp. 113–129). New York, NY: Peter Lang.

Maxwell, M. (1984). A deaf child's natural development of literacy. *Sign Language Studies, 44*, 191–224.

May, S. (2012). *Language and minority rights: Ethnicity, nationalism and the politics of language*. New York, NY: Routledge Press.

Mayer, C., & Akamatsu, C. T. (1999). Bilingual-bicultural models of literacy education for deaf students: Considering the claims. *Journal of Deaf Studies and Deaf Education, 4*(1), 1–8.

Mayer, C., & Wells, G. (1996). Can the linguistic interdependence hypothesis theory support a bilingual-bicultural model of literacy education for deaf students? *Journal of Deaf Studies and Deaf Education, 1*(2), 93–107.

McFadden, M. (1995). Resistance to schooling and educational outcomes: Questions of structure and agency. *British Journal of Sociology of Education, 16*(3), 293–308.

McIntosh, P. (2002). An archi-texture of learning disability services: The use of Michel Foucault. *Disability & Society, 17*(1), 65–79.

McRuer, R. (2006). We were never identified: Feminism, queer theory, and a disabled world. *Radical History Review*, (Winter), 148–154.

Mead, G. H. (1934). *Mind, self and society*. Chicago, IL: University of Chicago Press.

Meadow, K. (1972). Sociolinguistics, sign language, and the deaf subculture. In T. O'Rourke (Ed.), *Psycholinguistics and total communication: State of the art; a compilation of papers presented at a special study institute held at Western Maryland College, June 28-July 23, 1971* (pp. 19–33). Washington, DC: American Annals of the Deaf.

Meadow, K. P., Greenberg, M., Erting, C., & Carmichael, H. (1981). Interactions of deaf mothers and deaf preschool children: Comparisons with three other groups of deaf and hearing dads. *American Annals of the Deaf, 126*(4), 454–468.

Meadow-Orlans, K. P. (2003). Support for parents: Promoting visual attention and literacy in a changing world. In B. Bodner-Johnson & M. Sass-Lehrer (Eds.), *The young deaf or hard of hearing child: A family-centered approach to early education* (pp. 39–61). Baltimore, MD: Paul H. Brookes.

Mehan, H. (1993). Why I like to look: On the use of videotape as an instrument in educational research. In M. Schratz (Ed.), *Qualitative voices*, (pp. 93–105). New York, NY: The Falmer Press.

Mercer, J. (1973). *Labeling the mentally retarded: Clinical and social system perspectives on mental retardation.* Berkeley, CA: University of California Press.

Merton, R. (1968). *Social theory and social structure.* New York, NY: Free Press.

Mills, C. W. (1959). *The sociological imagination.* New York, NY: Oxford University Press.

Mills v. Board of Education of the District of Columbia, 348 F. Supp. 866 (1972).

Mitchell, R., & Karchmer, M. (2006). Demographics of deaf education: More students in more places. *American Annals of the Deaf, 151*(2) 95–104.

Moeller, F. (1909). Education of the deaf and dumb. In *The Catholic encyclopedia.* New York, NY: Robert Appleton Company. Retrieved from New Advent website: http://www.newadvent.org/cathen/05315a.htm

Monaghan, L. (1994). Comment on Turner. *Sign Language Studies, 83,* 139–144.

Monaghan, L., Schmaling, C., Nakamura, K., & Turner, G. H. (Eds.). (2003). *Many ways to be deaf: International variation in deaf communities.* Washington, DC: Gallaudet University Press.

Montagu, A. (1997). *Man's most dangerous myth: The fallacy of race* (6th ed.). Walnut Creek, CA: Alta Mira Press.

Montgomery, G. (1994). Comment on Turner. *Sign Language Studies, 84,* 211–227.

Moog, J. S., & Geers, A. E. (2003). Epilogue: Major findings, conclusions and implications for deaf education. *Ear and Hearing Monograph, 24,* 121–125.

Moore, J. A., Prath, S., & Arrieta, A. (2007). Early Spanish speech acquisition following cochlear implantation. *The Volta Review, 106*(3), 321–341.

Moores, D. (1992). An historical perspective on school placement. In T. Kluwin, D. Moores, & M. A. Gaustad (Eds.), *Toward effective public school programs for deaf students: Context, processes, and outcomes* (pp. 7–30). New York, NY: Teachers College Press.

Moores, D. (2010a). The history of language and communication issues in deaf education. In M. Marschark & P. E. Spencer (Eds.), *Oxford handbook of deaf studies, language, and education* (Vol. 2, pp. 17–30). New York, NY: Oxford University Press.

Moores, D. (2010b). Partners in progress: The 21st International Congress on Education of the Deaf and the repudiation of the 1880 Congress of Milan. *American Annals of the Deaf, 155*(3), 309–310.

Moores, D., & Martin, D. (Eds.). (2006). *Deaf learners: Developments in curriculum and instruction*. Washington, DC: Gallaudet University Press.

Moraes, M. (1996). *Bilingual education: A dialogue with the Bakhtin circle*. Albany, NY: State University of New York Press.

Mudgett-DeCaro, P. (1996). On being both hearing and deaf: My bilingual bicultural experience. In I. Parasnis (Ed.), *Cultural and language diversity and the deaf experience* (pp. 272–288). New York, NY: Cambridge University Press.

Nader, L. (2002). *The life of the law: Anthropological projects*. Berkeley, CA: University of California Press.

Nakamura, K. (2006). Deaf in Japan: Signing and the politics of identity. Ithaca, NY: Cornell University Press.

Napier, J. (2002). The D/deaf-H/hearing debate. *Sign Language Studies, 2*(2), 141–149.

Nash, J. E. (2000). Shifting stigma from body to self: Paradoxical consequences of mainstreaming. In P. E. Spencer, C. J. Erting, & M. Marschark (Eds.), *The deaf child in the family and at school* (pp. 211–227). Mahwah, NJ: Lawrence Erlbaum.

Nash, J. E. & Nash, A. (1982). *Deafness in society*. Lanham, MD: Rowman & Littlefield.

National Conference of Superintendents and Principals of Institutions for Deaf Mutes. (1888). *Proceedings of the (Gallaudet) Sixth National Conference of Superintendents and Principals of Institutions for Deaf Mutes, held at Mississippi Institution, Jackson, Miss., April 14–17.* Jackson, MS: Clarion-Ledger.

Neidle, C. (2002). Language across modalities: ASL focus and question constructions. *Linguistic Variation Yearbook, 2*(1), 71–98.

Nelson, K. (1998). Toward a differentiated account of facilitators of literacy development and ASL in deaf children. *Topics in Language Disorders, 18*(4), 73–88.

Nicholas, J. G., & Geers, A. E. (2008). Expected test scores for pre-schoolers with a cochlear implant who use spoken language. *American Journal of Speech-Language Pathology, 17*, 121–138.

Nikolaraizi, M., & Hadjikakou, K. (2006). The role of educational experiences in the development of deaf identity. *Journal of Deaf Studies and Deaf Education, 11*(4), 477–492.

Nonaka, A. M. (2004). The forgotten endangered languages: Lessons on the importance of remembering from Thailand's Ban Khor Sign Language. *Language in Society 33*, 737–767.

O'Brien, C. (2011). *The influence of deaf culture on school culture and leadership: A case study of a school for the deaf.* Unpublished doctoral dissertation, University of Missouri–Columbia.

O'Day, B., & Killeen, M. (2002). Research on the lives of persons with disabilities: The emerging importance of qualitative research methodologies. *Journal of Disability Policy Studies, 13*(1), 9–15.

Ohnma, S. (2003). Education of deaf children and the politics of recognition. *Journal of Deaf Studies and Deaf Education, 8*(1), 5–10.

Oliver, M. (1990). *The politics of disablement: A sociological approach.* New York, NY: St. Martin Press.

Oliverio, A. (1998). The state of terror. Albany, NY: State University of New York Press.

Oliverio, A., & Lauderdale, P. (2005). Terrorism as deviance or social control. *International Journal of Comparative Sociology, 46*(1–2), 153–169.

Padden, C. (1980). The deaf community and the culture of deaf people. In C. Baker & R. Battison (Eds.), *Sign language and the deaf community* (pp. 89–103). Silver Spring, MD: Linstok Press.

Padden, C. (2004). Translating Veditz. *Sign Language Studies, 4*(3), 244–260.

Padden, C., & Humphries, T. (1988). *Deaf in America: Voices from a culture*. Cambridge, MA: Harvard University Press.

Padden, C., & Humphries, T. (2005). *Inside deaf culture*. Cambridge, MA: Harvard University Press.

Padden, C., & Ramsey, C. (1998). Reading ability in signing deaf children. *Topics in Language Disorders, 18*(4), 30–46.

Peet, E. (1868). Initial signs. *American Annals of the Deaf, 13*(3), 171–184.

Peet, E. (1880). The combined method. *American Annals of the Deaf, 25*(3), 169–230.

Pettengill, B. D. (1872). The instruction of the deaf and dumb. *American Annals of the Deaf and Dumb, 17*(1), 21–32.

Phillips, D. (1999). On comparing. In R. Alexander, P. Broadfoot, & D. Phillips (Eds.), *Learning from comparing: New directions in comparative educational research: Vol. 1. Contexts, classrooms, and outcomes* (pp. 15–20). Oxford, UK: Symposium Books.

Pintner, R., & Paterson, D. G. (1915). The Binet Scale and the deaf child. *Journal of Educational Psychology, 6*, 201–210.

Pintner, R., & Paterson, D. G. (1916). A measurement of the language of deaf children. *Psychological Review, 23*, 413–436.

Pintner, R., & Paterson, D. G. (1917). Psychological tests for deaf children. *The Volta Review, 19*, 661–667.

Plummer, J. (2001). *Documents of life 2: An invitation to a critical humanism*. London, UK: Sage.

Power, D., & Leigh, G. (2000). Principles and practices of literacy development for deaf learners: A historical overview. *Journal of Deaf Studies and Deaf Education, 5*(1), 3–8.

Prichard, C., Jones, D., & Stablein, R. (2004). Doing research in organizational discourse: The importance of researcher context. In D. Grant (Ed.), *The Sage handbook of organizational discourse* (pp. 236–213). Thousand Oaks, CA: Sage.

Prinz, P., & Strong, M. (1998). ASL proficiency and English literacy within a bilingual deaf education model of instruction. *Topics in Language Disorders, 18*(4), 47–60.

Prison Talk. (2004). *Mohawk Correctional Facility* [Online forum comment]. Retrieved from http://www.prisontalk.com/forums/archive/index.php/t-83865.html

National Conference of Superintendents and Principals of Institutions for Deaf-Mutes. (1888). *Proceedings of the Sixth National Conference of Superintendents andPrincipals of Institutions for Deaf-Mutes Held at Mississippi Institution, Jackson, MS; April 14–17, 1888*. Jackson, MS: Clarion-Ledger.

Pugach, M. (2001). The stories we choose to tell: Fulfilling the promise of qualitative research for special education. *Exceptional Children, 67*(4), 439–453.

Qi, S. & Mitchell, R. (2011). Large-scale academic achievement testing of deaf and hard-of-hearing students: Past, present, and future. *Journal of Deaf Studies and Deaf Education.* Retrieved from http://jdsde.oxfordjournals.org/content/early/2011/06/28/deafed.enr028.full

Rabinow, P. (1984). *The Foucault reader.* New York, NY: Pantheon Press.

Ramsey, C. L. (1997). *Deaf children in public schools: Placement, context, and consequences.* Washington, DC: Gallaudet University Press.

Reagan, T. (1995). A sociocultural understanding of deafness: American Sign Language and the culture of Deaf people. *International Journal of Intercultural Relations, 19* (2), 239–251.

Reagan, T. (2002). Toward an "archaeology of deafness": Etic and emic constructions of identity in conflict. *Journal of Language, Identity, and Education, 1*(1), 41–66.

Rogoff, B. (2003). *The cultural nature of human development.* New York, NY: Oxford University Press.

Roulstone, A., & Mason-Bishop, H. (2012). *Disability, hate crime and violence.* New York, NY: Routledge.

Rowley v. Board of Education of the Gloversville Enlarged City School. 192 A.D.2d 814; 596 N.Y.S.2d 561 (1993).

Rubington, E., & Weinberg, M. (Eds.). (2008). *Deviance: The interactionist perspective* (10th ed.). Boston, MA: Pearson Press.

Ruby, J. (Ed.). (1982). *A crack in the mirror: Reflexive perspectives in anthropology.* Philadelphia, PA: University of Pennsylvania Press.

Ruiz, E. (2010). Who is Gallaudet? *Buff and Blue*. Retrieved from http://www.thebuffandblue.net/?p = 4083

Sacks, O. (1989). *Seeing voices: A journey into the world of the deaf.* Berkeley, CA: University of California Press.

Saussure, F. (2006). *Writings in general linguistics* (S. Bouquet & R. Engler, Eds.). Oxford, UK: Oxford University Press.

Sayer, A. (1992). Quantitative methods in social science. In A. Sayer (Ed.), *Method in Social Science: A Realist Approach* (pp. 175–204). New York, NY: Routledge.

Schein, J. (1968). *The deaf community.* Washington, DC: Gallaudet University.

Schein, J. (2002). *At home among strangers: Exploring the deaf community in the United States.* Washington, DC: Gallaudet University Press.

Schirmer, B. R. (2000). *Language and literacy development in children who are deaf.* Boston, MA: Allyn & Bacon.

Schorr, E. A. (2006). Early cochlear implant experience and emotional functioning during childhood: Loneliness in middle and late childhood. *The Volta Review, 106*(3), 365–379.

Scott, R. (1969). *The making of blind men: A study of adult socialization.* New York, NY: Russell Sage Foundation.

Seaver, L. (2004). *Hands & Voices: Supporting families without bias.* Retrieved from http://www.handsandvoices.org/articles/fam_perspectives/wo_bias_V8-2.htm

Sekula, A. (1981). School is a factory. *Exposure, 18*(3/4), 77–91.

Senghas, R., & Monaghan, L. (2002). Signs of their times: Deaf communities and the culture of language. *Annual Review of Anthropology, 31*, 69–97.

Simms, L., Rusher, M., Andrews, J. F., & Coryell, J. (2008). Apartheid in deaf education: Examining workforce diversity. *American Annals of the Deaf, 153*(4), 384–395.

Shapiro, J. P. (1994). *No pity: People with disabilities forging a new civil rights movement.* New York, NY: Three Rivers Press.

Shaver, D., Newman, L., Huang, T., Yu, J., Knokey, A-M., & SRI International. (2010). The secondary school experiences and academic performance of students with hearing impairments. Retrieved from http://ies.ed.gov/ncser/pubs/20113003/

Schirmer, B. (1994). *Language and literacy development in children who are deaf.* New York, NY: Macmillan.

Skelton, T., & Valentine, G. (2003). 'It feels like being Deaf is normal': An explanation into the complexities of defining D/deafness and young D/deaf people's identities. *The Canadian Geographer, 47,* 451–466.

Smith, D. E. (1990). *Texts, facts, and femininity: Exploring the relations of ruling.* London, UK: Routledge.

Smith, K., & Bienvenu, M J. (2007). "Deaf theory": What can we learn from feminist theory? *Multicultural Education, 15,* 58–63.

Smith, L. T. (1999). *Decolonizing methodologies: Research and indigenous people.* London, UK: Zed Books.

Snow, C., Barnes, W., Chandler, J., Goodman, I., & Hemphill, L. (1991). *Unfulfilled expectations: Home and school influences on literacy.* Cambridge, MA: Harvard University Press.

Spencer, P. (2000). Every opportunity: A case study of hearing parents and their deaf child. In P. Spencer, C. Erting, & M. Marschark (Eds.), *The deaf child in the family and at school* (pp. 111–132). Mahwah, NJ: Lawrence Erlbaum.

Spencer, P. E., Erting, C., & Marschark, M. (Eds.). (2000). *Development in context: The deaf child in the family and at school.* Mahwah, NJ: Lawrence Erlbaum.

Spencer, P., & Marschark, M. (Eds.). (2010). *Evidence-based practice in educating deaf and hard-of-hearing students.* New York, NY: Oxford University Press.

Spindler, G. D., & Spindler, L. S. (1987). *Interpretive ethnography of education: At home and abroad.* Hillsdale, NJ: Lawrence Erlbaum.

Steinke, E. M. (1891). The art of questioning. *American Annals of the Deaf and Dumb, 36*(3), 206–210.

Steinmetz, G. (2005). *The politics of method in the human sciences: Positivism and its epistemological others.* Durham, NC: Duke University Press.

Stewart, D. (2006). Instructional and practical communication: ASL and English-based in the classroom. In D. Moores & D. Martin

(Eds.), *Deaf learners: Developments in curriculum and instruction* (pp. 207–220). Washington, DC: Gallaudet University Press.

Stokoe, W. (1960). Sign language structure. *Journal of Deaf Studies and Deaf Education, 10*(1), 11–15.

Stokoe, W., Casterline, D., & Croneberg, C. (Eds.). (1965). *A dictionary of American Sign Language on linguistic principles.* Washington, DC: Gallaudet College Press.

Strauss, A. L., & Corbin, J. (Eds.). (1997). *Grounded theory in practice.* London, UK: Sage.

Strong, M. (1988). *Language learning and deafness.* New York: Cambridge University Press.

Strong, M., & Prinz, P. (1997). A study of the relationship between American Sign Language and English literacy. *Journal of Deaf Studies and Deaf Education, 2*(1), 37–46.

Sutherland, E. H. (1949). *White collar crime.* New York, NY: Holt, Rinehart & Winston.

Swanson, D. (2007). Silent voices, silent bodies: Difference and disadvantage in schooling contexts. In S. Springgay & D. Freedman (Eds.), *Curriculum and the cultural body* (pp. 63–78). New York, NY: Peter Lang.

Swisher, M. (2000). Learning to converse: How deaf mothers support the development of attention and conversational skills in their young deaf children. In P. Spencer, C. Erting, & M. Marschark (Eds.), *The deaf child in the family and at school* (pp. 21–39). Mahwah, NJ: Lawrence Erlbaum.

Switzer, J. V. (2003). *Disabled rights: American disability policy and the fight for equality.* Washington, DC: Georgetown University Press.

Tabors, P., Roach, K., & Snow, C. (2001). Home language and literacy environment: Final results. In D. K. Dickinson & P. Tabors (Eds.), *Beginning literacy with language: Young children learning at home and school* (pp. 111–138). Baltimore, MD: Paul H. Brookes.

Tagg, J. (1988). *The burden of representation: Essays on photographies and histories.* Minneapolis, MN: University of Minnesota Press.

Thomas, C. (2004). How is disability understood? An examination of sociological approaches. *Disability & Society, (19)*6, 569–582.

Tobin, J. J. (1999). Method and meaning in comparative classroom ethnography. In R. Alexander, P. Broadfoot, & D. Phillips (Eds.), *Learning from comparing: New directions in comparative educational research: Vol. 1. Contexts, classrooms, and outcomes* (pp. 113–134). Oxford, UK: Symposium Books.

Tobin, J. J., Wu, D. Y. H., & Davidson, D. H. (1989). *Preschool in three cultures.* New Haven, CT: Yale University Press.

Tomlinson, S. (1995). *Machine and professional bureaucracies: Barriers to inclusive education.* Paper presented at the Sociology and Disability conference, Royal Hotel, Hull, United Kingdom. Retrieved from http://www.leeds.ac.uk/disability-studies/archiveuk/tomlinson/machine.pdf

Traxler C. B. (2000). Measuring up to performance standards in reading and mathematics: Achievement of selected deaf and hard-of-hearing students in the national norming of the 9th edition Stanford Achievement Test. *Journal of Deaf Studies and Deaf Education, 5,* 337–348.

Turnbull, H. R., & Stowe, M. (2001). Five models for thinking about disability: Implications for policy responses. *Journal of Disability Policy Studies, 12*(3), 198–205.

Turner, G. (1994). How is deaf culture? An SLS print symposium. *Sign Language Studies, 83,* 97–126.

U.S. Department of Education, Office of Special Education and Rehabilitative Services, Office of Special Education Programs. (2006). *26th Annual (2004) Report to Congress on the Implementation of the Individuals with Disabilities Education Act* (Vol. 2). Washington, DC: U.S. Government Printing Office.

Valente, J. M. (2010). *d/Dumb: Vol. 10. Disability studies in education series.* New York, NY: Peter Lang.

Van Cleve J. V., (Ed.). (1999). *Deaf history unveiled: Interpretations from the new scholarship.* Washington, DC: Gallaudet University Press.

Van Cleve, J. V., & Crouch, B. A. (1989). *A place of their own: Creating deaf community in America.* Washington, DC: Gallaudet University Press.

Van Dijk, T. A. (Ed.). (1997). *Discourse as social interaction.* London, UK: Sage.

Van Dijk, T. A. (2003). Critical discourse analysis. In D. Schiffrin, D. Tannen, & H. Hamilton (Eds.), *The handbook of discourse analysis* (pp. 252–371). Malden, MA: Blackwell.

Vernon, M. (2005). Fifty years of research on the intelligence of deaf and hard-of-hearing children: A review of literature and discussion of implications. *Journal of Deaf Studies and Deaf Education, 10*(3), 225–231.

Vernon, M., & Makowsky, B. (1969). Deafness and minority group dynamics. *Deaf American, 21*(11), 3–6.

Vygotsky, V. V. (1997). *Educational psychology.* (R. Silverman Trans.). Boca Raton, FL: CRC Press. (Original work published 1926)

Waldschmidt, A. (2005). Who is normal? Who is deviant? "Normality" and "risk" in genetic diagnostics and counseling. In S. Tremain (Ed.), *Foucault and the government on disability* (pp. 191–207). Ann Arbor, MI: University of Michigan Press.

Wallis, J. (1699). *Grammar of the English language.* (5th ed.). Oxford, UK: L. Lichfield.

Washabaugh, W. (1981). Sign language in its social context. *Annual Review of Anthropology, 10,* 237–252.

Weber, M. (1968). *Economy and society: An outline of interpretive sociology.* Wittich, New York, NY: Bedminster Press.

Westervelt, Z. F. (1891). American Association to Promote the Teaching of Speech to the Deaf. *American Annals of the Deaf and Dumb, 36*(3), 222–224.

Wickham, G. (1986). Power and power analysis: Beyond Foucault? In M. Gane (Ed.), *Towards a critique of Foucault* (pp. 106–149). New York, NY: Routledge.

Wilbur, R. (2000). The use of ASL to support the development of English and literacy. *Journal of Deaf Studies and Deaf Education, 5*(1), 81–104.

Williams v. Smith, 131 N.E. 2 (1921).

Windsor, J. (2000). The role of phonological opacity in reading achievement. *Journal of Speech, Language, and Hearing Research, 43,* 50–61.

Wittgenstein, L. (1953). *Philosophical investigations.* Malden, MA: Blackwell.

Wixtrom, C. (1988). Two views of deafness. *The Deaf American,* (Winter). Retrieved from http://www.aslaccess.org/2viewsofdeafness.htm

Woodward, J. C. (1972). Implications for sociolinguistic research among the deaf. *Sign Language Studies, 1,* 1–7.

Woodward, J. C. (1975). *How you gonna get to heaven if you can't talk with Jesus: The educational establishment vs. the Deaf community.* Paper presented at the Annual Meeting of the Society for Applied Anthropology, Amsterdam.

Woodward, J. C. (1982). *How you gonna get to heaven if you can't talk with Jesus: On depathologizing deafness.* Silver Spring, MD: T.J. Publishers.

Zavella, P. (1993). Feminist insider dilemmas: Constructing ethnic identity with "Chicana" informants. *Frontiers: A Journal of Women Studies, 13*(3), 53–76.

Zinn, M. B. (2001). Insider field research in minority communities. In R. M. Emerson (Ed.), *Contemporary field research* (pp. 159–166). Boston, MA: Little Brown.

# Index

Figures, notes, and tables are indicated by *f, n,* and *t* following page numbers.